BRITISH POLICY
TOWARDS THE OTTOMAN EMPIRE
1908-1914

BRITISH POLICY
TOWARDS
THE OTTOMAN EMPIRE
1908–1914

Joseph Heller

The Hebrew University of Jerusalem

FRANK CASS

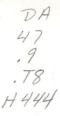
First published 1983 in Great Britain by
FRANK CASS AND COMPANY LIMITED
Gainsborough House, 11 Gainsborough Road,
London, E11 1RS, England

and in the United States of America by
FRANK CASS AND COMPANY LIMITED
c/o Biblio Distribution Centre
81 Adams Drive, P.O. Box 327, Totowa, N.J. 07511

British Library Cataloguing in Publication Data

Heller, Joseph
    British policy towards the Ottoman Empire 1908-
    1914
    1. Great Britain – Foreign relations – Turkey
    2. Turkey – Foreign relations – Great Britain
    I. Title
    327.41056   DA47.9.T8

ISBN 0-7146-3127-2

Typeset by John Smith, London

*Printed in Great Britain by
Page Bros (Norwich) Ltd*

To my parents

CONTENTS

PREFACE

The recent opening of the British archives for the years with which this book is concerned ended a long period during which historians were obliged to rely on Gooch and Temperley's *British Documents on the Origins of the War, 1898-1914*. Of course, use could also be made of the official publications of the other European governments which had taken part in the 'war-guilt' debate. But these, though independently edited, were too biased to produce a balanced picture. The voluminous material now available in the archives confirms this impression. The great number of documents makes it possible for the first time to reconstruct a picture of British policy towards the Ottoman Empire on the eve of World War I.

In his 1969 study on *The Young Turks: the CUP in Turkish Politics, 1908-1914,* F. Ahmad has used the correspondence between the British Embassy at Constantinople and the Foreign Office as a major source for the understanding of an internal Ottoman subject. In an earlier article, in 1966, on 'Great Britain's Relations with the Young Turks, 1908-1914' he attempted a new interpretation of what is, actually, the subject of this study too. However, the fact that he used only a relatively small number of the documents available and the necessary limits of an article left much room for new and more extensive research. Moreover, although he consulted the Lowther Papers and the Grey Papers, he did not refer either to the highly important Hardinge Papers in the Cambridge University Library or to the Nicolson Papers in the Public Record Office. Neither did he use the extensive correspondence between the Foreign Office and the British diplomatic missions other than Constantinople. F.H. Hinsley's *British Foreign Policy under Sir Edward Grey* (1977) only partly covered the subject of the Otto-man Empire.

Of the works which deal with the subject under discussion, only one has indeed tried to bring together all the aspects of the problem. It is an unpublished Ph.D. dissertation (Cambridge, 1957) by M. Heymann, *British Policy and Public Opinion on the Turkish Question, 1908-1914*. The author exhausted all the printed material available in western languages, but was unable to consult the archived material now available. Nevertheless his discussion of public opinion is still unsurpassed. Other authors single out questions like the Baghdad Railway or Macedonia, to take two examples, and neglect all other aspects.

Unfortunately, no attempt has yet been made to make any equivalent research into the Ottoman policies of either Germany (with the exception of Trumpener for the eve of the war), Austria or Italy where archival material is also available. Such research could further contribute towards an understanding of the policies of the Powers towards the Ottoman Empire. Most regrettable is the lack of any study of Ottoman foreign policy, except for an important aricle by Y.T. Kurat, 'How Turkey Drifted into World War I'.

The sources used in the present work are listed in the appended bibliography. All attempts to uncover further private material from relations and friends of such key figures as Lowther, Fitzmaurice, Tyrrell, Marling and Hohler proved unsuccessful. The enigma of the extent to which Fitzmaurice influenced Sir Gerard Lowther, the Ambassador, therefore, still remains. It is clear that Fitzmaurice's influence was indeed great, if not decisive, from the very beginning, but what remains unclear is the exact extent of and reason for this extraordinary impact. The discovery of new material affecting people who had been on the staff of the British Embassy during these years should lead to a re-evaluation of the subject. However, further research should be undertaken into the policies of Germany, France, Russia and Austria towards the Ottoman Empire as well as that of the Empire itself.

In writing this study I have incurred a great debt to my supervisor, Professor Elie Kedourie, for his constant help and encouragement and most valuable criticisms. I am also grateful to Professor Mayer Vereté, my teacher in the Hebrew University, Jerusalem, for his help and advice, and for having first encouraged me in this research. I would also like to thank Professor M.S. Anderson, who supervised me for one year, and my teacher, Professor J.L. Talmon, of the Hebrew University, for their assistance. I am also indebted to Dr M.

Heymann, who allowed me to read his Ph.D. thesis. I am thankful
to the Friends of the Hebrew University whose funds enabled me to
write this study, and also to their secretary, Dr W. Zander. I would
like to thank the staffs of the Public Record Office, the Cambridge
University Library, British Museum, School of Oriental and African Studies, Senate House and the London School of Economics, as
well as the Davis Institute of International Relations at the Hebrew
University, and the Faculties of Social Sciences and Humanities
who financed the publishing of this book. Finally, I would like to
thank my friend, Mr Barry B. Davis, for his valuable criticisms.
Last, but not least, I am grateful to Dr Stuart Cohen, who helped me
prepare this book for publication.

ABBREVIATIONS

BD	Gooch & Temperley, *British Documents on the Origins of the War, 1898-1914*, 11 vols
BP	Bertie Papers
CP	Crewe Papers
DDF	*Documents diplomatiques français*
GD	German Documents (*Die Grosse Politik*)
GP	Grey Papers
HP	Hardinge Papers
Int.-Bez.	*Die Internationalen Beziehungen im Zeitalter des Imperialismus*
LP	Lowther Papers
MP	Morley Papers
NP	Nicolson Papers
Öst.-Ung. Auss.	*Österreich-Ungarns Aussenpolitik*
VP	Vambéry Papers

INTRODUCTION

Throughout the half-century between the Crimean War and the outbreak of the First World War, few countries confronted successive British governments with the complexity of problems posed by the Ottoman Empire. The distinctive feature of Britain's Ottoman policy during this period was one of gradual change: the attitude of friendliness, which was evident in the Crimean War and the Eastern Crisis of 1877-8, and which was associated with such eminent British statesmen as Palmerston, Stratford Canning and Disraeli, turned to coldness and occasional hostility, epitomized in the person of Gladstone.[1] Enmity seemed to have reached its peak at Reval on the eve of the Young Turk Revolution of 1908. But the uniqueness of Britain's policy towards the Ottoman Empire does not lie solely in the gradual deterioration of relations, which is not an infrequent diplomatic occurrence. The significant factor was the bifurcate nature of Britain's aims. Britain advocated that the Ottoman Empire be reformed from within, a clear case of foreign intervention in another country's internal affairs; simultaneously, however, she claimed to defend its independence and integrity. As early as the Congress of Berlin, the pursuit of these two incompatible goals had demonstrably failed; nevertheless, it was not entirely abandoned.[2] Indeed, British demands for Reform became shriller and, from the Ottoman point of view, increasingly unpalatable and self-defeating.

One example was provided by insistent – and utopian – British proposals for the establishment of constitutional and parliamentary rule in the Ottoman Empire.[3] Another was the Government's attitude towards the Ottoman Empire's subject peoples in Europe. Britain was not the last of the European Powers to assent to the policy which condemned the Ottoman Empire of Abdul-Hamid to death by giving both direct and indirect encouragement to the

Balkan States. It had become an unshaken belief that Abdul-Hamid was the worst ruler Europe had ever known; moreover, nobody in authority in Britain was really prepared to reconsider the ambitions and political beliefs of the Bulgarians, Serbs, Greeks or Armenians, especially after the Bulgarian massacres of 1876 and the Armenian massacres of the 1890s. In such circumstances it was all too easy to justify an anti-Ottoman policy. Particularly was this so towards the end of the nineteenth century when the defence of the Straits became less of a priority in British strategy. The shift in the axis of British attention from Constantinople to Egypt ultimately brought about a change in diplomatic perspectives too.[4]

Other influences generated and then deepened the atmosphere of mutual enmity. There was the occupation of Egypt in 1882; the Baghdad Railway concession of 1903; the constant threat to British interests in the Persian Gulf; and the Anglo-Russian Convention of 1907.[5] Moreover, between these two crucial dates – 1882 and 1907 – it became fully apparent to British policymakers that the question of the Christian subjects of the Sultan could only be solved by cutting the Gordian knot, namely by further amputations of the Empire.[6] Abdul-Hamid's pleas that the Powers also make representations in Sofia and Athens were dismissed as irrelevant; he alone was regarded as responsible for the deteriorating situation in the European provinces. Antipathy was mutual; so much so that at the beginning of 1908 Sir Nicolas O'Conor, British Ambassador at Constantinople since 1898, drew a picture of near crisis:

> The relations between Great Britain and Turkey so far as they depend upon the Sultan are little more than tolerable. The policy of HMG with regard to Macedonia, Armenia and the other oppressed nationalities is objectionable and even hateful.

Consequently, O'Conor refused to predict the future course of events. On this point he felt too heavily the burden of his nine predecessors who had also served as Ambassadors to Abdul-Hamid. Their forecasts had not stood the test of time

> save insofar as these predictions have been based on general lines indicative of the obstructive policy of the Sovereign and the steadily increasing financial and administrative disorganization in all the Departments of the Government.[7]

However, O'Conor failed to mention that 'obstructive' as Abdul-Hamid might have been, he was, after all, acting within his legitimate rights. Besides, the Powers could always deal easily with such obstructions. The naval demonstration in support of the financial commission for Macedonia in 1905 and the dispute over the boundaries of Sinai in 1906 were not isolated examples. Contrary to British expectations, the Young Turks would prove less vulnerable.

The year 1908 happened to conclude a period which had witnessed a long and uninterrupted attempt to reform the Ottoman Empire. The immediate problem was that of Macedonia, with the Austrian project for a railway concession in Novibazar presenting an additional complication.[8] But the underlying issue remained what it had always been: the embittered and embattled relations between the Ottoman rulers and their Christian subjects. Sir Edward Grey, Britain's Secretary of State for Foreign Affairs since 1905, attempted to steer what had become a traditional course, favoured by both Conservative and Liberal governments. 'As to Turkish policy', he informed O'Conor only a few days after taking office, 'we want to pursue what I think was Lord Lansdowne's policy – keeping with the other Powers and getting them to go as far with us as we can.'[9] O'Conor advocated a more independent line; from St Petersburg, Sir Arthur Nicolson (Britain's Ambassador in Russia) called for more coordination with Russia. But Grey, both in his diplomatic correspondence and in his statements to Parliament, remained a firm believer in the European concert as a guarantee against European war. Only gradually did he become reconciled to replacing this alignment with the development of what became known as the 'Triple Entente'.[10]

Grey indicated the state of his thinking at the beginning of March 1908, when Britain launched a new diplomatic campaign. Seeking the support of the Powers, Grey warned that a division amongst them might raise the 'Turkish question' without solving that of Macedonia. He repeated his earlier proposal to reduce the Ottoman army in Macedonia, to guarantee the integrity and external security of this province and to press upon the Balkan States the need to prevent the passage of irregular groups of fighting men (referred to as 'bands'). It is significant that Grey believed that his proposals did not involve the disintegration of the Ottoman Empire.[11] But, although very keen to find a solution acceptable to all parties, he had soon to admit that the notion of the Concert had become a farce, a fact which threw a 'most unfair share of the disagreeable work in Constantinople' on the British Embassy.[12] The Powers, it transpired, were not prepared to agree with the British line, and Grey's policy was eventually to change accordingly.

Particularly was this so in view of the search for exclusive rights for British commerce in the Ottoman Empire. Concession-hunting was, in fact, the other side of the coin to the policy of reform. Significantly, the very first instruction issued to George Barclay, the Chargé d'Affaires at Constantinople, was to obtain an Iradé (concession) for the Quays Company; Hardinge (the Permanent Under-Secretary at the Foreign Office) told him that were he to succeed it would be 'a feather in your cap'.[13] Notwithstanding such exhortations, this aspect of Britain's Ottoman policy was also subject to mounting criticism, much of which emanated from Constantinople. Thus, Sir Adam Block, President of the British Chamber of Commerce at Constantinople, and formerly Chief Dragoman at the Embassy, informed Hardinge that so long as Abdul-Hamid was in power there was no chance of improvement and reform: 'As Caliph he cannot do otherwise. But the financial pressure may one day force him to yield to the necessity for financial control.'[14] Fitzmaurice, the Chief Dragoman of the Embassy, also pointed out the contradictory character of Britain's policy.[15] As long as the Macedonian policy prevailed, the British Ambassador 'must necessarily find himself in the equivocal, if not impossible position of having to goad the Sultan with the pinpricks of reform proposals while being expected to score in the commercial line successes which were dependent on the Sultan's goodwill.' After the Revolution, he also revealed that he had told both O'Conor and Barclay, his successor, that the Macedonian policy was 'insane'. He claimed that he had felt that the 'Turk' was 'in the hour before the dawn of his renewed national existence', which convinced him that the Macedonian policy was a 'potential anachronism'.[16]

But in the Foreign Office, the approach adumbrated in the Macedonian policy was still in the ascendant. Hardinge believed that the Concert could still be relied upon; Germany and Austria would be initially obstructive, but would later change their minds, albeit reluctantly (a process which Nicolson persistently wished to hasten by first achieving an understanding with Russia).[17] With its policy supported by the Balkan Committee and a large body of MP's,[18] the Foreign Office duly published a Blue Book which described in great detail the disorders in Macedonia.[19] Grey, in fact, appeared to measure the Ottoman attitude towards Britain solely through the perspective of the Macedonian situation. For this, he placed the blame entirely on the Ottomans. 'We had no bad disposition whatever towards Turkey', he told the retiring Chargé d'Affaires, 'but the Porte did not give us a chance of improving our relations with them.'[20] Altogether, Hardinge insisted on a strong line at Constantinople, otherwise Britain would suffer another defeat and the initiative would again be taken by Marschall von Bieberstein, the German Ambassador at Constantinople. Thus, the policy of coercion and pressure on the Sultan was implemented with regard to the Quays concession. ('The time will come when we and the French will have to tell the Sultan that it is not a privilege that we are seeking but our right.'[21]) It was simultaneously pursued with regard to the allocation of customs dues to the Baghdad Railway project.[22] Block was incensed: 'I sometimes think', he complained, 'that we want to hustle the East too fast ... we have deprived ourselves of all influence for good in the councils of the Porte, and have imperilled our own interests, commercial and political.'[23] Nevertheless, Grey and Hardinge vigorously followed Britain's traditionally contradictory policy. The latter was 'very glad' that Barclay had spoken to the Sultan about the Quays Concession; the grant would be a sign of goodwill towards Lowther, the newly-appointed British Ambassador.[24]

For the architects of British foreign policy, the rapprochement with Russia over Macedonia was a key to the revival of the Six Powers' Concert towards the Ottoman Empire which they greatly desired. They planned to accomplish the first step during a meeting with the Russian leaders at Reval on 9 and 10 June 1908, and then 'to get the assent of the Powers – a matter which will ... be extremely difficult.'[25] Both Hardinge and Grey were convinced that consideration of the European balance of power and Germany's growing naval might necessitated both a strengthening of Russia and a rapprochement with Germany over such questions as Macedonia.[26] Consequently, at Reval, Britain accepted the main Russian demand in Macedonia; she replaced the idea of a Christian governor with that of strengthening the position of Hilmi, emphasized her readiness to relax her anti-Ottoman policy, and promised to be 'anxious to meet the possible charge that might be made of an infringement of the sovereign rights of the Sultan', and at the same time to 'save the Sultan's face'. Britain could now rely on the 'full support' of Russia in Macedonian affairs.[27]

As far as the Ottoman Empire was concerned, Reval implied in fact a relaxation of the British reform policy. But the change had come too late. The myth already prevalent amongst the Young Turks, no less than the Sultan, was that Britain and Russia had actually hatched a new anti-Ottoman scheme during the Reval meeting and the revolutionaries therefore decided to strike earlier than originally planned.[28] Their assessment of the situation was not entirely incorrect. Although they had wrongly judged the Reval meeting, they had precisely gauged the tone of international politics. In particular, the eve of the Young Turk Revolution still found the makers of British foreign policy deeply committed to the traditional 'Turcophobia' of successive British governments. The relaxation of the reform policy was only a symptom of a new European realignment and not an admission that the reform principle had failed. British officials in the Foreign Office began, after Reval, to think increasingly in terms of a regrouping of the Powers, and the breakdown of the Concert was gradually admitted.[29] Moreover, no change occurred in the hunt for concessions; competition and jealousy were as strong as ever. The impasse over the Baghdad Railway provided a striking example. After Reval, Germany renounced the idea of discussions *à quatre* regarding the Baghdad Railway. Afraid of being in a minority against Britain, France and Russia, she naturally preferred to discuss that matter with Britain alone. The British Government objected, especially after the recent understanding with Russia.[30] Instead, balance of power considerations furthered the anti-Ottoman tendency in the Foreign Office. Mallet, realizing that Britain might be accused of 'uncompromising stiffness', blamed the Germans and their 'Bismarckian principles'[31] by which he probably meant the German policy of weakening the Entente, thus forcing Britain back into isolation.

Before July 1908, the Foreign Office had shown almost no interest at all in the Young Turks. Not surprisingly, therefore, the Revolution caught them completely unprepared. Moreover, the Embassy at Constantinople could not furnish Whitehall with any information whatsoever about the Young Turks. It was the Embassy at Paris that eventually supplied London with some sort of information about the Committee of Union and Progress (CUP). It did not mention the latter's anxiety as to the situation in Macedonia, and instead maintained that the Committee's principal aim was to oust Britain from Egypt, and to further Pan-Islamic ideas.[32] It was under these adverse conditions that the Foreign Office prepared to deal with the new situation.

The present work will attempt to attain three main objectives. The first is an analysis of the growth and development of British policy at two levels: the Embassy and the Foreign Office. The second is an assessment of the influence of various embassies on decision-making in the Foreign Office. The third is an estimate of the influence of European and Imperial considerations upon the formulation of Britain's policy towards the Ottoman Empire (and in particular the role played by Sir Louis Mallet, whose term as Ambassador at Constantinople has been the subject of debate).

1

HOPES, PROMISES AND DOUBTS

The Embassy, the Foreign Office and the 'Constitutional Movement'

The first report on the revolutionary events at Resna on 3 July 1908 was telegraphed from Constantinople on 8 July. It reached the Foreign Office on the same day, but was seen only the day after by the Eastern Department officials, the Permanent Under-Secretary, (Sir Charles Hardinge), and the Foreign Secretary himself, Sir Edward Grey.[1] Not until 14 July, after more detailed reports had reached the Foreign Office, were the first important comments made. The significance of the uprising was fully grasped by the lower echelons of the Foreign Office,[2] but was misunderstood by its head. Hardinge was entirely preoccupied with getting an agreement first with Russia and then with the Powers, and in mid-July did not even refer to the events in Macedonia in a private letter to Barclay, the Minister Plenipotentiary at Constantinople.[3] The latter, too, underrated the importance of the new situation and as late as 18 July could still not tell whether the rising was likely 'to fizzle out or spread'.[4] By the end of the third week in July, the Foreign Office was beginning to realize that the progress made by the Young Turks had 'a striking resemblance to revolution'.[5] But in the Embassy at Constantinople only Fitzmaurice saw that the Constitutional movement would win the day.[6]

The crucial events of 23-4 July, when Abdul-Hamid abdicated his absolute power, resulted in a radical change of opinion. In Constantinople, the first, apart from Fitzmaurice, to be convinced of a Young Turk victory was Block. On 25 July he suggested that Hardinge inaugurate a new pro-Ottoman policy and support Said and Kiamil in their efforts to reform the country. Otherwise, he warned, the new movement might turn to the Germans.[7] Something of the same feeling already prevailed in London. Consequently, and in view of the 'marked improvement' of the situation in Macedonia caused by the disappearance of the bands, the British Government on 27 July decided to suspend representations at the Porte for the creation of a mobile force.[8] On the same day, Britain congratulated Abdul-Hamid and Said on the establishment of a constitutional regime. At the same time, the end of the old Turcophobe policy and the inauguration of a new attitude, cautious but sympathetic, was officially announced by Grey in Parliament:

> If Turkey is going to improve the whole government of the country and ensure that the Mahomedans and Christians shall benefit equally by the improvement, then it is better that the Macedonian question should be settled by the Turks taking in hand and doing what for years we have been urging them to do, than by pressing partial reforms on reluctant, unwilling and obstructing authorities ... of course we must await events; but at the present time I can only say this: Our own sympathy must be with those who are trying to introduce reforms, and I should be the last to prophesy that they will fail. If they succeed, then they must succeed by their own efforts, but our sympathy is with them ... while not relaxing our watchfulness, while not becoming slack in our desire to do all in our power to promote improvement in Macedonia, we shall for the present preserve an expectant and sympathetic attitude.[9]

Grey's views were not shared everywhere. Barclay, the British Minister, remained sceptical about the success of the Revolution;[10] the Foreign Office was still confused. 'Events of the last few days', wrote Hardinge, 'have been so unexpected that it is impossible to say what will be our next step as regards the Macedonian reform projects.'[11] The old policy was only suspended and replaced by 'an expectant attitude' until it could be proved whether the bands had disappeared entirely or not. 'If only this Young Turk party can consolidate itself and introduce a really good administration into the country, they will have been playing our game entirely, but perhaps not the game of other more interested Powers.'[12] This was the real touchstone: a new policy was conditional on reforms being carried out by the Constitutional movement. The Foreign Office also hoped that the Revolution had caused a blow to German influence in Constantinople.[13] Meanwhile, it was decided to suspend the scheme for the mobile force, to bring the activities of the gendarmerie to a minimum and to refuse to give any help to the officials of the old regime.[14]

It was a matter of coincidence that Sir Gerard Lowther, the new Ambassador, arrived just at the beginning of the new era. Subsequently, he was to be blamed for the worsening relations between Britain and the Ottoman Empire. But in fact, by the time of his arrival on 30 July, fear, doubt and anxiety were already considerable in the Foreign Office.

Hardinge had already appreciated the negative repercussions which the Revolution might produce in Egypt, India[15] and the Balkan states, whilst Grey – although delighted with the enthusiastic popular reception accorded to Lowther[16] – was not ready to promise much to the new regime. He was careful not to commit Britain in any way which could involve her in actual intervention on the Ottomans' behalf. 'Our diplomatic attitude will be benevolent, and our influence used to secure fair chance for them,' was all he offered. Nevertheless, the trend of British policy was clear. Writing to Block, Hardinge promised:

> Whatever we can do to help and encourage the Turks in their present attempt at the regeneration of the Turkish administration will most certainly be done by us. We are very anxious to make use of this opportunity to improve our relations with the Turks. ... You may be quite sure that no external diversion on the part of Bulgaria or any other Balkan Power would be tolerated for one instant. I am quite convinced that the Russians, French and ourselves would do all we could to prevent such a development.[17]

The definite instruction which Grey conveyed to Lowther said that the Foreign Secretary's statement of 27 July, made in Parliament and reported by *The Times*, might serve as a text for explaining the British attitude. 'It is important that our attitude and views should become as clearly and widely known as possible.'[18]

Wider consideration further complicated the situation. Grey described the real dilemma for Britain: 'The delicate point will presently be Russia – we cannot revert to the old policy of Lord Beaconsfield, we have now to be pro-Turkish without giving rise to any suspicion that we are anti-Russian.'[19] Neither would it now be possible to maintain the tradition of intervention in Ottoman affairs. Grey himself detected quite early the true character of the Young Turks and the new regime. 'The new Turkish Government are not likely to be in a hurry to put themselves in the hand of any foreign Power. There is a nationalist feeling in the new movement in Turkey which would resent this.'[20] Thus, the tendency was to let the new regime alone. Both the Foreign Office and the Embassy thought that there was no necessity to despatch a warship to the Dardanelles,[21] and did not demand the suppression of the predominant German influence at Constantinople as a condition for her change of policy.[22] They were confident that the Revolution itself had been a blow to Germany since the latter identified herself with the Sultan; and the Foreign Office accepted Lowther's opinion that it should postpone a project to introduce British naval and financial advisers as counterweights to the German General von der Goltz.[23]

The development of British policy towards the new regime was considerably helped when two other interested Powers, Russia and Austria, assured the Foreign Office that the Ottoman Empire would be able to devote itself to internal reform without the distraction of external interference. In mid-August, Izvolsky[24] expressed Russia's willingness to work 'in full accord' with Britain. On 12 August, Aehrenthal declared that Austria-Hungary would favour non-intervention and the preservation of the integrity of the Ottoman Empire.[25] Since foreign intervention against the new regime seemed to be remote, in spite of the somewhat disquieting reports from Sofia,[26] the Foreign Office continued to devote its attention to the more immediate and urgent question of the reform administration. In essence, the policy was not new. Grey merely advised that the Young Turks should not try to go too fast, but should place the government in the hands of 'honest and capable' men. Financial consolidation seemed the second most important point. The chief motive in Grey's policy remained what it had always been: 'Just as we used all our influence, when Turkish Government was bad, to press reforms from outside, so now if reforms are being developed from inside we shall use all our influence to prevent their being interfered with from outside.' But he was not entirely altruistic. Grey also hoped that a consolidated Turkish regime would give British capital more openings – although he did insist that British firms should not impose onerous conditions.[27] Similarly, Mallet, the Head of the Eastern Department, was upset when the new regime selected a French expert to re-arrange their finances.[28]

Lowther was much more critical of the new regime. His scepticism was evident only one month after the Revolution. This coloured his official reports and was particularly apparent in his private letters, where he patronizingly referred to the Young Turks as 'a collection of good-intentioned children'. He did not expect the Young Turks (whom he foresaw were about to assume official power) to start playing the dangerous game of nationalism, but from the very beginning he doubted their radical and liberal statements. 'Just now the Committee are very anxious to obtain the applause of Europe and are constantly asking advice. ...'[29] The affinity of ideas between the newly arrived Ambassador and his knowledgeable Chief Dragoman, Fitzmaurice, was immediately clear. Fitzmaurice did have a better opinion of the Young Turks. ('They have many of the requisites of successful national leaders – are impersonal and have a great sense of responsibility.') But in view of the critical economic and social situation, he feared 'a desperate internal struggle accompanied by disorders' which would provoke Russian intervention. Fitzmaurice also warned that the Young Turks would raise the questions of Crete, Egypt, Macedonia, Bosnia, Aden, Lebanon, Cyprus, the special position of the British Residency at Baghdad and the 'irregular' status of Lynch's Navigation Company in Mesopotamia. But despite these anxieties, he still thought that this moment, when Britain was the most favoured nation at Constantinople, provided a golden opportunity for checking the progress of the German-sponsored Baghdad Railway and establishing British economic control over Mesopotamia, particularly through Willcocks' scheme for the irrigation of that area.[30]

Through Fitzmaurice, Lowther established his first contacts with the Young Turks. On 2 September 1908, he met with Mehmed Talaat and Dr Bahaeddin Shakir, the secretaries of the internal and external branches of the CUP. Lowther was impressed with their moderate ideas, and their realistic appraisal of future difficulties. They again professed their English orientation, and looked to the British Government for 'approval and sympathy'.[31] Lowther emphasized the importance of keeping Abdul-Hamid in his present position, but was careful not to exceed his instructions: 'It was to be anticipated that if matters went smoothly under the new order of things, British money would seek investment in the country; and that the British Government and this Embassy would encourage only sound and reliable people.'[32] In fact, Lowther was still suspicious and anxious. Thus, he reminded Grey of the national character of the Constitutional movement 'with a consequent tendency to restrict the privileged position of foreigners'. Lynch's steamers on the river Tigris might be regarded as an infringement of Ottoman sovereign rights. His demands that the Foreign Office hasten a loan for the new regime constituted more than a bona fide demonstration of goodwill, as there was a danger that the new regime might be driven into the arms of German financiers.[33]

Lowther's pessimistic reports soon grew more pronounced. Noting the impatience of the Young Turks and their increasing suspicions of Abdul-Hamid, by mid-September he feared that the CUP might turn the Empire into a military dictatorship. He also doubted, as he had done continuously since his arrival, the possibility of reconciling Moslem predominance with constitutional government.[34] Supplementary voices could also be heard in London. Thus Tilley, who had only recently served in the Embassy at Constantinople and was a veteran and staunch anti-Ottoman, advocated replacing the Ottoman Empire with the nation-state type of regime.[35] Professor Arminius Vambéry (a former British spy in Constantinople and Professor of Oriental Languages at Budapest University), also took a pessimistic view of the Young Turk Revolution. On 11 September he predicted that:

> The Young Turks may give the most alluring promise, they may exhibit the common danger from outside and show the greatest toleration, they will never succeed in blending the various elements into one body politic: an effort which has not yet succeeded even in civilized Austria-Hungary, in spite of more favourable conditions.[36]

Finally, Rothschild and Baring refused to take up part of a loan to the new regime, chiefly because they doubted the strength of Ottoman finance.[37] Nevertheless, Hardinge was not discouraged: 'In spite of our failure at the present moment, we intend to persist and to do all we can to improve our financial position in Turkey,' he wrote to Block.[38] The King received an even rosier picture:

> Everything appears to be progressing satisfactorily at Constantinople. The Turkish Government have applied officially for a

British Admiral to reorganize their fleet, for Mr Chitty to re-organize the Customs and have appointed Sir W. Willcocks as Adviser on irrigation and such questions.[39]

What was known as the 'Guéshoff incident' was already disturbing such equanimity. On the face of it, the issue seemed (in Hardinge's words) 'somewhat foolish', involving no more than an omission on the part of the Young Turks to invite the Bulgarian Agent at Constantinople to a banquet for diplomatic representatives.[40] In effect, however, wider issues were at stake. The Ottomans, it was feared, would exploit international sympathy with the new regime to 'recover hold over Bulgaria', a move which raised the threat of Russian counter-intervention on Bulgaria's behalf.[41] From Britain's point of view, such a development was fraught with danger. Judged by the standards of the European balance of power, Russia was inevitably a more important factor in British policy than was the new Ottoman regime. The need to preserve and consolidate Anglo-Russian amity – even at Ottoman expense – had already made itself evident in Britain's attitude towards the Turco-Persian boundary dispute;[42] Nicolson's warnings of an anti-Ottoman turn in Russian policy over Bulgaria merely furthered the trend. 'We want to act as much as possible in cooperation with Russia,'[43] was the official line. The new regime at Constantinople, not to mention the Ottoman Empire *per se*, was hardly taken into account. Britain did wish 'to safeguard Turkey from all external disturbances during the period which is necessary for her regeneration'. But the essential facts were baldly stated. 'Unfortunately Bulgaria is now at the zenith of her power, while Turkey, thanks to a long period of maladministration, is weaker than she has ever been before.'[44] There was perhaps goodwill towards the new regime at Constantinople, but Britain had totally committed herself to Russia just a few days after she had made her pro-Revolutionary statements.

This perspective manifestly dictated the shape and form of British policy during the early days of October 1908. The Foreign Office received prior notice of the Bulgarian declaration of independence and the Austrian annexation of Bosnia and Herzegovina.[45] But Britain rejected French offers to convene a conference of the Powers for the purpose of condemning Austria's action (not least because the Russian attitude was considered unreliable); she also resisted Ottoman efforts to elicit a strong line.[46] On the very eve of Bulgaria's proclamation of independence and the annexation of

Bosnia, Grey told Rifaat, the Ottoman Ambassador in London, that the new regime should accept both the independence and the annexation as they were merely 'injurious from the point of view of sentiment and prestige'. Grey advised the new regime not to go to war, because 'what Turkey most needed now was time and money. War would deprive her of both.' All he conceded was a promise that Britain would support any Ottoman claim for a financial indemnity, and an assurance that 'all' British sympathies were with the new regime.[47] Not even a midnight visit to Lowther on the night of 5 October by Tewfik Pasha, the Ottoman Minister for Foreign Affairs, could change this attitude.[48] Britain could not deviate from the policy of the rest of the Powers. In this respect, the realities of British policy were far removed from Ottoman expectations.

On the day of the proclamation of Bulgaria's independence, Grey, in an attempt to find an agreement and common ground with Russia, decided that the new regime should be content with protests and compensation. He realized that this was the only line which would be accepted in consultations with the Powers.[49] The Ottoman Empire once more became a pawn in an international game of power, and Britain had again to play a part. Britain's favourable declarations were not meant to represent a return to Beaconsfield's policy. To be pro-Ottoman without being anti-Russian was an impossible task in the state of increasing European tension, when Britain was becoming more and more dependent on the friendship of Russia and France.[50] The new regime had to pay a heavy price for the worsening European situation, which directly influenced British policy. Consequently, Britain's Liberal government could not give real support to the new regime at Constantinople. The balance of power and Imperial considerations determined the kind of policy Britain adopted – sympathetic declarations of a non-committal nature.

2

BETWEEN CRISIS AND COUNTER-REVOLUTION

October 1908 — April 1909

The Effect of the International Crisis

The Bulgarian proclamation of independence on 5 October, the annexation of Bosnia, and Crete's announcement of her unification with Greece, were all severe blows to the new regime and aroused great indignation in the Ottoman Empire.[1] A full-scale crisis was not avoided until an extraordinary meeting of the Ottoman cabinet had decided against military measures and Kiamil, the Grand Vizier, had suggested a conference to discuss the Bosnian and Bulgarian questions.[2] Throughout, British policy held to its course. Although prepared (on Lowther's advice) to reject Buchanan's recommendation for an immediate recognition of Bulgaria's independence,[3] Grey refused to enter into any further commitment respecting Ottoman territorial integrity.[4] Ultimately, the best the Young Turks could expect from the British Government was to arrange for some pecuniary compensation to the new regime and support for a loan guaranteed by, and demonstrating the goodwill of, the Powers.[5] On the main point, however, the British decided to recognize the Bulgarian and Austrian actions. Moreover, although the Foreign Office bowed to the Ottoman wish to exclude the Straits question from the agenda of the proposed international conference, it announced that it would not oppose in principle free passage to Russia.[6]

Nevertheless, the British did attempt to pursue an even-handed policy. They expressed fears over Macedonia and, despite Lowther's warnings of a future 'disagreeable anti-European movement' in Turkey,[7] on 13 October the Foreign Office was ready to show an even more favourable attitude towards the new regime. It now suggested the abrogation of Articles 23 and 61 of the Treaty of Berlin, which promised administrative reform for the European and the Armenian provinces respectively;[8] it also proposed that, as soon as a satisfactory degree of Ottoman administration had been attained, regular treaties between civilized states should replace the Capitulation treaties. In return, the Ottoman Empire was to recognize the annexation of Bosnia and the independence of Bulgaria, while Austria was to restore Novibazar, and the Porte was to be compensated for the other abandoned territories. In addition, Article 29 of the Berlin Treaty, which promised to settle border conflicts between the Porte and Montenegro, was to be abrogated in favour of Montenegro.[9] The Foreign Office regarded these important offers as a sign of 'considerable moral support' for the new regime. Provided the Porte agreed, their acceptance in a conference should avoid further threats to the Ottoman Empire.

However, when Lowther reported that Kiamil, the Grand Vizier, was proving uncompromising on some of the points raised by Britain,[10] the Foreign Office exhibited a stiffer attitude. Grey told Rifaat that the new regime should not dispute 'questions of form', and that Britain's policy 'was not due to any lack of sympathy, but to real considerations for the political interests of Turkey'.[11] He even went so far as to play down the Russian hostility to an Ottoman refusal to change the *status quo* of the Straits.[12] Hardinge, too, was annoyed:

> It is quite impossible to put back the clock and the *faits accomplis* in Bosnia and Bulgaria have to be eventually recognized on certain terms ... Kiamil Pasha should realize that even after a successful war against Bulgaria, Russia and Europe would not allow East Roumelia to go back to Turkey ... It is useless to reply ... to Kiamil Pasha's statements ...[13]

Mallet was even more ominous. He hoped that the Young Turks, whose power was over-estimated in the Foreign Office, had learnt their lesson 'otherwise Macedonia will follow'.[14] Neither was the British Government much more sympathetic to Kiamil's suggestion (communicated secretly to Lowther) that Bosnia become an independent principality governed by a Protestant prince from a neutral state, selected by the Powers and 'facilitated' by the Porte. Kiamil also suggested defensive and offensive alliances with Bulgaria,

Servia and Montenegro and hoped for the support of Britain, France, Russia and Italy.[15] Grey was pleased that Kiamil appeared to rely on Britain[16] and was ready to guard Ottoman interests in the Straits, since these were essential both to Britain's own interests in the Mediterranean and to the very existence of the new regime and the Empire itself.[17] Nevertheless, Hardinge dismissed Kiamil's recent plan as 'most extraordinary' and 'impossible', and the Ottoman Government as 'children'.[18]

Instead, and to secure the international position of the Ottoman Empire, the Foreign Office favoured the creation of an Ottoman-Balkan entente. The danger that Bulgaria might gravitate towards the Austro-German orbit was given more weight than Lowther's reports of Kiamil's lack of enthusiasm for the whole idea.[19] Rather, the impasse at which Austro-Ottoman relations had arrived made it all the more desirable that everything possible be done to bring about a Bulgaro-Ottoman rapprochement.[20] This implied a further shift in Britain's attitude towards the Porte. 'Mr Tilley is mistaken,' commented Hardinge, 'in saying that we are committed to Turkey to press for the taking over of a part of the debt by Bulgaria and the payment of the Bulgarian tribute. All that has been said is that we would endeavour to get as large a compensation as possible for Turkey.'[21] On the other hand, the very existence of the new regime was regarded as a guarantee for such a rapprochement because Bulgaria could not expect to obtain such good terms from a reactionary regime.[22] Despite Lowther's warnings that 'there will inevitably come a time when the Turkish worm will turn',[23] Hardinge remained convinced that his Bulgarian policy was correct. 'I am glad to say,' he wrote to Bryce, 'that the Young Turk regime seems to be going on all right at present, although it has yet many difficulties before it. If we can see the federation of the small Slav States of the Balkans with Turkey to support them, I do not think we need have much fear as to the future for some years to come.'[24] Could the Bulgarian question be solved, the British Government would agree to leave the Bosnian issue to the future.[25]

The failure of the negotiations for an alliance between the Ottoman Empire and the Balkan States forced Britain to modify her policy. Hardinge at last accepted that the 'difficulty of an "entente" or defensive alliance between the Balkan States and Turkey is largely due to their inveterate jealousy of each other and to the secret desire of each of them to eat up Turkey. I fear that such an agreement is still a long way off.'[26] Grey was even to see good reasons for Britain not promoting a Bulgaro-Ottoman alliance. 'If Turkey made it or would represent that she made it owing to pressure or advice from us, she would regard us as quasi-responsible for seeing that Bulgaria played the game well for Turkey.'[27] But despite Lowther's claims that Kiamil had all along merely been toying with the Servians and the Montenegrins,[28] the Foreign Office now exhibited a sympathetic attitude towards the Porte. Thus, in December 1908, Hardinge revealed to Buchanan that 'we shall probably have to give moral support to the Turks if they were the victims of Austrian aggression',[29] and – contrary to Bulgarian expectations – Britain refused to put further pressure on the Porte, instead favouring the Ottomans on the question of pecuniary compensation.[30] The direction of British policy became more evident early in 1909, when the negotiations between the Ottomans on the one hand and the Austrians and Bulgarians on the other reached an impasse. Sinister rumours reached the Foreign Office that Austria might provoke an attack on the Ottoman Empire, pushing Bulgaria into seizing the opportunity to attack the Porte too. In the latter case, the Foreign Office hoped that the Ottomans would inflict a 'thorough good beating' upon the Bulgarians.[31] 'It seems to me difficult to imagine,' wrote Hardinge, 'that we should be able to observe a neutral attitude in such a contingency. If we did so, I think we should lose our position in the Near East, and also amongst the Mahometan communities in Egypt, India and elsewhere.'[32] In consideration of Turkish feelings, the Foreign Office also accepted Lowther's advice that King Edward VII should not visit Greece at the present time.[33]

This favourable attitude could only be maintained, however, for as long as the Turks gave the impression of being in 'a very conciliatory and peaceful frame of mind', with regard to Austria and Bulgaria.[34] British policy reverted to its former course in February, when the Young Turks rejected the Russians' proposal that they take over a portion of the debt.[35] The British Government had regarded the Russian proposal as a 'very wise' way of bringing Bulgaria into the Russian orbit, and thus improving relations between the Porte and Russia.[36] A stubborn attitude on the part of the Porte, by contrast, might make war with Bulgaria inevitable, 'and might mean an end of the reformed administration'.[37] The Foreign Office did agree with Lowther that Bulgaria was 'very bellicose',[38] 'but added: 'For the strength of the feelings the Turks must blame the conduct of their ancestors from the beginning of the 14th century to last July.' Tilley, accordingly, objected to Lowther's claim for strategic rectifications in favour of the Ottomans, since the Empire could find safeguards only in 'her own strength and her good treatment of her Bulgarian subjects'.[39]

Much of this attitude could be attributed to the ingrained British belief that internal reform of the Ottoman administration was the cure for the Empire's ills. Even more decisive, however, was Britain's decision to support the Russian proposal as part of her European orientation, for sympathy towards the new regime was to be in accordance with the general framework of British policy:

> If I had refused to support the Russian proposal [Grey wrote to Lowther], the result would have been a diplomatic separation between Russia and us that would have reacted unfavourably on the whole of our relations. I should have thrown Russia back into the old belief that we were bent upon supporting Turkey against her, and disliked seeing her and Turkey drawn together. If I had insisted that I preferred the fixing by the Powers of the amount which Bulgaria should pay to Turkey direct I might have found that the other Powers had rallied to the support of the Russian proposal, and that Turkey and we had thus been put in the invidious position of disturbers of the peace. Or, at best, we should have had the support of only Germany and Austria, and this would have led to a new grouping of the Powers, affecting the whole international situation.[40]

The Ottoman Empire was thus the victim of power politics, and Britain did not feel any doubts or hesitations as to where her true interests lay. Admittedly, she had failed to foresee that Austrian and Bulgarian aggression would, so quickly, cause a change in her sympathetic policy towards the new regime. But this did not imply a contradiction or dilemma in British policy; the Foreign Office, Grey claimed, 'deliberately risked losing our influence with Turkey in the support of Russian Diplomacy, and in the cause of peace by pressing the Turks to go as far as they have done in accepting the Russian proposal in principle.'[41] He admitted to Lowther that it was not 'from blindness or for any light reasons that I risked our popularity at Constantinople'.[42] The friendship with Russia was too important an asset for Britain to risk for the sake of Ottoman 'obstructive' policy. Grey saw no clash of interests with Russia since the latter also favoured Ottoman-Balkan friendship. Nicolson, the Ambassador to Russia, persuaded the Foreign Office of Russia's sincerity although Lowther had strong misgivings, since he could not believe that an Ottoman-Bulgarian entente could ever be realized.[43] Fortunately, Russia's attention had gradually shifted from the Ottoman Empire to Servia and Montenegro. She was thus more anxious to keep her friendship with Britain, who had to assure her of 'full diplomatic support' for a peaceful solution.[44] But Tilley still envisaged a Russian seizure of Constantinople. He felt that Russia would never fight for Servia against Austria and Germany; that was why she displayed such stiffness towards the Porte and why Izvolsky talked of giving up the Entente.[45] But neither this, nor Lowther's story of the secret relations between the Russian Embassy and the CUP, made any impression upon London.[46]

The future of the Ottoman Empire depended on the kind of settlement she could achieve in the Balkans and the sort of regime that was established for the Empire. While the second question depended solely on the Ottomans themselves, the first was the concern and the interest of stronger, outside Powers. Ottoman spokesmen claimed that a secret agreement existed between Bulgaria and Russia which would be detrimental to their country's interests; hence they wished to guarantee themselves against the Bulgarian threat by making their consent to Ferdinand's new title conditional on his non-interference in Macedonia.[47] But since Bulgaria had become such an important factor in European politics, the Ottomans had little chance of obtaining Britain's support for their stand. At the Foreign Office, an agreement with Austria and Bulgaria was considered crucial to the future of the Ottoman Empire, and matters had to be viewed from the widest possible perspective. At this level, the important fact was that Russia was interested in winning over Bulgaria as the guardian of her own flank against Austrian expansion; British policy followed suit.[48] Indeed, political realities had caused the increasing cohesion of the Triple Entente. Hardinge argued:

> As to the anxiety felt by certain Russians as to a working understanding between G. Britain and Germany on the naval question, I do not think that Russia need have any cause for alarm ... It is far more essential for us to have a good understanding with

Russia in Asia and the Near East, than for us to be on good terms with Germany, and, since it is highly improbable that there can be any real improvement in the relations between Germany and France, it is absolutely vital to us to continue to support France, and to maintain what is now called the Triple Entente.[49]

Lowther and the Young Turks

Lowther had meanwhile extended his acquaintance with the Young Turk leaders and his knowledge of their political ideas. Familiarity, however, bred a degree of contempt. He described Ahmed Riza, President of the Ottoman Chamber, for instance, as 'too loquacious', immature, and unworthy of his exalted position. Altogether the Young Turks were 'visionaries'.[50] To an increasing extent, these views, often buttressed by Block's gloomy reports on the chronic financial situation,[51] were shared in the Foreign Office. Grey and Hardinge were particularly disappointed with their meeting with Riza and Dr Nazim in London on 13 November 1908. The representatives of the CUP had put forward the unacceptable idea of a Bosnian buffer state, and merely the 'civil' possession of eastern Roumelia by Bulgaria. The British regarded these suggestions as a recipe for war. 'The Turkish Government', Grey wrote to Lowther, 'will have a difficult job if all the Young Turks are like them.'[52] Meanwhile, the Foreign Secretary (acting on Lowther's advice) rejected the suggestion that Britain show her sympathy for the new regime by offering the Porte a large loan and extending her protection to the entire Ottoman Empire. Neither was he prepared to countenance any other form of alliance with the Young Turks. In public, both Grey and Asquith continued to speak most sympathetically about the new regime.[53] Private comment, as reflected in correspondence and memoranda, was however becoming increasingly critical.

Partly this was because Britain appeared to be losing her influence at the Porte. Kiamil did remain pro-British; but his ability to withstand the violent attacks of the organs of the CUP (reported to be 'under the inspiration of the German Embassy'), seemed doubtful. Instead, by December 1908 Lowther was beginning to discern the first signs of a German recovery at Constantinople.[54] The result was a barrage of invective against the 'chauvinism' of the CUP; and a run of strident despatches, each of which recommended that Britain withhold the grant of credit to the new regime for: 'If there is plenty of money going I fear the most violent ones will come to the front.'[55] The Committee, maintained Lowther, 'has no *raison d'être* ... it is a secret society responsible to none'[56]; he was getting 'rather sick of the Committee and wish them to disappear. They have given us a lot of trouble to keep old Kiamil on his, at one time, rather rickety seat and there are a lot of irresponsible young gentlemen amongst them.'[57] In view of the growing danger from the CUP, Lowther could see only one way to keep Kiamil in office: 'To let it be made clear to them that those who have money to lend will not do so unless the Government is in the hands of men of experience in whom some reliance can be placed.'[58]

The Foreign Office was similarly critical. 'I entirely share your view', Hardinge wrote to Lowther, 'that it is desirable that this Young Turk Committee should disappear in the near future, otherwise they will in course of time deteriorate, and assume precisely the same position as that held previously by the Palace camarilla.'[59] It should not be assumed that the Foreign Office was totally objective, while the Embassy lacked objectivity;[60] in fact, London no less than Constantinople, was staffed mainly by anti-Ottoman officials who shared the prejudices of the well-entrenched Gladstonian school. But even such an independent figure as Block, who had considered himself a pro-Young Turk from the beginning, was critical. He foresaw that the 'spirit of Chauvinism' rampant in the CUP would be detrimental to the work of the Public Debt Council.[61] This view was not entirely shared by Fitzmaurice, who (although sharply critical of the CUP) seemed to be content with the position Britain had achieved with the new regime, based as it was on Kiamil's favourable attitude.[62] But, far more pessimistic was the report signed by a War Office official, Lieut.-Col. F. R. Maunsell, a former Military Attaché to the Porte. He recommended the formation of a greater Bulgaria and an independent Albania, as bulwarks against the Austro-German *Drang nach Osten*. Of the new regime he was sharply critical: 'I am afraid from what I have seen that [the Turk] is hopeless, and that no real reform is intended. It is the same old Turk, although he has changed his coat, and made an effort to smarten himself up.' Tilley, not unexpectedly, accepted Maunsell's report quite enthusiastically. Hardinge sounded much less anti-

Ottoman: 'Happily this development will take some little time before it creates another Balkan question.'[63]

On 13 January, Kiamil won a unanimous vote of confidence in the Ottoman Chamber. Lowther regarded this as a severe blow to the CUP. The Ottoman rapprochement with Austria, and the first signs that Bulgaria too would come forward with a new offer, also strengthened the position of the Grand Vizier. Although he did not underrate the opposition of the CUP, Lowther saw these events as contributing to stability in the Empire. In an effort to strengthen this trend, he renewed his pressure upon the Foreign Office to offer Kiamil the GCB, since 'he can never be stronger than today.'[64] Indeed, Lowther supported Kiamil's policies in general – so much so, that Hardinge momentarily suspected him of being too pro-Ottoman.[65] But, as Hardinge himself said: 'The Turkish Government are now much firmer in the saddle.'[66]

Nevertheless, Britain's support clearly had well-defined limits. Thus, the Foreign Office was firm in rejecting another suggestion for an alliance made by the Ottoman Ambassador in Berlin. 'A friendly Turkey', wrote Hardinge, 'is a much more convenient situation for us than an allied Turkey.'[67] Moreover, enthusiasm was short-lived. Six months after the Revolution and less than a fortnight after Kiamil's victory in Parliament, Lowther sent a gloomy summary of the new regime's achievements. Although the most blatant abuses had been rectified, no change had occurred in 'the nature of the Turk', nor any major amelioration in the administration. Moreover, the law was now heeded less than it had been under the old regime. He admitted that external complications impeded the implementation of internal reform, and that Parliament had not been sitting for long; nevertheless, he was disappointed that he could not cite any constructive work. He criticized the Government for its failure to solve internal problems.[68] Tilley quickly noted the marked change in Lowther's attitude towards the new regime. He considered it 'startling' to receive such a report from Lowther who had hitherto been 'somewhat optimistic'. He did not deny that he himself had always been pessimistic about the possibility of reform, 'but any hopes on that subject would be dashed by this report'. He advised that

> we should at least be able in future to wash our hands of the internal affairs of Turkey, at any rate until something very

startling happened ... That the Turks will waste their money is more than likely, but how are we to prevent them except by 'meddling'? ... we have taken such a definite line in preparing to treat Turkey in future as a civilized state that we can hardly draw back now. We must take the risk of their coming to grief ... progress is scarcely what one would expect of Moslems, least of all of Turkish Moslems.[69]

Kiamil's resignation in February 1909, and his replacement as Grand Vizier by Hilmi Pasha, exacerbated Britain's problems and British prejudices. Despite the new administration's protestations of admiration for Britain, Lowther was immediately sceptical. 'We may take it for granted', he wrote to Grey, 'that this Government is compelled to [do] the bidding of the Committee. Hilmi is able and active, but I fear quite untrustworthy.' The CUP, he was sure, represented Turkish and not Ottoman interests; as such it would encourage the new Cabinet to be less favourable to Britain. The new situation might be welcomed by Russia, and would certainly be exploited by Germany.[70] Lowther was not alone in his sentiments. The Foreign Office approved when he told Riza, now President of the Ottoman Chamber, that the existence of the 'anonymous Society' (the CUP) was not in accordance with the Constitution.[71] Adam Block also agreed with the Ambassador that Britain's consent to an increase of 4 per cent in the Ottoman Customs should be made conditional on the improvement of the financial administration – otherwise 'stop supplies; that is the only way'.[72] The appointment of Rifaat, formerly Ambassador in London, as Minister for Foreign Affairs, now served as the only safeguard for the dubious British orientation of the new Cabinet; but his capacity to cope with the CUP was also in doubt. Hardinge concurred with Lowther that the new regime was 'gradually tending to a military despotism of a nationalist and chauvinistic character. In that case, we shall have to quietly bide our time until a more moderate system of government is introduced.'[73] 'The whole situation seems to be very critical', he told Block, 'as it is impossible for a country to be properly governed by an occult camarilla.'[74] Britain still hoped that the Young Turks would bring about some reform; they had, after all, deposed the Palace regime. But these aspirations were accompanied by some specific misgivings on whether Crawford, the recently appointed Customs Adviser, or Admiral Gamble, the Naval Adviser, could accomplish anything effective.

Thus the British Government found itself in a new dilemma, which had been created by the hasty and somewhat irresponsible expressions of enthusiasm articulated immediately after the proclamation of the Constitution. The Young Turks were far from being a success, but Britain found herself still committed by her earlier statements. Hardinge seems to have felt the difficulties of the situation particularly keenly. Responsive to Lowther's distrust of the new regime and its unconstitutional methods of government, he nevertheless pounced on the Ambassador's promise that 'on the slightest sign of their doing good work, I shall be more cordial'.[75] Thus, on 23 March 1909, he privately warned the Ambassador: 'You ought to be very careful not to show in any way that our feelings have changed towards the new regime, and not to do anything that might be interpreted in that sense.' Caution was advised: 'It is probable that this Committee will disappear in the not far distant future, and then our former position will undoubtedly be restored.'[76] Hardinge did not mean to dissociate himself from Lowther's scathing criticisms, but to warn him against giving the Ottomans any indication that Britain had indeed changed her policy.

Tilley was the one man in the Foreign Office who proved to be even more anti-Ottoman than the Ambassador. Doubtful of Hilmi's capacity to perform 'the miracle required to cure the "sick man"', he warned that the new type of Turk could be

> worse than the former ... What seems to me sad is that the Turk of the future who has lost his sense of superiority will lose his personal dignity, that if he is to remain on equal terms with the Christian, he is likely to vie with him in dishonesty, and that, in fact the Turk whom we are now hoping to create will not be the same Turk whose distinction has hitherto so often led travellers to think there was something to be said for his cause.[77]

Alone in the Foreign Office, Tilley even dared to foresee the end of the Ottoman Empire. He was sure that the Turkish element was bound to lose its position, since it was both intellectually and numerically inferior, and 'if it goes under is likely to lose such virtues as it possesses, particularly its dignity and what will be most to the fore will be the bad qualities of the Arabs, Greeks and Armenians'. His status as a junior official necessarily circumscribed Tilley's influence; but its weight was enhanced by his first-hand and comparatively recent knowledge of the Ottoman Empire. Although Hardinge rejected the possibility of an immediate disintegration,[78] Britain's estrangement from the new regime was growing steadily and perceptibly.

One indication of the process was provided by the manner in which the two governments appeared to disagree on an increasing number of issues of mutual concern. Thus, initially, Britain refused to agree to the Ottoman request that the financial commission for Macedonia be dissolved (a position which was not altered until September 1909 when R. W. Graves entered the Ottoman service as a member of a new Commission);[79] she also refused to sanction the despatch of an Ottoman High Commissioner to Egypt; was anxious that no changes be made in the Capitulations without the prior consent of all the Powers; and insisted on modifications in the Baghdad Railway Convention before considering the extension of credit to the Young Turks.[80] Increasingly, the Foreign Office – constantly goaded by Lowther's vilification of the CUP and by Block's gloomy predictions of impending bankruptcy – tended to measure success by the standards of specifically British gains. Thus, particular support was accorded to Cassel's National Bank of Turkey (provided the institution retained its predominantly British character);[81] and particular pride was taken in the achievements of Crawford and Gamble. Basically, however, there seemed nothing to do but await the march of events, in the hope that the passage of time would produce favourable results. In Hardinge's words:

> We may have to pass through a disagreeable period of one or two years, during which everybody's influence in Constantinople will be struggling for supremacy, while ours will occupy a back seat. Still, the fact that British influence is deeply ingrained in the sentiment of the Turkish population will ensure the eventual predominance of that influence.[82]

3

FROM CRITICISM TO OPPOSITION

British Policy and Interests from the Counter-Revolution to the Tripoli War (April 1909 – September 1911)

The Repercussions of the Internal Upheaval: The Alienation of the CUP

The attempted counter-revolution of March 1909 initially encouraged some rather far-fetched guesswork in the Foreign Office.[1] By the third week in April, the fear that the Constitutional regime had been terminated also elicited public expressions of concern from both Asquith and Grey.[2] Even more worrying, however, was the sharp reaction of the CUP. As early as 20 April, Hardinge could foresee the deposition of the Sultan with the final triumph of the CUP, and he did not conceal his antipathy towards the Young Turks:

> It is, I think, unfortunate that the Committee should have had this opportunity of showing how predominant is their position. They badly wanted a knock, and I thought at one moment that they had got it. I expect that they will now be even more arbitrary in their actions than they were before.[3]

Lowther reported that the 'violent members of the Committee did indeed wish to depose the Sultan, despite the absence of direct evidence against him'. He was sure that the bulk of the people supported the Liberal Unionists, but would have to give way to a long despotic period of rule by the CUP. 'All this', he wrote on the recent events, 'leads me to the conviction that these people are hopeless and that reform is out of the question for this wretched country.'[4]

Nevertheless, once Shevket Pasha had crushed the counter-revolution on 24 April, the Foreign Office was convinced that events at Constantinople were settling down quickly. It therefore decided to take the Young Turks more seriously. Thus there was no 'sorrow' or 'regret' expressed at the deposition of the Sultan. Grey and Hardinge quickly forgot their former attempts to support Abdul-Hamid as a constitutional monarch. Rather, he was now associated with 'absolute rule', 'corruption', the Armenian massacres of 1895 and the other failures of the Empire. Hardinge rejoiced that Abdul-Hamid failed to escape to Asia Minor where the 'bulk of Anatolia' might have stood by him, involving the country in a 'terrible' civil war.[5] Once more the Young Turks were deserving of respect since, as after the events of July 1908, they were gathering around themselves 'the best elements'. The former criticism expressed by the Embassy and the Foreign Office, Grey discovered, was an exaggeration:

> ... It is clear that we have greatly underestimated the strength of the force at the disposal of the Committee ... it seems clear to me that the best elements in Turkey are on their side, and we must back up those elements and be sympathetic to them. Whether the chance of really permanent reform is great or small, we must back the change as long as it exists ... I think that during the last three or four months we have let ourselves slide too much into a critical attitude towards the Committee and the Young Turks ... they have shown that there is real stuff in them, and we must be less critical and more sympathetic.

The ablest men were to be found in the Army, whose officers should place the work of administration in the hands of foreign advisers because of their own 'weakness' in this field.[6]

The implications of this change in policy were soon communicated to Fitzmaurice. Hardinge told him to

> adopt a sympathetic attitude towards the Young Turks and be neither critical nor even impartial towards them. He should try to show them that we are friendly and sympathetic and wish to help them. That is our feeling here, and the only practical line of policy to follow. Our only hope for a reformed Turkey rests now wth the Young Turks, and if they do not meet with sympathy and cannot lean on us they will soon learn to lean on some other

Power, and the splendid position which we had at Constantinople a few months ago will be lost.[7]

Lowther dissented, and cautioned the Foreign Office 'not to rush
into the arms of any group who happen to be at the top of the
wave for the moment'. Revolutionary turmoil was still rife in Asia
Minor; so too was the militancy of the Kurds and Armenians. On a
diplomatic level, he distrusted the affiliations of the regime ('It
would now seem as if the Committee has made up its mind no
matter how much they dislike and distrust Germany and Austria
to rely on their support as a counterpoise against Russia and
Bulgaria.')[8] On a personal level, he shrank from association with a
sinister bunch of 'Salonika Christians, Jews and freemasons' – an
aspect of the internal scene upon which Fitzmaurice laid particular
stress, and which attained further prominence when Djavid was
appointed finance minister (unwarrantedly, since Djavid was in fact
a Denmeh).[9] Lowther insisted that the Embassy was prepared to
cultivate 'intimate relations' with the 'mild chauvinists and
moderates' in the CUP;[10] but the general tenor of his reports was
unmistakably critical. 'The methods [of the Committee] are still
those of Abdul-Hamid, only instead of their being applied by one
man, they are applied by a few, the Committee.' He could not see
any forthcoming improvement in the lot of the Christians. The bulk
of the Young Turks meant well, but a group of young officers openly
threatening their opponents were the real troublemakers. Instead
of coming into the open and governing constitutionally, they preferred to control and criticize from behind the scenes claiming
inexperience in government.[11] By the beginning of August, the
Ambassador did realize that the existing Government was in
Britain's interest, since any other would be more chauvinistic.
Nevertheless, he maintained that the Foreign Office had 'overruled'
the Young Turks (the 'wild chauvinists') since April. He particularly resented the fact that this critical view of the CUP was not shared
by the Foreign Office.[12]

To an extent, Lowther's complaints were misplaced. The Foreign
Office was already less enthusiastic towards the new regime than he
feared. What had originally attracted the senior officials in London
to the regime was the hope that the Young Turks would provide the
Empire with stable, if not good, government. They had been prepared to suspend the policy of reform, believing that for the time

being military despotism was the only way to avoid chaos.[13] This explains why, contrary to Lowther's advice (but following Block's line), London had approved an increase in the Ottoman military budget in June 1909. 'Without an army the cause of the progressive party in the State is lost.' Further, as Mallet minuted, 'a strong Turkey will prevent further encroachments on the part of Austria and the army is the prop of the Constitutional movement.'[14] Nevertheless, what were considered to be Britain's vital interests in the region were not therefore abandoned. Indeed, when it came to making Britain's agreement to the customs increase conditional on compensations for the Baghdad Railway, the Foreign Office insisted on a line which was noticeably stiffer than that advocated by Lowther himself.[15] Where the Ambassador and the Foreign Office differed was in their estimate of the regime's chance of survival. Lowther, who was less concerned with concession-hunting than was the Foreign Office, repeatedly stressed that 'on all sides I hear the most pessimistic accounts of disorder, insubordination and discontent.'[16] The Foreign Office, by contrast, noted that the Law of Association (promulgated on 23 August 1909) would serve as a stabilizing factor since it was intended to abolish national differences within the Empire; and that the Young Turks had proved very adroit in 'nobbling' the Albanian Congress at Dibra into becoming an Ottoman one.[17] As Grey had earlier informed Izvolsky:

> The only thing we could do for the present, was to support the new regime in Turkey as long as there was any prospect of its success. Once or twice lately those who had been longest in Constantinople, and thought they understood the situation well had expressed the opinion that the Young Turks were failing, or had actually failed, but recent events had proved very clearly that it would have been a great mistake to accept any assumption of this kind.[18]

Ultimately, it was the Foreign Office which was compelled to modify its attitude. Partly, this was due to the high esteem in which Lowther was himself held (he was later to be offered – and to decline – the Ambassadorship at St Petersburg in succession to Nicolson);[19] of greater weight, however, was the increasing amount of unmistakable evidence that the internal situation in the Ottoman Empire was becoming 'critical'. In the autumn of 1909, the Foreign Office had still found it possible virtually to ignore a run of important reports on the possible effects of the Porte's proposed plans to separate Church and State;[20] such issues seemed to pale in importance beside the overriding need to obtain concessions in Mesopotamia. By the spring of 1910, however, the internal situation had clearly become paramount. For Lowther, the last straw was the murder, in mid-June, of the editor of *Sedai Millet* (the last remnant of opposition in the capital).[21] In Hardinge's case, there were a cluster of issues. As early as May 1910, he had disclosed to Cartwright, the Ambassador in Vienna, that:

> We are not satisfied with the situation in Constantinople. The CUP, with the best intentions in the world, appear to be gaining very little ground. At the back of them stands the figure of Shevket Pasha, as military dictator, and his word is absolute law. In addition to the fact that there is very little ability amongst the members of the Committee, there is, we hear, intense jealousy amongst them, and this, as anyone can see, must have a corroding and deteriorating influence. We hear that corruption is again rampant, although the monies obtained are said to be poured into the coffers of the Committee.[22]

In June, he and Grey also acceded to Lowther's request by fully endorsing his policy: Lowther was 'very glad you gave Rifaat some straight talk. He always seemed to imply that my criticisms went beyond what the Foreign Office would endorse. He will now know that it is not so.'[23] Once again, Hardinge agreed, and wrote to Goschen:

> The situation in Turkey is very bad at present, and our influence there is greatly dwindling, while Marschall has apparently recovered a great deal of his lost authority with the Turks. The CUP appear to have inaugurated a despotism even more drastic than that practised by our friend Abdul-Hamid. This, of course, suits the Germans very well. It looks to me as though there must be another explosion in Constantinople before long.

In fact what suited the Germans in the struggle for predominance at the Porte was Britain's vigorous stand over Mesopotamia, the Persian Gulf, Egypt and Crete, and the CUP sensitivity to these areas.[24]

Thus, by the end of Hardinge's tenure of office in 1910, Britain's relations with the Young Turks were already stagnating, if not

speedily deteriorating. Hardinge himself stated the reasons to be
the Ottoman refusal to grant monopoly concessions to Britain in
Mesopotamia, the boycott on Greek trade and the nature of the
regime established by the CUP in the capital and in the provinces.[25]
Lowther added that Britain's friendship was regarded by the Ottomans and the Germans as limited to words because of her attitude
to the question on Crete, the Persian frontier and the Egyptian
problem, and of Britain's refusal to sell warships to the Porte.
The Embassy now accused the Young Turks of substituting Pan-
Islamism for Ottomanism, using the Islamic fervour of the people
for their chauvinistic purposes. Lowther also saw an ominous
growth of German influence in the Army, because of the Baghdad
Railway and Russia's capitulation in the previous year over
Bosnia.[26]

Consequently, Britain took a markedly stiffer line. This was
particularly so once evidence was received that the CUP, at their
Congress at Monastir, had abandoned the former policy of granting
equality and liberty to the Christians in Macedonia. The revelation
shocked the Foreign Office, where the Christian elements in Macedonia were still regarded as Ottomans, with merely religious bonds
with the Balkan States. 'The playing off of one nationality against
another', remarked Grey, 'is the old policy of Abdul-Hamid and
would lead to the same result.' He began to give credence to the
stories about the brutal policy of the Young Turks in their dis-
armament policy in Macedonia.[27] Moreover, already biased against
the Porte's policy with regard to the Baghdad Railway, the Gulf,
Crete, Persia and Egypt, the Foreign Office now accepted rather
readily the Bulgarian and Servian rejection of the CUP policy of
'Turcofication' in Albania and Macedonia.[28] Grey was particularly
revealing when he wrote to Nicolson, his new Permanent Under-
Secretary, that

> Turkey is going to give trouble: the Turks are continually
> doing unreasonable things and they are on the brink of great
> financial difficulty. Overweening ambition, arbitrary conduct
> and financial straits combined are a dangerous mixture.

Himself a renowned Turcophobe and Russophile, Nicolson agreed
entirely. He suggested a serious warning to the Porte, adding:

> I am not a great believer in the new regime, and am sceptical that

any Turk, young or old or middle-aged, would really place the Moslem and Christian on an equal footing.[29]

Not everyone in London shared these views. Mallet, despite his suspicion of the CUP's inclination towards Germany and Austria and their fear of Russia's backing Bulgaria, was not yet as pessimistic as Grey, Nicolson and his own subordinates.[30] Moreover, Winston Churchill, the Home Secretary, who visited Constantinople at this crucial point, brimmed over with optimism. He saw Talaat and Djavid, and was strongly impressed by the 'quality, vigour, and practical character' of the CUP Government. They appeared to him both in their views and methods 'thoroughly modern indeed ... their relations as colleagues and their general manner reminded me more of our own way of doing business than of the Ministers of any other country I have seen. No higher praise is in my power!' He felt sorrow that the Porte and England had drifted apart at a time when 'great hopes' could be seen for their winning the battle for regeneration and territorial integrity, though he appreciated the obstacles presented by Egypt, the Entente with Russia and the furor aroused by Lynch's demands for the extension of his Tigris navigation concession. He also told Blunt that he would advise the Porte to abstain from all wars for the next five years, while improving their army and finances.[31]

Block, too, had offered the Foreign Office a more optimistic view of the situation than the Embassy. He claimed that although the new regime recently relied more on the Triple Alliance, it would not throw in its lot with the German combination, since the CUP were opportunists and would 'always play off one power against another and try to get as much as they can from any or all of them'. He encouraged the British Government to exert its good influence through its many friends in the country, and added, 'I still think the respect for England will in the long run allow us to get a hearing when we offer our sympathy.' He saw improvements where Lowther had not, in the administration, finance, navy, and, of course, in the army, but admitted that the crux of the question was money.[32] For this reason, he strongly warned of the consequences of Djavid's failure to secure an 'honourable' French loan in September. This would cause the fall of Djavid, and drive the Young Turks entirely into the arms of the Triple Alliance. He defended the Young Turks in their desire to free themselves from the French after their experience with the Ottoman Bank:

I do not suppose that England wants to see the break up of the Young Turkey party or a reshuffling of the cards in this country. We know that these men have got the desire and the determination to rehabilitate the country even though they are inexperienced and commit many faults but we are absolutely in the dark as to what would happen should they disappear.[33]

Babington Smith, the Director of the National Bank, also advised showing genuine friendship to the Young Turks in their efforts to reorganize their country.[34] Although Lowther advised that strict terms should be attached to any Ottoman loan, he basically agreed with Block and Babington Smith as to its necessity.[35] The latter, however, had not appreciated the extent of the change in the Foreign Office's attitude during the summer of 1910. As Parker summarized correctly:

[circumstances had] changed in Turkey, there has been harsh treatment of the subject races in Macedonia, a rather unfriendly policy towards Greece, and signs of a military preparation on a disquieting scale. When the National Bank was started we hoped that Turkey was entering on a period of regeneration, which British finance might further; now, although we did so much for them two years ago, the Turks seem to be set on working against our interests, and also on a policy of extravagance which must end in bankruptcy.[36]

Two additional factors further complicated the situation. One was the spectre of Pan-Islam – a force which Lowther ultimately considered to be the distinguishing characteristic of the Young Turk movement, and one which he feared might affect lands as far removed as Algeria and Persia.[37] The other was the possibility that the new regime would enter into a formal association with the Triple Alliance. Despite Marschall's denial of the rumours to that effect, the fact that the Ottoman Empire eventually obtained its much-desired loan in Berlin, rather than in Paris, did give them some credence.[38] In the Foreign Office, where suspicion towards Germany was already quite strong, Mallet was sure that Germany was making every effort to bring the Ottoman Empire into the Triple Alliance and that 'in the event of European complications, in which England was involved as one of the principals, we should probably have to reckon with Turkey'.[39]

It was at this point (October 1910) that Nicolson made his only effort to open a new chapter in Anglo-Ottoman relations. Although a strong supporter of the Triple Entente, and notoriously anti-German, he specifically asked Lowther to reconsider the wisdom of Britain's previous attitude. The Ambassador, however, was unresponsive. He had already admitted that he was

> at a loss to suggest a special line of policy. If we are nice to them as we have been they accept it as their due, as they imagine themselves Constitutional. If we threaten them with measures we may never carry out, we only encourage them to fall into the arms of the Triple Alliance.

Nicolson's advice that he establish some relations with the Committee and that he 'try to speak some words of sense and guidance to them' elicited an equally unbending reply. In fact, Lowther seems to have been rather put out by Nicholson's implied suggestion that he was out of touch with the Committee (he had only avoided association with 'the more violent members'); and could see no alternative to 'plodding on' week after week in the old manner with the hope of occasional satisfaction.[40] Nicolson never again mentioned his idea of re-establishing better relations with the CUP. Instead, with the plight of the Christians in Macedonia noticeably worsening, he reverted wholeheartedly to the critical attitude already adopted by his predecessor. Little remained of the sympathy once expressed towards the new regime.

The proceedings at the Annual Congress of the CUP, held at Salonica between 31 October and 13 November 1910, seem to have transformed what had hitherto been a trend into policy. Initial reports had not been unfavourable. Lamb (the Consul-General in Salonica), Marling (the Chargé), and Gregory (at the Foreign Office) were all misled by the CUP's official publication into believing that 'the Committee appears to be embarking on a more conciliatory policy'.[41] But, by 17 December, the Foreign Office obtained fully authenticated and contrary reports. These finally established that the CUP had decided to pursue and intensify its former policy of Turcofication and Pan-Islamism. Marling's summary was precise and contemptuous:

> Indeed, the whole report breathes precisely the spirit of intolerance at home, and Chauvinism abroad, that might be expected from the secret committee of young inexperienced semi-Asiatics

invested with what appears to them to be absolute power un-
accompanied by responsibility, but it throws lurid light on the
committee's ideas of constitutional government.

These revelations proved to have a very strong impact on the
Foreign Office, where Gregory, contrary to his first reaction,
regarded the CUP's secret programme as 'a very truculent one',
which differed considerably from their published manifesto. It was
to be 'entirely' pro-German, and 'markedly reserved' towards the
Entente Powers, quite apart from the continuation of their policy of
repression, 'possibly extermination', of the Christian elements and
active Pan-Islamic propaganda beyond the Ottoman frontiers.[42]
Grey considered these revelations so important that he passed the
reports on to Asquith, adding: 'I think it is premature to assume that
the new regime in Turkey will definitely adopt and pursue an
oppressive policy, but we must be on our guard against possible
developments.' Asquith accepted Grey's judgement and in turn
circulated Marling's two despatches on the subject to the Cabinet.[43]
By now, the aggressive character of the CUP, both at home and
abroad, seemed to be beyond doubt.

Significantly, however, there remained a gulf between attitude
and action. Despite the prevailing attitude of resolute hostility, the
Foreign Office deliberately adopted a cautious policy towards the
CUP. Thus, it decided not to interfere in Macedonian affairs (on the
plea that the other Powers were in any case apathetic);[44] it also
resisted the India Office's demands for a stronger line towards a
recent series of Ottoman encroachments in the Persian Gulf. Instead,
it worked for an equitable arrangement over Persian Gulf and
Mesopotamian problems. Nicolson made it quite clear that Britain
could not afford to quarrel with the Young Turks and preferred
agreement to warlike action.[45] Grey, too, disagreed with Marling's
suggestion that by withholding financial aid, Britain might encourage those elements within Turkey which opposed the CUP.

> To attempt to bring down the ruling authority in Turkey by
> quarrelling with it is a risky policy: if it fails we lose everything; if
> it succeeds it is not certain that we should gain very much from
> what succeeds it.[46]

Nothing was further from Britain's mind than participation in an
anti-CUP *coup*.

Pan-Islamism, especially, was considered to be too delicate an issue to be amenable to such a solution. Informed of the 'extent and force' of the movement by Professor Arminius Vambéry and, less stridently, by Hardinge,[47] the Foreign Office thought that the best line would be 'to lead the Turks into a better disposition towards us' by creating a better atmosphere for an understanding over the Baghdad Railway, the Gulf and Mesopotamia. Further quarrels with the Porte might affect the distribution of British naval forces and worsen the situation in Macedonia as well as in Egypt and India.[48] Nevertheless, Nicolson thought that the Porte should not be provided with too much money. Here he brought up a completely new argument:

> This would only assist towards the creation of a power which, I think, in the not far distant future – should it become thoroughly consolidated and established – would be a very serious menace to us and also to Russia. It would be curious if, in this twentieth century, we witnessed a revival of the Ottoman Empire of the seventeenth century, and there is the additional danger that it would be able to utilize the enormous Mussulman population under the rule of Christian countries. I think that this Pan-Islamic movement is one of our greatest dangers in the future, and is indeed far more of a menace than the 'Yellow Peril' ... Germany is fortunate in being able to view with comparative indifference the growth of the great Mussulman military power, she having no Mussulman subjects herself, and a union between her and Turkey would be one of the gravest dangers to the equilibrium of Europe and Asia.[49]

From his vantage point at Constantinople, Lowther was certainly able to supply the Foreign Office with further evidence of Pan-Islamic activity. Nevertheless, he felt it his duty to temper the anxieties of his Government. The Pan-Islamic movement, he advised, was less dangerous than Nicolson thought; it could only achieve a 'community of interests', not a 'community of religion'. The Shia Persian abhorred the Sunni and was unlikely to collaborate with the Ottomans. The Arab, claimed Lowther, had no respect for the Turk as a Moslem, and moreover felt that the Caliphate should be in Arab hands. Nor did he regard it as dangerous in India since the Indian Sunnis considered the Young Turks as 'sacrilegious revolutionaries' who had deposed 'God's elect' from the Caliphate and replaced him with a puppet.[50] Although he regarded a struggle between the moderates and the extremists within the Ottoman capital as inevitable, he thought that the CUP was not at present interested in a row and that Hakki, the new Grand Vizier, would be allowed to 'muddle' through. He was exceptionally optimistic that the thorny Albanian question could be arranged in 'the usual way – baksheesh, decorations, grants of land, etc.'[51] But Lowther's reports have to be compared with those simultaneously despatched by Fitzmaurice. It was the latter who had become the main channel of understanding for the complexities of Ottoman politics, and his letters were read with considerable interest by Grey, Morley, and often Asquith. His antipathy towards the CUP (which was reciprocated by a series of vicious attacks written by Jahid in his newspaper, the *Tanin*, the organ of the extremists) was throughout apparent. Fitzmaurice warned the Foreign Office against treating the Baghdad Railway question in the manner adopted during Abdul-Hamid's 'pre-economic system of "out of debt, out of danger"'. The CUP did not mind running into debt in order to complete the Railway. He foresaw the possibility of the Ottomans and Germans building the Baghdad-Basra line without Britain if they were unable to achieve a favourable arrangement over Koweit, which would restore Ottoman sovereignty there. He was ready to hand over Koweit to a liberal Ottoman regime like Hilmi's, but not to Dr Nazim or Ismail Hakki Bey. The general discontent in Macedonia, Albania, Yemen and Arabia might now bring about the disintegration of the Ottoman Empire. He regretted that the Young Turks did not realize the value of 'moral force' in conducting their internal policy and preferred 'brutal methods' which might lead to their downfall.[52]

The Question of Albania

Britain's attitude towards Albanian issues during the period clearly indicated the direction in which her policy was now moving. Initially, the renewal of the Albanian rebellion in March 1911 did not give rise to anxiety in London. On Lowther's advice, Nicolson expressed his confidence in the Young Turks' ability to crush their opponents in the provinces[53] and the British Government attempted to adopt an attitude of neutrality between Montenegro and the Porte.[54] It refused to join Russia's representations and preferred to wait until more interested Powers, such as Austria and Italy, did so.[55] By May, however, a more pessimistic view of the future of the Ottoman Empire had gained ground. The Foreign Office now believed more than ever that unless the Porte changed its policy of Ottomanization, disturbances would spread and could not be dealt with simultaneously, with the result that 'the Turkish Empire would find itself threatened with something akin to disintegration'.[56] Events moved even more unfavourably for the Porte after the Albanian Mirdites had broken into open revolt. The Foreign Office now paid increasing attention to the anti-Ottoman reports despatched by Miss Edith Durham, the *Manchester Guardian*'s correspondent in the Balkans. Nicolson's emotional reaction to her 'melancholic' letter was an outburst of characteristic Turcophobia: 'The Turk is always the same and will remain so.'[57] By late June, therefore, Britain was prepared to ensure that the Powers guarantee non-molestation in the event of the Albanians surrendering their arms, and fulfil their requests on the questions of language, schools and road improvements. This was obviously a step towards the Albanian demand for wide autonomy.[58] Although the Foreign Office denied any intention to initiate a formal collective representation to the Porte, and later rejected Cartwright's suggestion that the fleet be ordered to Mitylene, it did practically warn the Ottomans that the Albanian question, if not solved, might have repercussions outside the Ottoman Empire. War could be avoided only through an Austro-Russian understanding.[59] The Foreign Office had finally decided to abandon Britain's former friendly policy towards the new regime:

> We have during the last two or three years been exceedingly tolerant and gentle with the Turks and the result of our benevolent attitude has by no means been satisfactory [Nicolson wrote to Hardinge] and I do not see that a return to a firmer and less conciliatory attitude, is not likely to make more impression upon the Porte than the course which we have hitherto followed.[60]

Even the end of the Albanian rebellion was not interpreted as an Ottoman victory. On the contrary, the Foreign Office was now decidedly inclined to accept the most pessimistic reports as to the future of the new regime and consequently of the Ottoman Empire. The most significant example was the prompt manner whereby Nicolson confirmed the prognosis of Milovanovitch, the Servian Prime Minister, that the break-up of the Ottoman Empire would come from within and would be followed by a general attack upon the European provinces of the 'crumbling' Ottoman Empire.

> This is not a cheerful forecast, but I daresay it is not far from what may take place. Personally [wrote Nicolson to Lowther], I should view with great equanimity the break up of the Turkish regime and Turkish Empire in Europe. I have no desire to see either consolidated, for I consider that were they to become strong they could be a menace to every Power with Muhamedan subjects, and especially to us who hold Egypt and India. The Young Turks would never make the lot of the Christian a happy one or accord to him equal right with the Moslem, and the Young Turks have shown that their aims are but little dissimilar from old time methods as abominable as those of Abdul-Hamid.[61]

Significantly, Nicolson deliberately concealed from Lowther that Milovanovitch was the source of his information. The Ambassador himself was far less pessimistic.

> I see no cause for conflagration although discontent will be sure to reign ... I entirely agree with you that it is most undesirable that Turkey should become strong, and their very nature will always prevent their being a menace to us. But would it not bother us a lot to see Austria very strong here, and possibly in possession of Salonica, or do you count on Russia stopping that? The collapse of Turkey would offer so many possibilities in the future in the Mediterranean that I will not dare to touch on any of them.[62]

Thus, it was with some reservations that the Ambassador transmitted to the Foreign Office a very pessimistic report by Morgan, the Acting Consul-General at Salonica. The latter suggested that only the accession of a strong Sultan like Mahmud II could save the Ottoman Empire: 'This not probable; the sooner Turkey is taken over by a civilized Power, the better for the unfortunate population, of whatever race or creed.'[63] It was significant that there was no objection in the Foreign Office to Morgan's anti-Ottoman report. Officials found his report merely 'interesting' and did not comment on Lowther's remark: '... if Morgan thought the CUP was so shaky at Salonica, how do they still keep power at Constantinople?' The Foreign Office, indeed, under Nicolson's guidance, was moving fast towards the most pessimistic view of the future of the new regime.

The events culminating in the Tripoli War showed that Britain was much less concerned with the survival of the Ottoman Empire in September 1911 than she had been in April 1909.

Britain's Policy of Interests

Where the Foreign Office and the Embassy principally differed, then, was in their estimates of the Empire's prospects of survival. Their views of the ends of British policy more closely coincided. As much was indicated by their respective attitudes towards the increasing signs of Balkan nationalism. Of these, the most pressing was the question of Bulgaria. The Foreign Office was not prepared, immediately and unequivocally, to support the Russian demand for recognition of Bulgarian independence; to do so before the Porte had signalled its acquiescence would merely throw the Ottomans into the arms of Germany and Austria. Nevertheless, there was to be no question of acceding to the Ottoman request that Britain act independently with regard to Ferdinand's claim to a monarchical title in Bulgaria. 'We must not sacrifice our interests for the sake of Turkish friendship which is ephemeral', wrote Hardinge as early as the spring of 1909. The important thing was to preserve Anglo-Russian amity whilst also preventing Ottoman dependence upon Germany.[64] In an attempt to walk this tightrope, Britain recognized Ferdinand as Roi des Bulgares in May 1909; and yet at the same time fostered the establishment of an Ottoman-Bulgarian Federation with leanings towards the Triple Entente (in the hope that the Ottomans would eventually prove strong enough to resist the aggression implicit in Bulgarian nationalism).[65] Lowther dissented: he foresaw complications arising out of a rapprochement between the Ottoman Empire and Bulgaria, and was less alarmist with respect to the danger that the Germans might acquire the upper hand in Constantinople. Besides, the best way to counter German influence was to intensify Britain's commercial and financial activity in the Ottoman Empire.[66]

Ultimately, this was precisely what the Foreign Office was itself to attempt to do. Meanwhile, however, London had to define its attitude towards a range of subsidiary Balkan crises. Where these did not apparently affect Britain's interests directly, there existed a degree of residual sympathy towards the Ottomans. Thus, when the Cretan question created tension between Greeks and Turks in the summer of 1909, the Foreign Office demonstrated distinct impatience with Greek demands. Although deprecating too bellicose an Ottoman attitude, Mallet was convinced that a 'little severity' would do little harm, and was the only way to consolidate the Ottoman Empire.[67] Similarly, hints that a Servo-Bulgarian understanding would be in order before the collapse of the Empire were quashed, with the comment that 'the one hope is that all these aspirations may be knocked on the head by the existence of a strong and regenerated Turkey, who will be able to hold her own against them'.[68] Whatever the truth in the Servian and Bulgarian complaints that their 'co-religionists' in Macedonia were placed at a disadvantage by the new Law of Association, 'it is very desirable that brigandage should be stamped out'.[69] Although Grey's public statements on this issue did not go as far as either the Young Turks themselves or Buxton and the Balkan Committee may have wished, he did attempt to steer a middle course, by supporting an Ottoman rule which was firm as well as just. Thus, 'I shall be glad to give as much prominence as possible to any punishments inflicted upon officials guilty ... or to any steps taken to prevent the recurrence of cruelty when I am informed of them.'[70]

The relative stability achieved by 1909 meant that the struggle for concessions could be renewed. The Ottoman request for a customs increase met with a rigid British attitude. Britain decided that this should be used as 'a convenient weapon' with which either to 'force' participation in the Baghdad Railway or to obtain a rival concession in the Tigris Valley.[71] Hardinge told Djevad, the Ottoman Chargé, that British trade would greatly suffer from a customs increase. 'I pointed out [to Djevad]', Hardinge informed Lowther, 'that we had already done a very great deal to assist the Turkish Government since the revolution, that we were still working and doing all we could in their favour, but it was a little hard that we should also be asked to help them at the expense of injury to our trade.' At the time, the contradictions inherent in its policy were not apparent to the British Government; indeed, as far as the Foreign Office was concerned, no such contradictions existed.[72] But the Porte, encouraged by Germany, was certainly concerned; Rifaat was 'very depressed' by Hardinge's reply to Djevad on the customs increase. As Lowther warned, 'if we make the terms too severe they will round on us and say our sympathy is all froth'.[73]

During this period, the only issue on which the British felt it necessary to make representations at Constantinople concerned the Ottoman occupation of Zakhnuniya, an action which was considered to be a threat to Britain's position on the Gulf.[74] Nevertheless, Britain did seek to strengthen and consolidate her position in Mesopotamia by other means. This was shown by the Government's (premature) support for D'Arcy's British syndicate's request for an oil concession in Mosul and Baghdad.[75] More particularly, it was displayed by the British attitude towards the railway and navigation issues. Initially, the Government's policy was moderate. Responding to pressure from Block and Lowther, and acting in accordance with the decision of an Interdepartmental Committee on Mesopotamian Railways, the Foreign Office in July 1909 agreed to separate the question of railway concessions in Asiatic Turkey from that of the customs increase.[76] Lowther was instructed, accordingly, to request a concession for a railway *via* the Tigris from Baghdad to the Gulf and for an extension to the Mediterranean should the development of irrigation and trade in Mesopotamia render such a line desirable. By September, however, Hilmi had begun to express his reluctance to grant these concessions, and Hardinge therefore recommended that Britain use them as a lever against the Ottomans. Hilmi's final reply to the British application would be regarded as 'a good indication of the attitude of the Turkish Government' towards Britain. The Ottoman application for a customs increase could thus be used to re-establish Britain's position in Mesopotamia which had been 'seriously imperilled by the undisguised hostility of the late regime'. Britain's consistent support for the new regime certainly entitled her, so it was felt in London, to the railway concession, and Hardinge wrote: 'The moment seems to me an important one, since we have done a very great deal for the Turks during the past eighteen months, and so far have received absolutely nothing in return.'[77] As he was to reiterate some three months later: 'it is now time for them to show their gratitude in a practical form.'[78]

These attempts to re-establish British supremacy and prestige in Mesopotamia and the Gulf had to overcome two major obstacles. One was the suspicion of the Porte that underlying Britain's interest in railway concessions lay a desire to partition the Ottoman Empire.[79] The other was the objection of the Germans to the construction of an independent British railway to Mesopotamia which would compete with their own line there. The Foreign Office did not link these two obstacles; indeed, Hardinge denied that there yet existed a systematic tendency on the part of the Porte to lean towards the Triple Alliance.[80] Nevertheless, the degree to which the German and Ottoman positions complemented each other was unmistakable. Metternich, the German Ambassador in London, as early as October 1909 left Grey in no doubt of Germany's objections to British control of the southern part of the Baghdad Railway, which he described as the 'most valuable part of the whole line'. Von Schoen, German Foreign Secretary, some months later, demanded a *quid pro quo* from Britain in return for Lynch's monopoly of navigation on the Tigris and British control of the Baghdad-Gulf railway.[81] But the Foreign Office was adamant. According to Hardinge, it had every reason to be so. Britain, he estimated, held two important cards: a quotation on the Paris Bourse and the Turkish request for a 4 per cent customs increase. Hence she could demand either an independent line to the Gulf or control over the southern section of the Baghdad Railway. Ottoman objections to the former had to be met with a stiff attitude in regard to the customs increase (the only point on which the Foreign Office was prepared to give way concerned Egyptian borrowing powers);[82] German objections to the latter had to be rebuffed by the claim that the concession for the Baghdad-Gulf line would merely compensate for the 'damage' to be suffered by British navigation interests below Baghdad, should the Germans obtain the exclusive right to build the railway. After Cassel's conversation with Gwinner, the German financier, in December 1909, the British Government insisted that Britain's share in the Baghdad-Gulf line be at least 55 per cent.[83]

The British determined to be equally firm on allied questions. In response to Lowther's pleas for time and patience, the Foreign Office did agree not to press the Porte on the point of the status of the Sheikh of Koweit.[84] But it did fully support the claims of Lynch's Euphrates and Tigris Steam Navigation Company for a renewal of their concessions under the new regime. Particularly noteworthy was the reaction to reports that Sassoon Effendi and the Arab deputies in the Chamber, together with Halajian, the Minister of Public Works, who was under German guidance, were threatening to block the concession; Mallet then suggested that the only possible response had to be an unofficial hint to the Porte that consent could not be given to the 4 per cent customs increase.[85] Similarly, when Willcocks administered 'a stab in the back' to Lynch by stating publicly that the Euphrates would dry up as a result of the projected irrigation works, the British Government insisted on compensation in this eventuality.[86] Ultimately, once Hilmi had tendered his resignation on 28 December, Britain found herself supporting him and the CUP against the machinations of the German Embassy.[87]

The Hakki Cabinet, which replaced Hilmi's on 31 December, presented further difficulties for British policy in Mesopotamia. Hardinge was now 'very sceptical' as to the possibility of obtaining the Porte's consent to British control and construction of the Baghdad-Gulf line. But, together with the abolition of the embargo on Egyptian borrowing power, it was to be a *sine qua non* of Britain's consent to the 4 per cent customs duties increase.[88] At the same time, Britain also opposed the Porte's scheme to grant the German company the excess of the tithes for the kilometric guarantees for the Helif-Baghdad section, as this would damage British trade. The result was an impasse in the negotiations. The Germans were prepared to give way on the railway only in return for a wider Anglo-German agreement. This suggestion the Foreign Office dismissed as an attempt to isolate Britain from her Russian and French friends.[89] The situation also brought an aggravation of Anglo-Ottoman relations. The Ottoman Ambassador was told that the Porte was acting in 'complete disregard' of British interests and was not fulfilling its promise to modify the 1903 Convention, 'in spite of all that HMG had done to assist the new regime, and of the friendly and even enthusiastic support, both moral and material, which had been extended by this country to Turkey, more especially during the crisis of 1908-9'. Grey was ready to give the Porte the most binding assurances that Britain had no political designs in Mesopotamia. But he could not, he commented in April 1910, remain indifferent to the threat to Britain's economic position in Mesopotamia, the political situation in the Gulf, or the 'important influence' the latter would have on India. Lowther was therefore instructed to renew the application for the Tigris Railway to be built nominally by an Ottoman Company.[90]

This move gave rise to another difference of opinion between the Embassy and the Foreign Office. Lowther pointed out that the Ottoman Army, influenced by the Germans, was determined to complete the railway line to Baghdad. That being the case, he doubted whether financial pressure on Britain's part would be helpful. In fact, Britain's policy seemed to be self-defeating: 'Germany's threats seem to carry a good deal more weight than our protestations of a friendly attitude.' But these criticisms merely earned Hardinge's reproach.[91] The Foreign Office believed that a strong line would strengthen the hands of those like Djavid who did not favour the continuation of the Baghdad Railway on the conditions laid down in the 1903 concession. Eventually, when Lowther did apply again for the Tigris concession, on 3 May, Rifaat promised merely to try and obtain the right to build the southern section from the Germans. But the chances that this rather 'childish' move would succeed became even more improbable when, according to Block, Djavid gave way to the military party.[92] The crux of the problem was that Germany had also put pressure on the Ottomans to complete the Baghdad Railway and the Porte claimed that two parallel lines in Mesopotamia would not pay. The extent to which the German and Ottoman positions now openly coincided was revealed when Metternich berated the British Liberal Government for being more imperialist than the former Conservative one, which had merely asked for a port on the Gulf.[93]

The CUP's policy of centralization threatened not only Britain's interests in Mesopotamia, but also her more important position on the Persian Gulf where the Porte was determined to re-establish Ottoman prestige and authority. Thus the quasi-autonomous status of the Sheikhs of Koweit and Mohammera was challenged and the privileged position of the British Residency at Baghdad encroached upon. These moves convinced both the India Office and the Foreign Office that Hakki's regime presented even more of a threat to British interests than had Hilmi's. Mallet appreciated that Britain had to respond; but he could not recommend the adoption of forceful measures. Instead, pending a final settlement, a *modus vivendi* had to be found:

> There may be inconvenience in this course, but we have hitherto gained nothing by complaisance to Turkey, whereas Austria, who filched from them two provinces, is on the best terms with them, as Sir G. Lowther points out. On the other hand, Austria is a powerful and dangerous neighbour and is able to put pressure on Turkey whereas we cannot do anything beyond occupying the Customs houses of an island or two.[94]

It was agreed in the Foreign Office that, if possible, ships-of-war should not be sent to the head of the Gulf, in order not to give to 'the Turkish chauvinists' a pretext for the immediate purchase of gun-boats for the Gulf. But the situation worsened when the Vali of Baghdad appointed a Mudir at El Odeid on the Trucial Coast. Parker,[95] in response to pressure from the India Office, demanded that the Admiralty should make preparations for landing forces for 'the effect of unhesitating action at Odeid may be salutary else-where'. A serious clash was only avoided when it was discovered that the Government of India had been misinformed.[96]

The Foreign Office continued to advocate a policy of limited response at the end of October, when the India Office again pressed for a firm line. One reason, as Marling pointed out, was the 'very anomalous nature' of Britain's relations with the local chieftains.[97] Another was the feeling, shared by Grey and Nicolson, that Britain had to adopt a moderate line in the Gulf for fear of Pan-Islamic propaganda. Nicolson admitted that the India Office and especially the British Resident in the Gulf were clamouring for action in view of the waning British influence, but

> ... any action of a determined character which we might take in those regions would produce a very far-reaching effect and, were we to alienate the Turkish Government by any acts of force, we might feel the effects pretty soon in Egypt and Persia, and perhaps even in India.[98]

Ultimately, it was decided that British policy should combine a mixture of financial pressure and military demonstration in the form of occasional visits by British ships to the Gulf. In any case, the storms looming ahead of the new regime led Nicolson to doubt the possibility of Britain's ever obtaining absolute control over the Baghdad-Gulf section of the Baghdad Railway. Instead, he suggested that Britain should now concentrate her efforts in fortify-ing her position at the terminus at Koweit.[99] This was a reflection of the change which had taken place in the Foreign Office's position on 27 July 1910: no monopoly to Britain, but none to Germany either. Moreover, Britain's position was further weakened by the Potsdam agreement of November 1910, between Germany and Russia, which gave the latter a free hand to build a railway between Tehran and Khanikin (thus bypassing the traditional commercial route to Persia via Baghdad, which was a British monopoly) in return for

Russian consent to Germany's completion of the Baghdad Railway to Basra.[100]

On 1 March 1911 Rifaat presented the Ottoman counter-proposals on the Baghdad Railway. These offered Britain only a 20 per cent share in the Baghdad-Gulf line, and demanded direct Ottoman control over the terminus at Koweit. The Porte's stand was now much stronger in view of the loan granted to her by Germany.[101] The Foreign Office considered those terms disappointing. As Nicolson pointed out, it would obviously be regarded as a diplomatic defeat for Britain were a 60 per cent share in the line to go to the Porte and Germany.[102] Thus, little notice was taken of British supporters of the new regime like Noel Buxton and Block, who sided with the Porte in these matters.[103] Nevertheless, neither was the Foreign Office prepared to adopt the sharp anti-Ottoman line proposed by the Government of India. Rather, it tended to regard the negotiations *per se* as important. This was in marked contrast to Hardinge, who was 'very sick' at the Ottoman reply, and demanded a firm attitude on the Gulf, especially at Koweit, where Germany stood behind the Porte. Any concession, he claimed, would encourage the latter towards further encroachments in the Gulf area. The Foreign Office, however, continued to advocate caution.[104] Parker warned that in the event of a disagreement between the Porte and Britain, the Ottoman policy of 'pinpricks' in the Gulf, accompanied by Moslem agitation in Egypt, would become more frequent:

> We may be in a situation bordering on war with Turkey. To judge by the recent Turco-Italian incident in the Red Sea it seems that Turkey would climb down if we really showed our teeth, as she did at the time of the Akaba incident: but we are not in quite such a good position as Italy, because of our large Mussulman population ... before very long we may be faced with a Fashoda incident with Turkey or continual submission to her claims

The Foreign Office did move slowly towards the idea, recommended by both the Board of Trade and the India Office, that Britain demand no less than 50 per cent participation in the Baghdad-Gulf line, on condition that Koweit and not Basra, was the terminus.[105] Nevertheless, it rejected Lowther's suggestion that Britain change the *status quo* at Bahrein in retaliation for the arrest of some Bahreinis in Basra on the charge that they had refused to take out Ottoman passports as demanded by the local Vali.[106]

It was against this background that Anglo-Ottoman relations were discussed in detail by the Committee of Imperial Defence on 4 May 1911. General W. Nicholson, the Chief of the Imperial General Staff, warned that the Ottoman Army was 'very large' and was rapidly improving. Moreover, British naval or military operations in the Ottoman Empire could only be 'temporary', since it could not be imagined that British ships or troops could be kept there permanently. The Porte could meanwhile retaliate by creating trouble in Egypt. Kitchener said that if Britain allowed the Porte to take over Koweit it would have a 'serious' effect on India. But he thought that all really depended on the campaign in troubled Yemen. Grey took the most bellicose line when he argued that Britain could exploit the precarious Ottoman situation in the Yemen by interrupting the flow of reinforcements. He recognized that this was an act of war, 'but war must be faced if necessary.' The CID, however, concluded that the Porte could not be coerced.[107] The Foreign Office, too, wished, if possible, to maintain the *status quo* in the Gulf, which might be achieved if the moderates obtained the upper hand at Constantinople. Lowther, who also favoured a moderate line, warned that the 4 per cent customs increase could not be refused for much longer without causing a breach with the Porte.[108]

Thus, by mid-1911, relations between Britain and the Ottoman Empire could be described as hostile, but not critical. Lowther reported that the sympathy shown towards the Ottoman Empire by Britain at the beginning of the new regime no longer counted – especially, as the Turks reportedly put it, since 'it did not come out of British pockets.' The British refusal to concede the 4 per cent, the *temettu* tax and a loan made the British Government 'the principal offenders' and 'obstructionists' to the regeneration of Ottoman finance and consequently the enemies of the new regime.[109]

Hardinge in India claimed that he was not at all worried about any danger from the Indian Moslems in the event of war between Britain and the Ottoman Empire. He regarded the current Pan-Islamic policy of the Porte as a 'fallacy', although he did warn that unless checked it might turn out to be 'a dangerous political factor'. He suggested that Britain first declare her protection over Bahrein, then send a ship to Basra, seize Ottoman vessels and remove the Ottoman posts in the Gulf. Once the Bahrein crisis had blown over, he suggested spreading the rumour that Britain was sending one or two warships to Hodeida to prevent reinforcements reaching the Yemen. This would be enough to deter the Porte since the presence of a British warship would bring about a general rising of the tribes. Altogether, Hardinge wished that the Ottomans would 'get a knock. It would do them a world of good', and he was upset that the time was not opportune.[110]

The Persian Gulf remained, therefore, the main problem for the British Government in formulating its policy towards the Porte. The standing sub-committee of the CID, which had been appointed under Morley's chairmanship by the Prime Minister on 8 May, finally decided on Britain's policy on 14 July: Basra was preferable as the railway terminus since it would avoid many awkward questions; Britain was ready to admit Ottoman suzerainty over Koweit and the Sheikh as an Ottoman Kaimakam, but would expect the Porte to recognize her arrangements with the Sheikh in 1899 and 1907. The southernmost limit of Ottoman jurisdiction acceptable was to be Ojair in El Katif. A few days later, on 26 July, it was decided, at an interdepartmental level, that the British Government should ask for a 20 per cent share of the Baghdad-Gulf line provided that Russia and France received the same share; this would create a majority of 60 per cent for the Entente in the railway. Since the Ottomans, backed by the Germans, offered only 40 per cent for the Entente and excluded Russia, the Foreign Office expected the negotiations to be long and difficult. But it would maintain a 'very firm' attitude on these questions, linking them to the consent to the increase of the customs dues to 15 per cent and the removal of the restrictions on the borrowing powers of Egypt. The proposals were submitted to the Porte and to the Germans on 29 July 1911, and regarded as a concession by Nicolson.[111]

Henceforth, the struggle for British interests in Mesopotamia was to be mostly restricted to the Persian Gulf, and to a lesser extent to the Gulf-Baghdad section of the Baghdad Railway. The Foreign Office in 1911 largely abandoned its interest in navigation and in irrigation. When Willcocks resigned from his position as an adviser in the Ottoman Ministry for Public Works, the Foreign Office was happy that he had been employed by the Porte without taking Britain's advice.[112]

4

ON THE EVE OF CATASTROPHE

Britain, the Tripoli War and the Formation of the Balkan League (September 1911 – October 1912)

The Tripoli Crisis[1]

The threat to Ottoman rule in the Vilayet of Tripoli stemmed from Italy's economic penetration of the province and her complaints of ill-treatment to her citizens there. It increased once the Moroccan question had been settled in France's favour. Italy now demanded a similar position in Tripoli. The Foreign Office appreciated the implied difficulties for British policy. 'If the Powers of the Triple Entente wish to secure the goodwill of Italy, they must acquiesce in her designs on Tripoli. If they do this they must presumably *pro tanto* alienate the sympathy of Turkey and throw her more and more into the arms of Germany.'[2]

Britain had decided upon her attitude a few days before the outbreak of hostilities between Italy and the Ottoman Empire in September 1911. Should the Porte appeal for British intervention, in Rome, Grey proposed to refer the Ottomans to Italy's allies, Germany and Austria. 'It is most important,' he maintained, 'that neither we nor France should side against Italy now.' He accepted the Italian version of the situation in Tripoli, and was even prepared to tell the Porte that 'any action Italy took to defend her interests had been brought by the Turks upon themselves'.[3] British policy had to be one of 'expectancy and neutrality', and principally designed to avoid throwing Italy 'into the arms of Germany and Austria'. Grey did admit that an Italian attack on Tripoli might cause 'great embarrassment' to Britain, because of her numerous Moslem subjects. It might also impair her position in the Ottoman navy.[4] Yet, there was no doubt as to where British sympathies lay. Mallet and Nicolson deplored the critical line of the majority of the British press on the Italian action. They were anxious lest Britain should lose Italy's friendship which had been firm ever since Italian unity,[5] and, in Nicolson's words, thought it

> ... exceedingly foolish that we should displease a country [Italy] with whom we have always been on most friendly terms and whose friendship to us is of very great value, in order to keep well with Turkey, who has been a source of great annoyance to us and whose Government is one of the worst that can well be imagined ... If, as I imagine, the second Turkish appeal for European intervention does not succeed, the Turks will then set to work to cause us all as much trouble as they possibly can.[6]

Kitchener's assessment of 'complete tranquillity' in Egypt further reassured Nicolson as to the correctness of his policy.[7] Hardinge demurred: 'I have never heard of a worse case of brigandage than the seizure of Tripoli by Italy.'[8] But even after Said Pasha had replaced Hakki in Constantinople, the Foreign Office did not modify its tone. Rather, as early as 16 October, the Porte was advised to accept the fact that Tripoli was practically lost. The 'obscure' situation at Constantinople served as another excuse for British rejection of Ottoman pleas for intervention in Rome.[9]

The British did oppose the Italian suggestion that the Porte should be granted the 4 per cent Customs dues increase as part of the future settlement between Italy and the Porte. ('We have our own ends to gain by any such concession.'[10]) But they were not worried about any advantage the Triple Alliance might gain by Italy's occupation of Tobruk: 'So long as we maintain our naval supremacy, the possession of Tripoli must weaken Italy.'[11] On the contrary, the greater fear was that the Ottoman Empire might score some military success in Tripoli:

> ... they would [then] become perfectly impossible, and we should find them exceedingly difficult to deal with in cases which are pending between us, and also probably a great impression would be made on the Mussulmans in Egypt and possibly in India.[12]

Thus, the Foreign Office refused to intervene when warned by the Porte of a possible Italian attack on the Dardanelles.[13] Moreover, although Nicolson did consider the annexation of Tripoli and Cyrenaica on 5 November 'premature', he was more concerned about the 'most unfortunate' anti-Italian attitude of the British press: 'I am afraid that this will affect our friendly relations with Italy, which it is most desirable to promote and maintain.' He soon realized that the extension of the area of hostilities might create internal complications and encourage the Balkan States to exploit the opportunity. But, basically, the British Government wished to remain passive spectators,[14] and this attitude could not be altered by either Lowther or Churchill.[15]

The British came closer to 'strict neutrality' when Grey expressed his criticism of Italy's policy on 14 November: 'The Italians have been very foolish in putting out their foot so far in this Tripoli business; they had a fair case for squeezing guarantees for economic interests in Tripoli and the reversion of Tripoli out of the Turks.' Nicolson also doubted the astuteness of the Italians, since he could not see how Italy could inflict a severe blow on the Ottomans: 'I am afraid Italy will weary of the war before Turkey, and that the latter will be able to continue passive resistance indefinitely.'[16] Moreover, the possibility of prolonged Ottoman resistance to an Italian attack on the Dardanelles occupied the attention of the Foreign Office more than ever before. As Grey stated: 'I think our interest in the grain trade and commercial shipping connected with the Black Sea is such that we could not stand the Black Sea trade being stopped by this wretched war.'[17]

The possible effect of the War on Moslem opinion elsewhere was another moderating factor. Hardinge, on 30 November 1911, spoke of 'considerable effervescence' among the Indian Moslems (although he also admitted that they were too preoccupied with their hostility to the Hindus to involve themselves fully in the 'Turkish question');[18] Lowther also reported the view that an Ottoman withdrawal from the Tripoli vilayet would produce 'a frightful row' in the Yemen, Assyr and 'other Arab provinces'. Sir Mark Sykes, MP, raised the Pan-Islamic question in the House of Commons on 27 November (albeit only to deny its importance).[19] Even in the Foreign Office, where the Turks were generally held in low esteem, some voices expressed the fear that 'Italy's aggression will tend to unify Moslem feeling'.[20] These fears increased early in 1912, when British officials also began to worry lest a continuation of hostilities in Tripoli might give rise to complications in the

Balkans.[21] Speaking for the Government of India, Hardinge advised that Britain should not take a back seat in any future mediation between Italy and the Ottomans:

> It is most important for us to be able to show to the Muhamma-dans of India that we have been doing what we can to put an end to the war with Italy which they resent very much and regard as the beginning of the end of Islam in Europe. They think also that we might have stopped it.

Nicolson was sympathetic; under these circumstances, pressure on the Porte was out of the question.[22]

More especially was this so once the Tripoli War extended beyond Africa. The Italian bombardment of the Dardanelles on 17 April was deplored both at the diplomatic level and (by Lord Morley) in Parliament, particularly since it raised British fears as to the effect of the closure of the Straits on trade.[23] The Italian occupation of Rhodes (and then of all twelve Dodecanese islands) in May, posed further difficulties. In the event of war with the Triple Alliance, admitted the Admiralty, Italian naval bases in the Aegean Sea and the eastern Mediterranean would constitute a threat to Egypt and also to the Levant and Black Sea trade.[24] So serious was the warning that the Foreign Office feared that the Cabinet might be persuaded to evacuate the British Fleet from the Mediterranean – an eventuality which would have a crucial effect on Britain's position both at Constantinople and at Rome.[25] The Foreign Office ultimately won the battle with the Admiralty since the CID decided to maintain the one-power standard in the Mediterranean, which meant a British Fleet equal or superior to that of Austria.[26] Never-theless, preference was given to the North Sea in the event of war, and it was decided to risk further dependence on the French Navy. On the whole, this implied a weakening of Britain's position in the area.

Meanwhile, Britain's attitude remained uneasy. The Govern-ment repeatedly claimed that it would never enforce unacceptable conditions on the Porte out of consideration for the Moslems of India; yet it opposed the German suggestion that the Tobacco Regie should advance a loan to the Porte. The reason, said Mallet, was that such 'mischievous advice' might be an obstacle to peace with Italy. Cassel's refusal to lend money to the Porte was also approved on the same grounds.[27]

The Coming of the Balkan Wars[28]

Meanwhile, clouds had once again begun to gather around the Balkans. Initially, they seem to have escaped British attention. Thus, officials at the Foreign Office did not pay much notice to the first reports that the 'seed of a future entente has been sown' between Sofia and Belgrade. They considered the Balkan Federation still 'very far distant' since the Balkan States distrusted both the Porte and each other.[29] They therefore dismissed Izvolsky's warning that serious trouble might very shortly occur.[30] Even when Bax-Ironside informed the Foreign Office that serious negotiations were taking place between Bulgaria and Servia with the intention of dividing up Macedonia in the event of the disintegration of the Ottoman Empire, the Foreign Office was still unmoved. Moreover, Lowther had no idea of what was going on between Sofia and Belgrade.[31]

In fact, events in the Balkans were developing faster and more ominously than in Tripoli. Servia and Bulgaria signed a secret treaty of alliance and friendship on 11 and 13 March 1912 respectively. Since the engagement was backed by Russia, it was interpreted in the Foreign Office as an anti-Austrian move, and therefore much regretted since it lessened the chance of Russo-Austrian rapprochement in Balkan affairs.[32] Indeed, it was the increasingly anti-Ottoman attitude adopted by Russia, as exemplified by the controversy on both the Ottoman-Persian and the Caucasian frontiers, which chiefly concerned officials. Britain was, understandably, most unwilling to annoy Russia, and yet officials in the Foreign Office could not deny that Russia had put British policy into a 'mess'. Britain was thus again caught between her need to retain the firm friendship of Russia and the bogey that an anti-Ottoman policy would arouse the danger of Pan-Islam.[33] She would far rather have preferred a rapprochement between the Porte and the Balkan States which would have guaranteed peace: 'Such a rapprochement', in Mallet's words, 'would relieve us of any difficulties which might arise with Russia, if she pursued a policy hostile to Turkey.'[34]

But that was precisely the policy which the Russians seemed intent on pursuing. By the end of April, Russia's friendship towards the Italians was particularly conspicuous, and her itch to take advantage of whatever tensions might arise in the Balkans was suspiciously apparent. Nicolson, as always, was the most sensitive to the change – and the most worried:

> I do not know if at the back of his [Sazonov's] mind he has any desire that trouble should ensue in the Balkans which might justify Russian intervention on behalf of the Balkan States and therefore gradually lead perhaps to the expulsion of Turkey from those regions. In any case I think he is playing a dangerous game.... I think, however, that it is absolutely essential that we should at all costs maintain to the full our understanding [in Persia] with Russia. I should view with absolute dismay were it to be in any way seriously impaired and if our relations with Russia were to become cold.

Grey added a further dimension to Nicolson's apprehensions: 'If Russia comes out heavily against Turkey it will not suit us, because of the Mohammadans in India.'[35] Lowther also felt that the change of Russian Ambassadors at Constantinople was more than a personal one: 'I should not be surprised to see a succession of pinpricks with the eventual intention of bringing about the collapse of Turkey.'[36]

By May, Nicolson had discovered through the Embassy in St Petersburg, that the Bulgaro-Servian treaty was of 'a more serious and far-reaching character than we originally supposed' and that the division of Macedonia had in fact been decided upon. This he considered to be a result of Sazonov's 'adventurous' policy. Nevertheless, he instructed the British Chargé in St Petersburg not to disclose his apprehensions to Sazonov, since 'at the present moment it is exceedingly necessary for us to keep on the best possible terms with Russia.' Initially, however, he was confident that no trouble would occur in 1912.

This attitude became increasingly untenable once an Albanian revolt was seen to be imminent. In May 1912, in fact, the Albanians submitted to Ghazi Moukhtar's Government a programme which amounted to autonomy,[38] and which was independently propagated by both Austria and Russia. Sazonov hoped that autonomy in Albania would serve as a 'stepping-stone' for the introduction of 'serious' reforms in Macedonia; he pressed the scheme on Britain as 'the only way' to keep Bulgaria and Servia quiet. Mallet, once again the Porte's chief advocate in the Foreign Office, disagreed. He preferred to give Ghazi Moukhtar's Government a chance to prove itself and told the Russian Chargé in London that he 'personally' was much afraid to give 'so much' advice to the Porte just now. Grey expressed the prevailing thought as late as August: 'Justice and good government is really all that is wanted in Macedonia.' Mallet was therefore allowed to carry on with his policy of non-intervention in Ottoman internal affairs as illustrated by his remarks to the Bulgarian Minister: 'It was unnecessary to say that I was strongly in sympathy with administrative reforms, but precipitation might throw things back and lead to a recrudescence of chauvinism in Turkey.'[39]

Meanwhile, the unsettled situation in the Ottoman European provinces and the growing ferment amongst the population convinced the Montenegrin Government that the time was ripe to strike at Ottoman rule. Contacts with Bulgaria were established in May when the Porte had decided to renew its annual subsidy to King Nicholas of Montenegro. On 11 June a joint commission signed an Ottoman-Montenegrin Protocol which promised to settle the controversial frontiers of the two countries. Delayed ratification on the Porte's side, because of anxieties as to Albanian reaction, led the Montenegrins to seize the opportunity to fulfil their long-delayed national goals. In July they launched a series of attacks on Ottoman border positions which culminated in a serious clash at Berana early in August.[40]

The frontier incident at Berana convinced Mallet that it was necessary for Marling to use strong language at the Porte. On this occasion, he did not challenge Norman's assertion that the Ottoman behaviour was 'a return to Committee methods'. Nevertheless, Britain was not ready to take the initiative or to act outside the European Concert. The Foreign Office and Marling accepted Miss Durham's anti-Ottoman view of the Berana incident, and not the conflicting interpretation of Summa, the Vice-Consul at Scutari. 'Nothing is trustworthy', Grey commented, 'except the account of a British eye-witness and even that is not always trustworthy.' Miss Durham's influence in the Foreign Office was increasing, although only her testimony of the events was accepted, and not her conclusion that the Powers should put an end to Ottoman rule in Europe.[41]

The Policy of British Interests

A few days after the outbreak of the Tripoli War, the India Office, at the behest of the Indian Government, suggested that the Foreign Office demand the Porte's recognition of British rights in the Gulf and Mesopotamia. Nicolson emphasized that an ultimatum, designed to take advantage of the Porte's difficulties with Italy, would be 'most unwise', but he agreed that Lowther should take the first favourable opportunity to urge 'very strongly' a settlement of British claims on the demolition of British property at Baghdad. Nevertheless, the Foreign Office regarded consideration of these demands as proof of the Porte's moderation.[42] Similarly, although the Foreign Office determined to adhere strictly and rigidly to the policy of defending British interests in Mesopotamia, it was eager to come to an agreement before the Baghdad Railway reached Baghdad. Thus, when Assim, the Ottoman Foreign Minister, told Lowther that the Porte could not agree to Britain's proposals regarding the distribution of the railway shares, the Foreign Office prepared to climb down. Its conditions were that British trade be assured against any discrimination on rates on all railways in the Asiatic provinces, and, above all, that the Porte agree to all British demands in the Gulf.[43]

Nevertheless, the reply which, on 15 April 1912, the Porte submitted to Britain's proposals of the previous July was disappointing. The Turks rejected the idea that the shares of the Baghdad Railway be equally distributed amongst the five interested Powers (which would have given the Entente a majority holding), and insisted on a quadruple division which excluded Russia. They were equally, and more seriously, intransigent on Gulf questions. This was an area which – as Lord Lansdowne had told the House of Lords in May 1903 – the British regarded as their own sphere of influence and in which they would regard the establishment of a naval base or fortified port as a 'grave menace' to their interests. Yet the Turks demanded the right to share in the policing of Gulf waters and to a degree of control over the internal administration of Koweit. They also proposed that the islands of Babiyan and Warba be excluded from Koweiti territory and disputed the British view of the status of El Katr and El Bidaa.[44]

In considering the terms of their own counter-proposals to the

Ottoman message, the various organs of the British Government were divided. Even before the receipt of the reply from the Porte, the Foreign Office had conducted lengthy and tedious negotiations with the Board of Trade and the India Office and – through the latter – with the Government of India. Initially, both Crewe and Hardinge had advocated the pursuit of 'strong measures' against the Ottoman Empire, for the consideration of which a special Government of India committee had met in January 1912. But any possible idea of military action had to be abandoned as impractical, once the committee decided that there was little that the British forces could do to harm the Turks beyond occupying Fao or El Bidaa.[45] Thereafter, the British attitude had become more conciliatory. The India Office, admittedly, did continue to advocate a firm stand: Lord Crewe demanded that, since the Ottomans had rejected the idea of a quintuple participation in the Baghdad Railway, the British revert to their original claim for 50 per cent of the shares in the line; Hirtzel initially wanted to 'chuck' the Ottoman reply 'into the fire'; he later insisted that the Turks recognize the boundaries of a greater Koweit.[46] But these proposals (the last of which was described as 'preposterous' by the Foreign Office, were all overruled. Grey's aim, by this stage, was Ottoman recognition of British interests in the Gulf and the avoidance of a rupture with the Porte – not the cessation of the negotiations. To these ends, he was prepared to modify his earlier stand. In this respect, he was helped by Hardinge, who did not care much about control over the Baghdad Railway provided that it did not continue beyond Baghdad. There still remained, of course, the risk of German participation in the Basra-Gulf section of the railway; but that was a danger which could be averted by the acquisition of compensatory safeguards with regard to the Gulf as a whole.

On 18 July 1912, the British counter-proposals were conveyed to the Porte. In deference to the Porte's opposition to a quintuple share in the Baghdad-Gulf railway, the British were prepared to withdraw their claims. In return, however, they demanded the exclusion of any differential treatment in all railways in the Asiatic provinces, the admission of two Britons to the board of the future Baghdad-Basra railway company, a guarantee that no branch lines be built beyond Basra without British consent, and Ottoman permission for another three British steamers to navigate between Baghdad and Basra. Britain hoped that the Porte would appreciate her 'sacrifice' over the Railway and satisfy British demands on El Katr and Koweit. She also insisted on an exclusive right to control and police Gulf waters. Were the Porte to agree to these conditions, and to the removal of the veto on the borrowing powers of Egypt, the British Government would agree to the increase of customs duties on British goods to 15 per cent for seven years.[47] Nicolson was of the opinion that the present moment was favourable for 'inducing' the Ottomans, who were 'rather deserted and isolated and in sad need of funds and in considerable difficulties in the interior', to accept the British proposals. But he realized that the establishment of a new administration at Constantinople might cause considerable delay in the Gulf and Railway negotiations.[48]

Britain and the Young Turks

As early as the autumn of 1911, Mallet had believed that nothing could prevent a further deterioration in Anglo-Ottoman relations. He did not seem to share the view, expressed by Leon Ostrorog (until recently legal adviser to the Porte) and 'many' others, that Lowther was responsible for alienating the Young Turks. The situation was far too complicated to be thus easily explained, and was principally the outgrowth of the behaviour of the Young Turks themselves:

> ... short of telling Italy that HMG will not allow the annexation of Tripoli, I do not see that we can take any active line for the present. What good did we get from our Balkan policy 4 (sic) years ago? ... no one remembers that we got 1 million for Turkey and the moral is obvious. Far from alienating Turkey from the Triple Alliance, it drew her closer and the result of Italy's action may [be] the same ... I should not be surprised at any develop-ments in the direction of closer understanding with Germany. But everything depends on the internal situation in Turkey and that is an unknown quantity.[49]

Notwithstanding this unfolding antipathy, in October 1911 the Porte made a 'curious' but 'interesting' offer to enter into an alliance, first with Britain and later with the Triple Entente. It also again requested British intervention in Rome. Both suggestions were rejected by the Foreign Office as 'quite out of the question'.

Nevertheless, it was decided not to slam the door in the Ottomans' face, but to react in a 'very courteous and friendly manner' in order not to jeopardize Tcharykov's overtures to Constantinople. In his reply to the Porte, Grey stated that Britain had decided on 'strict neutrality' in the Tripoli War and therefore could not enter into any negotiations which would lead to a departure from that policy. Once the war was over, however, both countries could renew the search for better relations (the dangerous term 'alliance' was carefully avoided).[50] The Young Turks did possess one strong advocate in the British Cabinet: Winston Churchill, the First Lord of the Admiralty, who disliked Lowther and who claimed that the members of the Cabinet had taken the question of an 'arrangement' with the Porte too lightly. He pressed Grey not to consider the matter from an 'Armagadon [sic] point of view' since the situation had greatly changed of late and would do so again in the future. Besides:

> Turkey has much to offer us ... we must not forget that we are the greatest Mahometan power in the world. We are the only one who can really help her and guide her. And if she wants to turn to England and to Russia and if Russia is herself anxious for association we should carry Turkey in some sort of way into the system of the Triple Entente ... Turkey is the great land weapon which the Germans could use against *us* [Churchill's italics]. Italy is not likely to be worth much for or against anyone for some time to come.[51]

Hardinge, the Viceroy of India, also counselled moderation. For one thing, as he complained to Nicholson, 'In all these wars against Turkey it is we out in India who in reality have to pay the piper.' For another, the Ottomans did have a case:

> Had I been a Turk I should have strongly advocated an invasion of Thessaly, and I would have told the Powers that I should be ready to clear out as soon as the Italians cleared out of Tripoli.[52]

Finally, note must be taken of the views expressed by Kitchener, always an independent figure, and one who had aspired to the post of Ambassador to the Porte after the 1908 Revolution. When, in June 1912, Assim again appealed to Lowther for an alliance (only to be rebuffed), Kitchener appealed for a reconsideration of the offer. He advised Asquith that such an alignment could be of considerable value to Britain after the Tripoli War. Somewhat naïvely, however, he proposed giving a categorically limited *quid pro quo* to the Ottomans: 'We should of course take no responsibility for complications in Turkey in Europe; but we might be very useful to Turkey in Arabia, Syria and the Far East.'[53]

Ultimately, however, all three suggestions were rejected. The Foreign Office, together with Lowther, considered that the Young Turk advances were prompted more by temporary desperation than by a sincere interest in a long-term improvement in Anglo-Ottoman relations. That, indeed, seemed to be the lesson of recent history. 'There is not much reason for us to thank the Committee for their behaviour to us in the past.'[54] Besides, a favourable response to the Ottomans would have depended upon the fulfilment of three essential conditions. One was the cessation of the Tripoli War (of which the formal end was not yet in sight); the second was a firm Ottoman commitment to take Britain's side in the rivalry with Germany (which was not forthcoming); the third was a substantial improvement in internal Ottoman administration. Of the latter, there were, it is true, some signs. In February 1912, the Foreign Office was itself encouraged by the appointment of an Ottoman Mission of Enquiry and Reform into the European provinces of the Ottoman Empire under the presidency of Hahji Adil Bey, the Minister of the Interior. Hence, some small gestures were in order on Britain's part.[55] Nevertheless, Foreign Office criticism of the new regime was not abated. It supported an unsympathetic Memorial to the Sultan, published in *The Times* on 3 February 1912, calling upon the Turks not to waste the unique opportunity of convincing the West that the new regime was not a failure.[56] It was also critical of the 'big stick' elections to the Ottoman Chamber later that month. Despite Lowther's support of the CUP victory, the general view was that 'the Committee have triumphed but by methods which might have been expected under the old regime but are unbecoming in the new'.[57] At best, the Foreign Office was prepared to let matters take their course, and – whilst not accepting the Ottoman overtures – to attempt not to antagonize the Porte on the eve of the renewed Baghdad Railway and Gulf negotiations. Hence no Blue Books on Macedonia and Albania were published and the 'topographical' work of the British Vice-Consul at Mosul was ordered to be stopped.[58]

The limits thus placed on the manoeuvrability of both sides were nicely demonstrated late in June 1912, when the Porte requested Britain's consent to the appointment of an Englishman as a president of an Inspection Commission, with two English assistants, to reorganize the Ministry of the Interior. Mallet welcomed the chance to extend the work of administrative reform initiated by Crawford and Graves. His enthusiasm was not shared by either Lowther or Grey. Although the latter did admit that the Porte should not be discouraged, he was far more cynical in his estimate of the cause of the Ottoman move:

> When the devil was sick
> The devil a saint would be,
> But when the devil was well
> The devil a saint was he.[59]

Ultimately there was considerable relief in both the Embassy and the Foreign Office when the new liberal Government under Ghazi Moukhtar decided to withdraw the application, on the grounds that the inspectors could not be engaged in administrative functions without being involved in political matters. Mallet alone expressed regret that the opportunity for 'a real improvement' in the administration could not be taken, though he admitted the 'great difficulties' involved. He was convinced that the application for British advisers constituted an opportunity for Britain to recover her 'lost credit' at Constantinople. 'If Turkey continues to exist as a Power to be reckoned with, the importance of maintaining cordial relations with her is obvious, but a necessary condition of our friendship must be reform.' But on the next day he added another reservation to the above: the hope that the Tripoli War would not cause a general conflagration.[60]

Meanwhile, dramatic changes took place at Constantinople, leading to the temporary defeat of the CUP. The crisis of July 1912 had its roots in the formation of the Liberal Union party in November 1911. Soon thereafter, the latter won an important victory in a by-election where the CUP candidate, the Minister for the Interior, was defeated. Sensing a threat to their grip on the country, the members of the CUP tried to bolster their shaky position by dissolving Parliament and appointing Talaat, Djavid, Adil and Said Halim to the Cabinet. There followed the 'big stick election' of 1912, in which the CUP secured an overwhelming parliamentary majority. But this triumph contained the seeds of failure. The undemocratic manner of the CUP's rule, and the un-satisfactory state of the Porte's foreign relations, led to the creation of the Group of Saviour Officers. These the CUP attempted to pacify by acceding to their demands that new legislation be intro-duced in order to prevent the army's intervention in politics. But the discontented officers were not satisfied with this concession and Shevket had to relinquish his position as Minister of War (9 July). Despite the crisis, Said managed to secure a vote of confidence in Parliament on 15 July. Nevertheless he submitted his resignation two days later after the army had launched threatening moves and the Saviour Officers had issued a declaration to the Sultan and to the press.[61]

Throughout these proceedings, the Foreign Office had made it clear that Britain's position could only be that of a spectator. The Embassy, too, had discouraged appeals for assistance from the Saviour Officers. Ghazi Moukhtar's appointment as a Grand Vizier on 22 July was received with little enthusiasm in the Foreign Office, even though his Cabinet was anti-CUP in nature, including both Kiamil and Hilmi, and its declaration of policy promised the appli-cation of the Constitution and a more amiable policy towards the Entente Powers. Nicolson considered the new Cabinet to be merely transitory. It had been formed, he thought, chiefly to deal with the dangerous situation and to eliminate the CUP from any inter-ference in the administration of the country. He was glad that Tewfik had declined to form a Cabinet, as this was a 'risky' task when the CUP might act in desperation.[62] When Giers, the new Russian Ambassador to the Porte, later suggested that the British Chargé should try to bring Kiamil to power, as a replacement for Ghazi Moukhtar's weak Cabinet, Marling rejected the suggestion. With the Foreign Office's approval, he argued that this might burden the British Government with great responsibility whilst she could give the Porte only moral support. Moreover, after Ghazi Moukhtar's fall, Britain might well be identified with the new Government's opponents. He also very much doubted Kiamil's ability to cope with the Balkan crisis. But he welcomed the recent *coup* : 'This is really the counter-revolution, not the tragi-comedy of April 1909.' The Foreign Office concluded that it would be better to leave the present Government to face the crisis and to keep Kiamil in reserve, though it was admitted that the situation at Constanti-nople was 'very obscure and uncertain'.[63]

Britain's attitude towards Ghazi Moukhtar's Government was one of expectancy and doubt. The Grand Vizier's promise of fair elections and a purge of CUP adherents from the administration was received with mixed feelings: 'This is a step in the right direction but there is a danger that the party of the present Government may in the end err in precisely the same way as has the Committee.' Nevertheless, the predominant view in the Foreign Office was that expressed by Mallet: 'Any drastic attempt to solve the problem [of reform] is bound to make the situation worse.'[64]

From Crisis to War

Early in August 1912 the situation in Macedonia worsened. A bomb thrown by Macedonian revolutionaries at Kochana resulted in a reprisal massacre, in which 700 people were killed and wounded.[65] In the absence of any eye-witness reports, the Foreign Office found it difficult to apportion blame for these events. Grey agreed with Parker that the Porte be informed of 'the extreme importance' of punishing 'severely' all officials found guilty. But he accepted Mallet's view that the Bulgarians should also be warned that they would lose Europe's sympathy were they to abandon a pacific policy.[66] In effect, Britain's policy was both sympathetic towards the Porte, and optimistic. Thus, the Foreign Office rejected Berchtold's claim for the 'political' decentralization of Albania, and supported the Porte's view that autonomy was out of the question. 'What is wanted is good government with special arrangements suited to different districts, such as Albania', was Grey's view. His attitude was that Ghazi Moukhtar's anti-CUP Government deserved another chance; moreover, in return for Ottoman self-reform, the Powers would use 'all' their influence to secure peace in the Balkans. Largely on Mallet's advice, Russia and France were accordingly informed that Britain could not join any formal representation to the Porte which might create difficulties for Ghazi Moukhtar's Government 'by exciting the chauvinism of the reactionary party.'[67] Similarly, when Guéshoff, the Bulgarian Prime Minister, told Barclay that he had lost all faith in the Porte, Mallet dismissed the announcement as an attempt to frighten Britain. His moderate view predominated: nothing in the nature of collective intervention should be undertaken for fear of weakening the liberal government. He was sure that Sazonov did not want war and that the crisis could be solved peacefully.[68]

Mallet's attitude towards the Porte at this phase in Ottoman history stemmed not only from his belief that the new regime was still capable of reforming itself but also from a revival of the Pan-Islamic nightmare:

> The chances against a violent end coming to Turkey in Europe are much the same as in the past. As a Mussulman Power, a catastrophe of this nature would probably be to our disadvantage whereas her gradual decay would not affect us so prejudicially.[69]

Nevertheless, on 4 September Mallet informed the Ottoman Chargé that intervention would have to come sooner or later, since the position of the Christian population was 'intolerable'. The Kochana massacre was a black mark against the Ottoman Government, and Mallet hoped that the Porte would publicly announce that it intended to extend to the Christians of Macedonia those reforms which had already been granted to the Albanians.[70]

The British attitude towards the related question of parliamentary representation for the Christians of Macedonia provides a good index of general British policy on the eve of the Balkan Wars. At this stage, Grey was still hopeful that the situation was remedial. Admittedly, on 4 September, he did agree with Berchtold's view that the recent elections to the Ottoman Chamber, managed by the CUP, had been unfair. But he rejected Berchtold's support for the principle of representation for Christians by nationality; this would merely lead to a revival of old feuds. 'Impartial elections should be enough.' It would be inaccurate to state, as did Temperley, that Grey on this occasion, when a liberal Cabinet was in power at Constantinople, lost all confidence in the success of Constitutionalism in the Ottoman Empire. Mallet's subsequent comment that the Porte was already working for impartiality in the elections was welcomed by Grey: 'We would comment favourably to the Turks on this and encourage them.'[71] Only the Balkan Wars destroyed Grey's belief in Ottoman self-reform in Europe, while in Asia his optimism survived even longer.

Nicolson seems to have been less sanguine. But he had two good reasons of his own for not pressing the Porte too much: the 'astonishing' interest with which the Moslems of India were watching Britain's behaviour during the Balkan crisis; and the damage which might be caused to the progress of the Baghdad Railway and Persian Gulf negotiations. The first was the more important, and the more frequently expressed. As Nicolson told Grey:

> If the Balkan States win our Moslems will reproach us with allowing the Ottoman Empire to be dismembered; while if Turkey wins we shall be reproached for not insisting on Europe permitting her to reap the fruits of her victories as Europe would certainly not do.[72]

This argument could not, of course, be used against the Balkan states. At this level of diplomatic exchange, Nicolson had to revert to other themes. That is why he preferred to refer to reform when speaking to the Bulgarian Minister on 20 September. He claimed that the Ghazi Moukhtar Government was the 'best' that the Ottomans had enjoyed for 'generations', and was animated by the 'most honest' intentions with regard to the realization of reforms. Moreover, he could promise that the Powers would 'cordially and sincerely encourage Turkey in this excellent direction'. He told the Bulgarian Minister that the Bulgarians were deluding themselves by believing that they were powerful enough to cope with the Ottoman army.[73] At this stage, the Foreign Office expected the Porte to publish at least an outline of proposed reforms and an announcement that those guilty of the Kochana massacre would be punished. Both moves would help the Powers to prevent the Balkan States from commencing hostilities. The Foreign Office now considered the question of reform as a means to avoid war rather than as an end in itself.[74]

But the whole situation was entirely changed when the Balkan States decided to mobilize their armies on 30 September 1912, an act which 'depressed if not alarmed' the Ottoman Cabinet. By 1 October, it was clear to the Foreign Office that the Porte would now rather fight than grant the concessions demanded by the Balkan States. Vansittart, still only a Junior Clerk in 1912, felt that the Ottomans should mobilize all their troops. He ruled out any possibility of the Porte giving in to the Bulgarian ultimatum which included the application of Article 23 of the Berlin Treaty, and the appointment of a Christian Vali for Macedonia, under Great Power guarantee. The Foreign Office clearly allotted blame for hostilities to the Bulgarians rather than the Porte.[75] Peace, was the opinion, could only be preserved by Sofia.[76] The Porte would be expected to do no more than declare its intention of introducing reforms and discussing them with the Powers, and signing an immediate peace with Italy to calm the situation.[77] Otherwise, however, it was the Balkan States who (as Poincaré, the French Premier, suggested) had to be cautioned against war and against territorial benefits. The Foreign Office, for its part, suggested informing the Porte that the Powers had taken note of its intention to introduce reforms in accordance with the spirit of Article 23 and the laws of 1880. Were the Porte's own reforms to be 'effective', the Powers would guarantee the Ottoman provinces in Europe.[78]

But the British line towards the Porte became less favourable when the moderate elements in Ghazi Moukhtar's Government – Kiamil and Gabriel Effendi – were overruled as a result of the increased enthusiasm for war generated by the CUP. The shift in policy was presaged by Nicolson:

> The great question now is ... who will get the upper hand in Constantinople – the Moderate party or the fanatical and extreme party? I think that the former would assist us in every way in the measures to preserve the peace, but I am afraid that the latter party is gaining ground daily and that they may sweep away all elements which are of a pacific and moderate character. The danger point, therefore, in my opinion, lies just as much at Constantinople as at Sofia.[79]

Montenegro's aggression against the Ottoman Empire on 8 October was regarded by Vansittart as a 'cat's paw' to force hostilities before the Powers' diplomatic initiative gathered momentum. But the change in attitude thus apparent did not yet possess operative implications. On the day Montenegro began to act aggressively against the Ottomans (8 October), the Foreign Office still rejected Berchtold's suggestion that the Porte be pressed to agree to European supervision of the fulfilment of the reforms.[80] Neither was it prepared to participate in any action on the part of the Powers designed to coerce the Porte to secure the peace.[81] Nicolson, as ever with an eye on St Petersburg, feared that:

> We shall have before long to make up our minds whether we will take up the Balkan cause in cooperation with Russia, and risk offending our Moslem opinion and Turkey: or whether to

placate the latter [in which case] we shall imperil the Triple Entente and probably break it.

But Grey considered these apprehensions premature.[82] A more relevant consideration was the shortcomings of the Ottoman army and the impoverished state of the Ottoman treasury.[83] Under these circumstances, what the Porte had to do was conserve its energies, not succumb.

Accordingly, the Foreign Office pressed the Turks to come to terms with the Italians over Tripoli, and rejoiced when they did so, especially since the prolongation of that conflict might have brought with it the closure of the Dardanelles once more. The final peace treaty was signed at Lausanne on 18 October, and was followed on the 25th by Britain's recognition of Italian sovereignty in Tripoli and Cyrenaica.[84]

5

CATASTROPHE AND CHANGE

British Policy during the Balkan Wars
(October 1912 – October 1913)

The Balkan Scene and the Future of the Asian Provinces

Until 24 October 1912, the Foreign Office hoped that neither side
to the Balkan Wars would obtain a clear-cut victory over the other;
a decisive military result might make any settlement very difficult. But attitudes changed after the first Ottoman defeats at
Komanova and Kirkilisse. Gabriel Effendi, the Ottoman acting
Minister for Foreign Affairs, immediately feared a general collapse
and suggested to Lowther that England take the initiative in bringing about the intervention of the Powers. Grey's reply was that, if
the Porte wished to avoid further defeats, it should unconditionally
place the question of a settlement in the hands of the European
Powers.[1] The situation had deteriorated even further by the
28th, when the Bulgarians occupied Drama and the Ottoman army
surrendered at Lule Burgas. On that day Grey informed the
German Chargé that Britain would not object to the demands of the
Balkan States if their victory were final. His one exception was that
Constantinople should not be transferred to the control of the
Allies. Britain was even prepared to support the aims of the Balkan
States, provided Russia and Austria agreed to declare their 'dis-
interestedness'. Grey did still not exclude the possibility of Ottoman
successes; but Nicolson had lost faith in the Ottoman army and
regarded any projects for reforms as a waste of time. What is more,
the British Government was henceforth not inhibited by any fears
as to the attitude of the Moslems of India, since Hardinge reassured
the Foreign Office that even were the Ottomans to lose Albania and
Macedonia, he could still keep his Moslem subjects in hand.[2]

On 1 November, it became quite clear that the situation was 'utterly disastrous'. Vansittart expressed the fear that the demoralized Ottoman army might not be able to check the rapidly advancing Bulgarians before the Chataldja lines. The Admiralty decided to send a ship to Besike Bay and the foreign Missions called upon the Porte to protect them from a possible influx of the retreating hungry and fanatical troops.[3] By 5 November, the collapse of the Ottoman army was so total that Fitzmaurice envisaged the imminent occupation of Constantinople, or 'Tzarigrad', as he now called it, to the Bulgarians.[4]

This danger forced the British Government to define its attitude. The resultant reassessment was indeed drastic, even though it was geographically restricted. The makers of Britain's policy were now prepared to support the claims of the advancing Balkan States, but did not seek territorial concessions for themselves. Thus, contrary to Kitchener's advice, Grey was opposed to exploiting Ottoman weakness by pressing the Porte for a settlement consolidating British rule in Egypt. 'Our position would be very much weaker if we were trying to get anything for ourselves', Grey replied, 'and there would be a general scramble.' Furthermore, and contrary to rumours in the press and at Constantinople, Britain had no intention of running the Khedive for the Caliphate. 'I would rather stake my money', Nicolson commented, 'on a young Arab Caliphate if the Sultan goes under.'[5] It must also be noted that the Foreign Office rejected any suggestion of weakening Ottoman rule in Asia. Lowther did predict the possibility of a 'movement of emancipation' in parts of Asia Minor and Syria, and Fitzmaurice prophesied that Arabia might be 'semi-automatically' detached and link up with Cairo. But these sentiments found no echo in London. There, Grey approved Consul-General Cumberbatch's message to 'leading Moslems' from Beirut that an extension of Egyptian rule to Syria was 'neither practicable nor desirable'.[6]

The end of Ottoman rule in Europe, however, was quite another matter. Here, the Foreign Office was now ready to confirm the dissolution of the Ottoman Empire – and indeed even to welcome that eventuality since it might enable the Turks better to manage their Asiatic dominions.[7] Hence Britain's agreement to the Bulgarian demand for Adrianople (which necessitated a rejection of Berchtold's suggestion that the Treaty of San Stefano – which omitted that provision – constitute the basis of preliminary peace proposals).[8] Hence, too, Britain's support for Greek claims to the Aegean Islands.[9] Hence, finally, the fears that Ottoman successes before the Chataldja lines (after 17 November) might induce the Porte to be more rigid.[10] Although apprehensive that Austro-Russian rivalry in the Balkans might lead to a general conflagration, Grey generally sympathized with Russian support for Balkan demands. The only exception was Constantinople and its vilayet, for which the British (in response to the Russian idea of internationalization) suggested neutralization and the establishment of a free port. Grey was, however, prepared to seek a solution to the Straits problem on the pro-Russian lines suggested by Izvolsky in October 1908.[11]

The pro-Balkan sentiments, of which these moves were an expression, were rife throughout the Government. In the Cabinet, nearly all Ministers were 'anti-Turk, Grey being perhaps the only one who [would] like to hold the balance even, and that because he despises the Greeks and the Servians'.[12] Elsewhere, pro-Balkan sentiments were less qualified. In his Guildhall speech, on 10 November, Asquith said that the 'victors were not to be robbed of the fruits which cost them so dear'.[13] Even more extreme was Churchill's speech to the Eighty Club on 30 November, when he paid tribute to 'that great man' Gladstone who had predicted the course of events 'in extraordinary precision and detail'. Despite Asquith's disclaimers in Parliament that Britain was exhibiting 'complete indifference' to the fate of the Turks,[14] his reply was hardly satisfactory. The fact was that Britain, while agreeing that serious acts of violence had been committed against the Moslem population during the recent campaign, refused to intervene. Vansittart admitted that:

> The conduct of the Allies, from the moment when they obtained the upper hand, has been just as bad as anything the Turks have ever done ... one cannot help regretting that nothing has been done to check them or let Europe know the real [sic] of these people on whom a deal of sympathy has been wasted.[15]

Nevertheless, British policy did not change.

At one level, British policy could be attributed to the strength of pro-Balkan public feeling. This was the point made by Grey as early as mid-November 1912, in response to Kiamil's desperate appeal that Britain give the same degree of support to the Moslems as Russia was according to the Slavs. Grey did sympathize with Kiamil's plight, but:

> ... it must be borne in mind that the effect upon public opinion here of the long years of Abdul-Hamid's iniquities was inevitable; then came a wave of sympathy with the hopes of the Young Turk revolution, followed by a reaction to disgust when the CUP rule turned out badly; the flicker of hope that we felt when the CUP fell could hardly counteract this and no doubt the general feeling is that the Turks are reaping what they have sown.[16]

That, however, was not the entire story. British policy can also be attributed, firstly, to the fact that the Ottoman defeat had been 'very calmly' received throughout the Moslem world,[17] and, secondly, to Russia's behaviour. The maintenance of the Anglo-Russian alignment, as Nicolson never tired of pointing out, was in any case more important to Britain than the effect of the possible fall of Constantinople on the Moslem subjects of the British Empire. The Anglo-French Entente and the Anglo-Russian Convention were cornerstones of British policy. 'Were these understandings to be in any way weakened we should find ourselves in a most awkward international position.'[18]

At the end of November 1912, Fitzmaurice was asked by Kiamil to mediate between the Porte and the Balkan States. He advised the Porte to start immediate and direct negotiations with the Balkan States and warned against following the CUP's advice to continue the fighting. Fitzmaurice's appeal to the Ottoman statesmen was unknown to the Foreign Office at the time. Nevertheless, he doubtless expressed the general attitude of both the British Government and public opinion when, in a private letter to Tyrrell, Grey's Private Secretary, he congratulated the Balkan States for having 'cleared up a mess which defeated the ingenuity of European diplomacy'.[19] An armistice was eventually signed on 3 December, but peace was still a long way off. Both the Foreign Office and the Embassy accused the Central Powers of 'stoking up' the Porte, whose suggested terms Vansittart regarded as 'ridiculous'. Lowther and Fitzmaurice, together with the French and Russian Ambassadors, intimated to the Porte the 'expediency' of being 'reasonable and moderate', but no direct British intervention was planned for the present. Grey suggested that this option should be kept in reserve for use in case of a possible deadlock in negotiations at the coming London conference.[20]

The crux of the situation proved to be Adrianople, whose retention the Ottomans claimed was a strategic necessity. Parker assumed that the negotiations would reach an impasse and that the war would be renewed. In that case he dreaded the complete collapse of the Ottoman Empire as a result of possible outbreaks in the Asiatic provinces which might lead to the active intervention of Russia in Armenia, France in Syria and Germany in Anatolia. Grey, however, refused to press the Porte to yield to the terms of the victorious Balkan States. Indeed, since London provided the venue for the peace conference, Grey wished to avoid supporting either side.[21] However, he did consent to a joint advice to the Porte on the grounds that the financial straits of the Ottoman Empire had made it imperative for her to make peace, otherwise the Powers might be provoked to interfere to an extent which might considerably impair the sovereignty of Constantinople. He also agreed with Russia that if hostilities did recommence, Britain could no longer maintain her neutrality.[22]

The impasse over the peace negotiations continued into 1913. British officials, too, were divided. While the Foreign Office fully supported the Balkan Allies, Lowther did not hesitate to call their peace terms 'preposterous'. He warned that by supporting the Allies' 'very severe' terms, Britain would be 'instrumental' in restoring the CUP to power, and was very much against the Foreign Office's proposal to hand over Lemnos and Mitylene to Greece. He also sharply criticized the attitude of both the Foreign Office and the British press towards the massacre of Moslems by the Allies:

> Although we know that in this case Bulgars and Greeks have been worse offenders than Turks in the way of massacres, not a word is said in our press against them. Of course, this makes my position now and in the future impossible, but will it not also have a very bad effect in India, where we must depend to a great extent on Moslem opinion?[23]

Fitzmaurice took a different view. He suggested that the Powers put pressure on the Porte to make concessions, as had been done during the Akaba crisis of 1906. Contrary to Lowther, he dismissed the feared effect on Moslem feeling in India as 'tiresome' and 'sectarian' and described the atrocities against Moslems as a 'fiction' of the sort spread in Tripoli. But he had his own fears: unless the Porte hurried up it might be faced both with '*big* [Fitzmaurice's italics] Arab' and Armenian questions, as well as the prospect of 'the international Shylocks' taking control of Ottoman finances.[24]

This was very much the line taken by the Foreign Office. Nicolson did regret Bulgaria's refusal to be satisfied with the demilitarization of Adrianople (which in any case he hoped would soon fall). None-theless, he was forced to accept that in the interests of European peace, the Porte had to be pressed to abandon everything.[25] Britain therefore supported the decision of the Powers to send a few ships to defend their nationals and interests, hoping that this might also help the démarche concerning Adrianople.[26]

In fact, the Foreign Office ignored Lowther's lament that: '… we have successfully thrown Turkey into the arms of the Triple Alliance, for they have been very mild in their advice and pro-digious [sic] of what Turkey "might do" if they continued the war.'[27] It was far more worried by two other possibilities. One was that hostilities in the Balkans would be resumed, thus provoking Russian intervention and – in turn – Austrian action against Serbia. It was to offset this eventuality that Lowther was repeatedly warned not to make any suggestion to the Porte which might compromise Allied territorial claims.[28] The other British fear, however, was that the Allies might make such heavy financial demands on the Porte that the entire Ottoman administration would be crippled. Britain now wished for the Ottoman Empire to consolidate and strengthen itself as an Asiatic power, and anything which might prevent this eventuality had to be challenged. Were Ottoman rule in Asia to be liquidated, observed Nicolson, 'we shall then come face to face with facts which to my mind will be still more formidable and difficult than those with which we are at present confronted in Europe'.[29]

Kiamil was quite determined to stop the war by sacrificing Adrianople. But he was careful not to assume sole responsibility. He therefore summoned a Grand Council comprising the leading figures of the country, which supported him on the need to reach peace. The CUP, however, seized the opportunity to launch a *coup de main*. On 23 January 1913, at 3.00 pm, while the Cabinet was drafting its conciliatory reply to the Powers' Note, a body of about forty to sixty people, 'mostly, apparently, of the hooligan class' (Lowther) appeared at the entrance to the Sublime Porte. Led by Enver and Jemal, and later joined by Talaat, waving liberty banners and Moslem emblems, they cried, 'Death to Kiamil Pasha!' The 'conspirators' had previously cut the telephone lines and arranged for a pro-CUP battalion to guard the Porte, while the anti-CUP battalion had been sent away on military exercises. They were resisted by Kiamil's aide-de-camp, but overcame and killed him, as well as General Nazim Pasha, the Minister of War and his aide-de-camp. Enver forced Kiamil to resign at gunpoint, claiming to speak, in Lowther's words, in the name of the army and the people. That evening, at 8.00 pm, Shevket, the CUP's nominee, was appointed Grand Vizier.

Lowther later claimed to have foretold this sequence of events. Kiamil's readiness to surrender Adrianople, he had predicted on 16 January, would lead to a return to power of the 'committee Jacobins', and their resumption of activity on 'carbonary' lines. But even he had to admit that the impact of the CUP's reappearance was 'almost seismic'.[30] At the Foreign Office the *coup d'état* was regarded (in Vansittart's phrase) as 'deplorable ... The leading members of the CUP ought to have been adequately dealt with in advance.' The CUP, it seemed certain, would renew the war. Lowther, who had already warned the Foreign Office against the policy of the German Ambassador (Wangenheim), before the *coup*, now reported that the new CUP Cabinet had a 'distinct' German character.[31] In London, there was some confusion concerning the possibility of a counter-*coup* against the Shevket Cabinet.[32] But in Constantinople, Lowther continued to report tidings of an unmistakably ominous character; before the *coup* took place, the conspirators had been in close contact with the Triple Alliance embassies.[33] Not even he, therefore, concealed his antipathy to the new administration and – for once – did not attempt to temper his Government's criticism of the Young Turks. On the contrary, it was he who now forecast that the CUP, having formed the National Defence Committee on the lines of the French Revolutionaries in 1793 and the 'Communists' in 1870, would now launch the 'Terreur'.[34] This was regarded in the Foreign Office as 'the most depressing report which we have yet received'.[35]

Despite Lowther's novel warnings of collusion between the CUP and the Triple Alliance (which he attributed to British support for the Balkan States), the basic policy pursued in the Foreign Office did not change. Britain, it was felt, had to support Russia in the Balkans in order to preserve the Triple Entente.[36] Similarly, Britain had also to discourage talk about a possible division of Asiatic Turkey into spheres of influence. To that end, Grey assured the Germans that there was no ground for the suspicion that the Entente Powers had agreed to form 'Arabian, Armenian and Syrian spheres of interests'.[37] He also impressed upon France and Russia the need to avoid any agitation.

> The French must not make another Morocco of Asia Minor. Germany has been shut out of the whole of North Africa because she did not choose to enter the field in time and France has absorbed Tunis, Algiers and most of Morocco. But if there is to be European spheres in Asia Minor Germany must be recognized as entitled to ask as much say as France in the matter.[38]

Finally, the Foreign Office took care not to promote dissension within the Ottoman Empire. It did welcome the tendency towards decentralization in evidence in both Beirut and Basra, but rejected the request of the Reform Party of Beirut for European intervention on behalf of their cause. Rather, it was relieved when the Porte stated its objection to the Beirut delegation, and when the French also preferred not to grant official recognition.[39] Neither was there any sympathy whatsoever in the Foreign Office for Zionist aspirations in Palestine. Mallet did not believe that the Jews could be 'good agriculturists' and regarded the question of Jewish immigration to Palestine as an internal Ottoman problem. The Foreign Office was informed that the Arabs and the 'old Turks' detested the Zionist movement. Lowther convinced the Foreign Office that the Zionists were aiming at creating another national problem for the Porte.[40]

Nevertheless, the Foreign Office was not sanguine as to the future of Ottoman Asia. Unlike Hardinge, who considered that Turkey could still become 'a great Asiatic Power', Nicolson could see only continued and extended difficulties.

> My own belief [he wrote to Cartwright] is that it will not be possible for the Turks to maintain a hold in Asia. They are so thoroughly discredited as a fighting force and so disunited among themselves that the various non-Turkish races in Asia are not likely to lose an opportunity of furthering their own aims. This would produce a general welter in Asia and a consequent scramble among European Powers over the debris of that Empire ...[41]

Grey, as late as June 1913, did assure the Commons of his hope that the Porte would manage to consolidate its Asiatic provinces by introducing 'justice and sound finance', with European help. Within the Foreign Office, however, the general prognosis was that 'as long as the CUP remains in power [the] anti-Turkish process would seem likely to grow until Turkey proper is reduced to the western half of Asia Minor'.[42]

It was in this spirit that the Foreign Office approached the renewed Ottoman offer of a defensive alliance with Britain in June 1913. Contrary to the situation which had been apparent in October 1911, not one of the officials concerned could see any reason to support the notion. Even Mallet, who had already been chosen as Lowther's successor, considered the alliance to be 'impractical'. It would merely unite 'all Europe' against Britain and be a 'source of weakness and danger' to both countries. The Triple Alliance might regard it as a 'challenge' on the part of the Triple Entente, and it would particularly arouse German 'jealousy'. Mallet had another suggestion.

> A less risky method would be by a treaty of declaration binding all the Powers to respect the independence and integrity of the present Turkish dominion, which might go so far as neutralization; and by participation by all the Great Powers in financial control and the application of reforms.

Grey, too, favoured the continuation of the Concert policy towards the Porte: unless all the Powers were united, Turkey 'would, when her fears subsided, resist efforts at reform and play off one ... against another'.[43] Consequently, the Turkish offer was turned down. But this refusal did not indicate, as one historian has suggested, a turning-point in British policy from one of encouraging the Porte to look to Britain for sympathy and inspiration to one of keeping the Porte neutral. The 'sympathetic' policy had already ended in the latter part of 1910, and the advice to the Porte to remain neutral between the European alliances was already implicit in Britain's attitude of refusal in 1911.[44]

Later that summer, however, attention reverted to the battlefield. Dissensions amongst the Balkan Allies provided the Porte with an opportunity to recover some of its territory; Adrianople (which had fallen on 26 March 1913) was reoccupied on 22 July.

The Foreign Office considered it 'very natural' for the Porte officially to order the Ottoman Comander-in-Chief to reoccupy former Ottoman territory. Nevertheless, Grey found it necessary to warn the Turks not to advance beyond the Enos-Midia line agreed upon in the Treaty of London. Such action would increase the risk of European intervention and might again raise the question of Constantinople.[45] But Britain was not ready to back her warning by strong measures; hence, Sazonov's suggestion of a naval demonstration was disregarded. Crewe and Hardinge, but not Asquith, feared the danger that 'a very strong' outburst of feeling might take place amongst the Moslems in India were Britain to attempt to deprive the Porte of recovered territory.[46] Nicolson, for instance, was prepared to exert pressure only through the Financial Commission in Paris, but not to break off negotiations with Hakki. The Foreign Office also objected to a Russian demonstration in the Caucasus designed to induce the Porte to give up Adrianople, since this might induce the break-up of the Ottoman Empire in its entirety. On the contrary, at one stage Grey was even prepared to consider 'reasonable' modifications in the Enos-Midia line in the Ottomans' favour.[47]

Hakki Pasha was therefore incorrect in accusing Britain of favouring a pro-Bulgarian and pro-Greek policy. Asquith, it is true, was a Turcophobe; but his influence in the detailed formulation of policy in this question was slight. Even more so was that of the Balkan Committee, 'a collection of busybodies and nobodies'.[48] In fact, the Foreign Office was embarrassed by Sazonov's aggressiveness towards the Porte,[49] and rejected Marling's suggestion that it suspend conclusion of the Persian Gulf and Mesopotamian agreements with Hakki until the Porte promised not to violate the Treaty of London. Parker, sensing that his negotiations with Hakki were nearing a successful conclusion, opposed any idea that Britain's 'material interests' be sacrificed for the sake of 'the most barbarous State in Europe [Bulgaria]'. Marling proved similarly unsuccessful in his attempt to agitate the Foreign Office against the Young Turks who, in order to enhance their prestige, would not hesitate to 'embroil Europe into a general war'. The Embassy was blamed for being out of touch with the Porte, and Marling in particular for becoming 'exceedingly anti-Turkish'.[50] Even after the Ottoman Army had crossed the Maritza, Britain refused to accede to Russia's suggestion that the Entente break off relations with the Porte. She was only prepared to protest 'strongly' with the rest of the Powers but not with the Entente alone.[51]

Once it was realized that the Powers, including Russia, were not going to compel the Porte to withdraw, the Foreign Office did not have any qualms about the Turks 'squeezing' the Bulgarians. Nicolson even stated privately that he was 'really pleased' that the Porte had retained Adrianople, and that it was 'perhaps natural' that the Ottomans were defying the Powers.[52] At the end of September, the Powers were faced with the *fait accompli* of the Treaty of Constantinople which was more advantageous to the Porte than the Treaty of London had been. Even when the Greco-Ottoman peace negotiations reached deadlock, the attitude of the Foreign Office did not change. The Government did protest that the delay in peace had 'considerably' affected British trade and shipping. Yet, Britain refused to depart from its principle of acting with the Concert in the event of the Porte using force, contrary to the Russian wish to act with the Entente alone.[53] Neither was anyone in the Foreign Office prepared to re-open the Macedonian question.[54] The peace between Greece and the Ottoman Empire was finally signed in Bucharest through Roumanian intervention on 14 November.

The Armenian Question: First Phase[55]

The Armenian question was the last of all the nationalities problems to be brought to the fore by the failure of the Young Turks to govern the Ottoman Empire. Indeed, at the Foreign Office the Armenian issue was regarded as an internal Ottoman matter until well into the Balkan Wars of 1912-13. Thus, in 1909, Sir Edward Grey had rejected a suggestion that the Powers intervene in the question. A warning to the Young Turks that a recurrence of the Adana massacres would involve the Powers, he claimed, would serve no purpose. Indeed;

> ... such a declaration ... might be a direct incitement to the Armenians to create disturbances which might provoke retaliation on the part of the Turks in the shape of massacres with a view to bring about the intervention of the Powers on behalf of the Armenians.[56]

This remained Britain's official policy until 1912. Reports from consular officials in 1910 and 1911 did present an increasingly gloomy picture of tension, 'widespread ill-feeling', Armenian approaches to the Russians, and CUP inability to deal with the situation.[57] In the Foreign Office, however, officials continued to rely on Kiamil's Government to protect the Armenians. This basic attitude was not affected by the outbreak of the Balkan War ('We cannot do anything practical on behalf of the Armenian population in Asia Minor'), and differed sharply from that of Atkin, a 'busybody' clerk in the War Office, who suggested nothing less than the intervention of British and Russian cruisers on behalf of the Armenians.[58] Thus, the Foreign Office rebuffed an attempt on the part of the Balkan Committee to draw it into a new initiative with the suggestion that the system of government which had been established for the Lebanon in 1864 should now be applied to the Armenian provinces. 'The Balkan Committee', Maxwell commented, 'are obliged to seek some other vent for their energies now that their *raison d'être* in Macedonia has ceased to exist.' Instead, as Sir Arthur Nicolson wrote: 'it would be but fair ... to give the Ottoman Government in their present serious difficulties time to deal with pressing questions and not worry them on other matters.'[58] Occasionally, Mallet did admit that were a conference for the revision of the Treaty of Berlin to take place it would be 'necessary' to reconsider Article 61. Nevertheless, he too rejected the opinion of the Friends of Armenia that the situation demanded the appointment of a Christian governor, independent of the Porte and controlled by the Powers. The British Government thought that at present such a step might do 'more harm than good' and was not 'practical'.[60]

Ottoman disasters during the course of the Balkan Wars altered the picture. Outwardly, the Foreign Office continued to regard the Armenian question as an internal Ottoman matter; but its underlying attitude towards Ottoman rule in Asia Minor underwent a considerable change. In mid-January 1913, serious concern was aroused when Lowther surmised that the Armenians would no longer be satisfied with 'palliatives', and would expect more drastic solutions such as autonomy under the auspices of Russia. Mallet felt that this 'might inaugurate the division of Asia Minor between the Powers'. Nicolson forecast more ominously: 'The annexation to Russia of the vilayets mentioned is but a question of time.' The Foreign Office no longer set store by Kiamil's Government, and

Grey now found it opportune to defend Britain's claims in view of those of Russia. 'The open door for trade and a good arrangement about the Persian Gulf and below Baghdad are our ambitions.'[61] In fact, the Foreign Office in general now found itself nearer to the point of view of the Friends of Armenia,[62] and admitted that nothing could be done for the Armenians as long as the Porte possessed executive power: foreign control was 'no doubt' the only solution.[63] Diplomatic representation, it was further admitted, would be useless since the CUP Government was unable and probably unwilling to improve the conditions of the Armenians. The Foreign Office could understand the Armenian anxiety about the rumour of Europe's intention to guarantee the integrity of the Ottoman provinces in Asia without insisting on the introduction of reforms.[64]

Nevertheless, forceful intervention remained out of the question. As long as the Balkan problems remained unsettled, the British Government had to be content with advice. Thus, it continued to express the hope that the Porte would take the question of reforms into 'urgent consideration' and instruct the Valis to take 'every means' in their power to defend the Armenians. Fitzmaurice was careful to demonstrate Britain's impartiality to Shevket when he told the Grand Vizier that the Adana massacres of 1909 were the consequence of 'an exaggerated state of mind' on both sides. Britain ruled out any possibility of intervention in order to deal with the growing unrest in the Armenian provinces. As in other parts of the Ottoman Empire, Britain was prepared only to protect her own subjects along the Ottoman littoral.[65]

The entire question took a new turn late in April 1913 when the Porte, acting independently of Germany, asked the British Government to supply inspectors for the gendarmerie, agriculture and public works, gendarmerie officers, and an adviser and inspector-general for the Ministry of the Interior. Norman and Mallet reacted enthusiastically and suggested that Britain immediately comply. Mallet even regarded it as 'very important':

> We want Turkey to remain a Power in Asia and we want reforms for the Armenians. Unless reforms are introduced, it is certain that Turkish Power will decline and that there will be massacres and troubles of all kinds in these provinces ... We are the only people who could undertake the duty and carry it

through successfully and the only Power who would be allowed by the other Powers to undertake it, as it is recognized that we have no territorial and political ambitions in these Provinces. This proposal offers us the only opportunity which we have ever had of doing anything for the Armenians and if we shirk it, and allow others to take our place, our influence and prestige must decline – and we shall be much criticized here.

Nicolson was less enthusiastic since he saw the dangers of such compliance for both the Porte and the British Government. He was disappointed that the proposed reform did not cover the whole of Asia Minor, and felt that by furnishing advisers for the Ministry of Interior, Britain might arouse the 'jealousy' of the Powers. Afraid that by monopolizing the supply of advisers to the Porte, Britain would merely enhance the struggle for 'spheres of influence' among the Powers, he wished to widen the arc of participation. Thus, he suggested that Russia, France and Germany should also be called upon to furnish advisers, and that particularly Russia, as she bordered on the vilayets in question, should be fully consulted.[66]

Lowther objected to this scheme;[67] so too – and more vigorously – did Sazonov. Late in May 1913, the latter made clear his objections to the appointment of British gendarmerie officers in the Armenian vilayets; Russia would not play 'second fiddle' there. Sazonov's stiff opposition was more than the Foreign Office had bargained for, because it was believed that the British contribution had been reduced to the 'very narrowest possible limits'. Norman, Maxwell and Mallet thought that Britain should not give way to Russia's demand, for if Britain refused the Porte might turn to Germany. Nicolson, however, realized that Sazonov was under 'pressure' from the Armenians to introduce 'effective' reforms, and that Britain ought carefully to avoid any friction between Russia and the Porte. He concluded, therefore, that he had better leave the initiative to Russia and consent to the Armenian question being discussed by the Entente Ambassadors at Constantinople on the basis of the 1895 scheme. This was to be followed by consultation with the Porte and the Triple Alliance Powers. Nicolson was not prepared to withdraw the consent already given to the Porte concerning the gendarmerie officers. But he was ready to postpone their actual engagement by the Porte until the general scheme of reform was ready.[68]

Whilst the Foreign Office was inhibited by the desire to prevent an Ottoman-Russian conflict in order to assure the success of reform, the Embassy tried to tempt the Foreign Office to accept the realities of spheres of influence. Lowther felt that the Ottomans meant to create 'a maximum of friction and antagonism' amongst the Entente Powers by asking for British officials in what was clearly a Russian sphere of influence. This, he maintained, might lead to the engagement of German officials in reforming Mesopotamia. He therefore suggested a more equitable arrangement: the foreign advisers for the Armenian vilayets should be Russian, those for Mesopotamia, British, those for Syria, French, and those for Adana and West Asia Minor, German or others. In order to buttress his point of view he warned that the matter must be seen in terms of the European alliances. The Ottoman project backed by Germany, now in the ascendancy at Constantinople since the CUP had regained power, was intended to exclude Russia. This would never succeed, since the Armenians themselves favoured reforms only under Russian auspices. Any other project, which must be anti-Russian in character, was 'almost certain to be fraught with disastrous instead of beneficial results'. Fitzmaurice spoke even more freely and explicitly than Lowther on the necessity to end Ottoman sovereignty in the Armenian vilayets. He had already suggested that Russia be given the actual control of these vilayets as Austria had been given the actual control of Bosnia and Herzegovina in 1878, or as had been the case with Britain and Egypt in 1882, (although he admitted that in such a case Germany might attempt a second 'Agadir' at Alexandretta or a 'Kiaschiao' [sic] at Mersina-Adana).[69] But the Foreign Office could still not accept Fitzmaurice's and Lowther's 'radical solution' of 'cutting the tie of Turkish direct rule'. It hoped that the Ottoman project was fuelled by a 'genuine desire' to avoid Russian intervention, even though it might have been intended to generate Anglo-Russian friction. The Russian frontier authorities need not make the task of the British gendarmerie officers more difficult by intriguing with Kurds and Armenians.[70] The official attitude was that the consolidation of the Ottoman Empire necessitated the avoidance of 'spheres of influence' and the implementation of reforms.

Subsequently, however, the vigorous anti-Ottoman attitude adopted by Russia (who wished to appoint a Russian Governor-General for the Armenian vilayets) caused some differences of opinion in the Foreign Office as to what British policy should be. Mallet's attitude was more pro-Ottoman than ever before:

> ... one cannot but assume that a statesman taking up the attitude of M. Sazonov at this juncture in Turkish history, is making for the disruption of the Empire. ... I should like to remind him that the Armenian question is an interest of all the Powers (see Berlin Treaty). It is an especial and vital interest of ours, as the partition of Asiatic Turkey would have the most serious effect on our position in the Mediterranean and disastrous results in India.

Nicolson, on the other hand, was anxious to avoid a clash with Russia. Extremely sensitive to the importance of preserving the Entente with Russia, he was, accordingly, ready to admit that Russia had a 'more immediate and direct interest' than any other Power in the Armenian Vilayets. His strategy was to work together with Russia 'calmly and temperately'. He laid down the basic line of British policy when he proclaimed that he was prepared for concessions provided Sazonov agreed to two conditions which alone could assure the success of the reform scheme: 'unanimity amongst the Powers' and 'acceptance of their scheme by Turkey without coercion'.[71] In fact, Nicolson shared Mallet's apprehensions, even though they still differed as to the future success of Ottoman reform. He wrote to Cartwright:

> Our policy is to endeavour to maintain and consolidate Turkish dominion in Asia [but] I should not if I were called upon to do so defend such a policy upon any higher ground than simple expediency and an unwillingness to be parties to any measures which might alienate or disappoint our moslem population in India. In my heart of hearts I have the very gravest doubts, apart from any question of morals, whether it will be possible to maintain Turkish dominion for any great length of time. The prestige of the Turk as a fighting machine and also as a soldier of Islam has entirely disappeared and there are many indications to show that the spirit has gone out of the Turks and that they are really no longer capable of maintaining the position they have hitherto enjoyed. This fact will, I doubt not, soon become general throughout the Asiatic provinces and will I expect lead to movements tending to disintegration.[72]

Mallet was hardly as pessimistic as Nicolson, but even he had to warn Hakki that 'if the integrity of Turkey was to be maintained' the 'terrible state of affairs' in the Erzeroum vilayet must be terminated. Mallet insisted that 'Europe would not stand this any longer', and that the Porte 'must' find some way of controlling the Kurds. He justified the British suspension of the gendarmerie officers by the need to prevent the participation of Russian officers in the vilayets in question.[73] In the final analysis, all the Foreign Office officials were united in the wish to reconcile the different points of view of the various Powers.

This was not the case in the Embassy at Constantinople, now directed by Marling, and/or Fitzmaurice. There, anti-German and pro-Russian feelings ran high. Marling dismissed the German threat to demand an established sphere of influence in Cilicia, and considered that the Russian project was 'essential if anything really good is to be done'. He also warned the Foreign Office that the Armenians would not accept the Ottoman project (which he thought was really German) and, being in a state of unrest, they might provoke Russian intervention. Mallet rejected Marling's arguments since he had no intention of quarrelling with the Germans. The aim of the Foreign Office was to bring about a compromise between the different points of view and not to establish whether Russia or Germany possessed the greater interest in Asia Minor. Nicolson, however, accepted Marling's view as 'sound and practical'.[74]

Proceedings at the Armenian Reform Commission, composed of the Powers' Dragomans, further indicated that the differences between Russia and Germany were part of a much wider issue. This was a question which stood between the representatives of the Triple Entente and the Triple Alliance in their respective entirety. Fitzmaurice naturally supported the Russian scheme, though in a 'general and non-committal' way, and thus Mallet's opposition to Russia proved to be of negligible effect.[75] More especially was this so in view of Grey's attitude. Claiming that a compromise could still be reached, the Foreign Secretary informed the Commons that the representatives of the Powers who were discussing the Armenian question did not have in view 'the establishment of different spheres of interest in the Turkish Empire'. But his statement was based more on wishful thinking than on established facts. He spoke more frankly in Cabinet, where he was reported to have revealed that the Russian scheme of 'reforms' in Armenia ... would practically make it an autonomous province which could, when the time was ripe, be swallowed at leisure by Russia. Grey was inclined to yield to all the Russian demands on the ground that the regeneration of Turkey is impossible, and that though it was inexpedient now to partition her, yet the sooner, in decency, it is done the better for everyone.[76]

While the Eastern Department felt that Russia's claim for a privileged position in Armenia would open the door wide to 'spheres of influences' and then to partition, the Embassy considered that it was Germany which would be only 'too pleased to dismember Turkey'. In part, the latter attitude was due to the hatred which Marling and Fitzmaurice harboured towards Germany and towards Wangenheim, the German Ambassador to the Porte. Thus, they maintained that the Armenian vilayets were a legitimate Russian interest which would not create a 'sphere of interest', while Cilicia could never be justified as a German 'sphere'. They were also convinced that Wangenheim would not risk 'Germany's present paramount influence' with the CUP for the sake of implementing an efficient scheme, by which they meant that proposed by the Russians. The Germans, for their part, regarded the Russian plan as the genesis of the partition of the Ottoman Empire. Not only did Russian ambitions in the Armenian provinces collide with German aspirations, but the annexation of the Armenian provinces by Russia would be followed by the annexation of Syria by France. In any case, the Germans realized that the British Embassy's views did not harmonize with those of the British Foreign Office.[77]

It was at this point that the anti-Russian element in the Foreign Office on Ottoman questions lost its main protagonist. Mallet, shortly to leave for Constantinople as the new Ambassador, was replaced by Eyre Crowe as head of the Eastern Department. Thus, Norman was left alone to face the full-scale attack launched by Marling and Fitzmaurice on the official attitude of the British Government. Crowe, as expected, supported the Embassy's view. German consent to regional military service and to the establishment of a single united province under a Governor-General appointed by the Sultan with the Powers' consent, strengthened Crowe in his conviction that the German diagnosis was 'false'; an 'earnest' effort should be made to make Germany 'see reason' and adopt a 'true view of the situation'. He also took the opportunity to present his interpretation of events during the preceding five years: Germany and Austria, Crowe claimed, had 'frustrated reform in Macedonia because they thought Russia would take advantage of it'. This was the only reason he could find for the outbreak of the Young Turk Revolution and the wars which followed it.[78]

Towards the end of September 1913, Russia and Germany finally reached agreement. They called upon the Porte to agree to the appointment of two Inspectors-General for the two *secteurs*, to select and dismiss the high officials, to establish an elective council for each *secteur* consisting of Moslems and Christians in equal numbers, and to accept equality in all other offices and supervision by the Powers, through the Ambassadors.[79] But shortly after the agreement was reached, Talaat, now Minister of the Interior, suggested that Crawford and Graves, who were still serving as advisers to the Porte in the Finance and Customs Department, accept the office of Inspectors-General in the two *secteurs* for five years. Neither the two British officials nor the Foreign Office were enthusiastic about the suggestion. Crowe regarded it as a 'device' inspired by Wangenheim to cause friction between Russia and Britain, and also to 'water down' the reform scheme which had already been agreed upon. He felt that the idea was to replace Crawford and Graves by German officials in posts 'where foreign influence is most important and has the maximum of effectiveness'. Moreover, Crawford and Graves would be transferred to an area where they would 'probably' be faced with difficulties, achieving nothing but friction with Russia.[80]

Britain's Policy and Interests in Mesopotamia

In July 1912, it will be recalled, Britain had withdrawn her earlier demand to participate in the construction and control of the projected railway between Baghdad and Basra. This concession did not, however, imply that she was prepared to abandon her interests in Mesopotamia. Admittedly, in the negotiations towards a settlement priority was given to the Persian Gulf.[81] Nevertheless, Britain not only kept a watchful eye on her interests in Mesopotamian navigation and irrigation, but also cultivated a growing interest in the oil-fields of the Mosul and Baghdad vilayets.

The question of Mesopotamian oil had become prominent when the Admiralty found oil important for fuelling. Hence the anxiety felt at every sign of German attempts to gain predominance in this sphere. As Nicolson put it: the Germans already controlled the Baghdad Railway, and were seeking the control of river navigation too: 'If they also get the oil-concessions in Mesopotamia and Persia they cannot fail to acquire enormous political influence at British expense, in regions which are of supreme importance to India.'[82] The Foreign Office was therefore perturbed when it discovered that the National Bank was negotiating with Shell, the Deutsche Bank and the Asiatic Petroleum Company to establish a new company for the discovery and working of oil wells in the Ottoman Empire. It feared that the only British financial house in the Ottoman Empire was prepared to go over to 'the enemy's camp'. On these grounds, the Foreign Office rejected the National Bank's request for official backing; it would support only such totally British groups as D'Arcy's, and would make 'every endeavour' to obtain the Mosul and Baghdad oil-fields for the 'purely' British Anglo-Persian Oil Co.[83] One suggestion was that on the conclusion of the Balkan War, the Government offer £1 million in cash to the Porte in return for a fifty years' concession to the Anglo-Persian Oil Co.[84]

A more immediate concern, as expressed by the Interdepartmental Committee on the Question of Oil-fields in Mesopotamia and Persia, was that the Shell Company (predominantly Dutch) and the Deutsche Bank might absorb the Anglo-Persian Oil Company. The British wished the Porte to promise that the concession for Mesopotamian oil-fields would not be given to any one but D'Arcy, and claimed that the Germans had no legal option to the fields, rights in which had been promised to D'Arcy in 1909.[85]

But this was a weak argument; the Turks showed themselves sympathetic towards German counter-claims, and at one stage denied that they had ever made an earlier promise to D'Arcy.[86] The causes for this antipathy were clearly to be found in the Balkan situation; more precisely, in the contrast between Britain's leanings towards the Balkan Allies and Germany's financial assistance to the Ottoman Government. No progress at all in the negotiations was made until April 1913, when Shevket offered to give Britain the predominant share in an amalgamated Anglo-German company.[87] Even that was not the end of the story. Nicolson seriously doubted whether Shevket could fulfil his side of the bargain and Lowther questioned the legal premise on which it had been offered. In any case, Shevket himself later quibbled over the exact meaning of the term 'predominant'. Thus the only alternative was that which Parker had suggested earlier, to keep up pressure on Hakki. But it was decided not to add the oil question as another condition for Britain's assent to the 4 per cent customs increase. Rather, Britain was to rely upon the Porte to make 'arrangements' without delay which would ensure, through a purely British Company, British control of the Mesopotamian oil-fields.[88]

Meanwhile, negotiations were opened between the Anglo-Persian Oil Company and the more powerful rival German company. The Foreign Office, still furious over the 'very unpatriotic' manner in which the National Bank had behaved,[89] insisted that it come to a 'proper' working agreement with the D'Arcy group, and follow the directions of the British Government in matters affecting British interests. Further complications ensued. As late as March 1914, the Porte formed an Ottoman group for the exploitation of oil in the vilayets of Mosul, Baghdad and Basra. An urgent representation was made to Hakki reminding him that the Porte was already pledged to D'Arcy; Britain would not be satisfied with less than 50 per cent of any company formed. Mallet (by now Ambassador at Constantinople) was instructed to tell the Porte 'categorically' that if D'Arcy would not obtain at least 50 per cent, the British would be compelled to break off all negotiations with Hakki, and reconsider their consent to the customs increase and monopolies.[90] Ultimately, both the Porte and the Germans were conciliatory. On 19 March 1914, an agreement was signed which divided the interests – 50 per cent for D'Arcy, and 25 per cent each for the Deutsche Bank and the Anglo-Persian Petroleum Company. Four days later, Mallet and Wangenheim made a joint application to the Porte for oil production in Mosul and Baghdad vilayets.[91] But the negotiations with the Porte were still in progress on the outbreak of war.[92]

The National Bank of Turkey also threatened long-established British interests in Mesopotamian navigation. Here, too, the Bank was prepared to take part in a consortium – consisting of Lynch, the Deutsche Bank and a Belgian group – and to negotiate with the Porte for the formation of an Ottoman Company to take over the steamers presently owned by the Porte, Lynch and the Deutsche Bank. The Foreign Office anticipated the opposition of the Board of Trade and the India Office, and shared their view that the Rivers concession was essential for maintaining competitive rates against the Baghdad Railway. The British felt that they were on safe ground since, according to Parker, Lynch held the rights of navigation through the British Government. Nevertheless, Grey preferred to be realistic. He held that Britain could never obtain 'purely' British control over the navigation, and that a majority for British interests would be 'safer'.[93] But Lynch was not to be supported. He was suspected of trying to cooperate with the Deutsche Bank and of 'playing false' with the Foreign Office. Consequently, the three additional steamers demanded from the Porte were not to go to Lynch, but to an 'independent' company.[94] The concession eventually went to Lord Inchcape.

Ultimately, it was the CUP Government which decided to finalize this issue, together with all other Mesopotamian and Gulf questions. To this end – and notwithstanding the continuation of hostilities in the Balkans – Hakki Pasha, the ex-Grand Vizier, was sent to London within a few days of the January 1913 *coup d'état*. Initially, there was some doubt about both the scope of his authority and the extent of his skill ('He is a windbag and chatterbox who loves good cheer of any kind', was Fitzmaurice's unsympathetic warning).[95] But Hakki soon made excellent progress. First, he concluded a Rivers Navigation Agreement, signed *ad referendum* on 16 May 1913. This incorporated several crucial suggestions put forward by Kühlmann, the German Chargé in London (notably that in return for a British agreement to allow the Baghdad Railway Company to build the Baghdad-Basra line, Germany would agree that the section to the Gulf be postponed; that two British directors join the Board of the Konia-Basra Railway; that no German subject make any claim to participate in the Rivers navigation; and that the Shatt-el-Arab be open to give all flags access to Basra). Nicolson regarded Germany's readiness to give Britain a 'free hand' in navigation to be 'the most satisfactory' feature of the suggestion. Lorimer, the Consul-General and Resident at Baghdad was decidedly less enthusiastic. The exchange of railway for navigation interests he considered to be 'imprudent ... to me it seems probable that railway will kill navigation'. But this view was overruled.[96] As Parker stated, the agreement was better than had ever been expected, 'all that was necessary was to tie the Germans down as soon as possible to their undertaking about the river navigation, lest they should whittle it away.'[97] Once Lynch had been excluded from the entire arrangement, the final agreement between the Porte and Inchcape was signed on 12 December 1913.[98]

Substantial progress was meanwhile achieved in the negotiations with Hakki on the Shatt-el-Arab question. Here the Porte accepted the British demand that the two chief officials on the Navigation Commission be British subjects recommended by the British Government, that the Sheikh of Mohammera entrust his interests to a British Commissioner and that the frontier be demarcated according to Britain's demands. With regard to Koweit, no agreement could be reached over the terms of 'suzerainty' and 'sovereignty'. Hence it was agreed that Koweit be defined as 'un caza autonome de l'Empire ottoman.' Nevertheless Britain did not give up her predominant position there. She rejected the Porte's claim to regulate the succession in the Sheikh's family and kept her 1899 agreement with the Sheikh (according to which he would not receive foreign representatives without Britain's consent).[99] Moreover, and in accordance with a separate agreement, the Porte was evicted from Bahrein and El-Katr. In exchange, Britain had agreed to give the Porte the island of Zakhnuniya and a small strip of coast. Thus the safeguards required by the Government of India had been secured and Britain could undertake not to annexe Bahrein.[100]

More complicated was the question of the renunciation of the veto by the Ottoman Empire on the borrowing powers of Egypt. Hakki considered this to be the most difficult issue of all, since the Porte could not abandon its right without parliamentary consent. But this was always Britain's 'principal' condition of her assent to the 4 per cent customs increase, Parker pointed out. Hakki suggested that the Porte might agree to one 'very large' loan to be raised in instalments over a number of years. Parker repeated that nothing short of complete renunciation would be accepted by Britain.[101] Various other matters also had to be settled. The Ottomans wanted British consent for the customs increase from 11 per cent to 15 per cent *ad valorem* not only for seven years, but for an indefinite period. They also demanded consent for the substitution, in due course, of a specific tariff for an *ad valorem* one, agreement to the *temettu* tax, the abolition of foreign Post Offices (which caused a 'serious' loss of revenue to the Porte), and the British Government's promise 'to study' the possibility of abolishing the Capitulations. Neither the Embassy nor the Foreign Office was enthusiastic about the last two suggestions; but Parker advised against returning a 'flat refusal' on the Capitulations question since the Porte had been so 'accommodating' in the negotiations, and in any case Britain was asked only to 'study' the question.[102] As Grey informed the Russian and French Ambassadors, on the whole he was very satisfied. The settlement with Turkey was necessary since nothing could be done to prevent the Baghdad Railway from reaching Basra. The chief aim of British policy was to safeguard the *status quo* in the Persian Gulf, and to safeguard British trade on the route from the Gulf to Asia Minor, through the two British directors and by keeping navigation in British hands.[103]

The final British Draft Memorandum was presented to Hakki on 5 June 1913, and led to an interview between Parker and Hakki on the 11th which made it clear that the two sides were very close on most of the controversial questions. Even the India Office and the Government of India agreed that the settlement was 'eminently satisfactory', and the final agreement with the Porte was signed by Parker and Hakki on 24 July 1914.[104] It was facilitated by the Anglo-German agreement on 15 June 1914, and the Porte's readiness to meet British claims regarding oil, irrigation and local lines to serve as feeders for the river navigation. Britain's consent to the customs increase and to Ottoman monopolies had as its preconditions concessions from the Porte.[105] Parker, as the person principally responsible for the agreement, naturally considered it a great success and a great boon to the Ottomans too.[106] 'Turkey has for the first time secured a large and certain prospect of financial assistance for the development of her own resources.' The Ottoman side claimed to be less enthusiastic. As Djavid, the Minister of Finance, stated, what the Porte really wanted was not just a free hand in the question of the Customs administration but complete economic independence. Said Halim informed Beaumont, the British Chargé, that the present situation whereby the Porte had to go around 'begging permission' to alter various financial arrangements was 'intolerable'. But Britain was not prepared to go any further.

If the Mesopotamian and Gulf agreements are to be viewed in a correct political context, Britain's attitude towards Mesopotamia must be examined in wider terms. There was no doubt that Britain regarded the Persian Gulf as her 'sphere of influence' though she preferred to define her position as 'maintaining the *status quo*'.[107] The Mesopotamian interior, however, presented a more complicated case. One interesting test case occurred in March 1913, when Arab tribes on both sides of the lower Tigris (from Gart to Gurna) begged 'protection and assistance' from Crow, the British Consul at Basra. The motive of their action was a conflict with the Ottoman authorities regarding their land contracts. In accordance with established precedent, Crow had refused this invitation to interfere in Ottoman internal affairs, but he did warn his superiors against alienating the tribes in a manner likely to detract from British 'local interests'. Mallet expanded on this theme:

> My point is that it will be a pity to alienate finally these powerful Sheikhs, who will turn to some other country. We are always talking of our prestige and interests in Mesopotamia. We do not know what may happen in that part of the world during the next few years – there have been talks of an Arab revolt and declaration of independence. It is a question whether without committing ourselves, we might not find some way of showing the Arabs that we are not entirely indifferent to their interests.[108]

But these sentiments with regard to Basra did not presage the formal implementation of an 'annexationist' policy elsewhere in Mesopotamia. On the contrary, when Britain's local representatives did suggest such a course, they were sharply cut short. In April 1913, the Foreign Office poured cold water on suggestions emanating from Hony, Vice-Consul at Mosul, that steps be taken to ensure that the region should become a British sphere of influence once the Ottoman Empire 'disintegrated'.[109] Even more specific was the reaction, during the following summer, to Lorimer's repeated advice that Britain make clear the claim to a Mesopotamian sphere of influence by 'consolidating' her position there. In view of the 'possible ultimate dissolution of Turkey', the Resident was critical of the Hakki-Parker agreement, which he regarded as a sacrifice of British interests. Instead, he advised strengthening all Britain's existing establishments in Mesopotamia, where her stake was 'most large' and her claims 'greatest'. The reaction in the Foreign Office, after some initial uncertainty, was critical. Mallet, by now fearful of the implications of Russian policy in Armenia, minuted sharply: 'There is a strong tendency on the part of our Consuls to talk of spheres of influence which if it continues must be discouraged.' Parker, somewhat tartly, wanted Lorimer informed that it was official British policy to uphold the integrity of the Ottoman Empire.[110]

There was certainly no official sympathy for the prospect of self-government in the area. Seyyid Talib's incitements to the local populace in Basra to rebel against the CUP were dismissed as unimportant and irresponsible.[111] Elsewhere, too, the local populations were considered to be absolutely unprepared for self-government. 'I think', wrote Lorimer to Hony, 'that if the Turkish Government falls short of the ideal, an Arab Government would fall even shorter.' Hony 'entirely' agreed with Lorimer, as he wrote to Marling:

> Societies are being formed, agitations are being fomented, to save this people from the Turk. What is more needed is someone to save them from themselves. The Government is no doubt responsible for many abuses, but it must be acknowledged that it is the people themselves who are most ready to avail themselves of opportunities thus afforded. The corrupt members of the Administrative Council are local Arabs. The most corrupt members of the Department of Justice are local Arabs.[112]

The Foreign Office, meanwhile, was haunted by considerations of a wider sort:

> We shall see [Nicolson wrote to Cartwright on 8 July 1913] the liquidation, should it of necessity come to pass, of the Turkish succession in Asia a far more delicate and difficult performance than that which has recently taken place in Europe. It will not be the small countries like Balkan States which will be filled with the desire of acquiring rich provinces, but it will be the Great Powers who will be scrambling to obtain their share of the spoils. We shall certainly do our best to cooperate in any measure which may help in maintaining Turkish rule surrounded naturally by all limitations and safeguards for the welfare of the subordinate races. I think that a very long time will elapse before we have done with these matters and they will afford us many months if not years of very anxious work and anxiety.[113]

About this time, on 1 July 1913, Lowther left Constantinople for good. He had served as Ambassador during one of the most crucial periods of Ottoman history and had been confronted by circumstances which no other British Ambassador accredited to that Empire had ever experienced. Previous British Ambassadors had faced the problem of dealing with the Sultan-Caliph as the only source of government; Lowther was confronted with a number of bodies: the CUP, the army, the Porte and the Parliament. Ryan's defence of his former chief, based on the claim that the Young Turks were 'chauvinistic', and that 'no British diplomat was likely to make much headway against them', is clearly unsatisfactory.[114] Nevertheless, and despite its limitations, this kind of apologia might still serve as the starting-point for an understanding of Lowther's political attitudes. For Lowther did have strong views as to what should be the character of the new Ottoman regime. As a man who had previously served in Constantinople, he thought of the Ottoman Empire in terms of a 'dictatorship' so long as Abdul-Hamid was in the saddle.[115] The kind of regime he found after the Revolution filled him with deep suspicion and doubts both as to its philosophy and leadership. In both respects, he was distrustful. From the first, he questioned whether the Young Turks could live up to their motto of Liberty, Equality and Fraternity; the Moslem could not be expected suddenly to drop his Islamic notions and embrace those of the Christians, who had for generations been regarded as both enemies and inferiors. Nor did he have any trust in the CUP's leaders. Here, it seems Ryan's judgment was correct: 'It must be admitted that he lacked elasticity. A rich man and very much of a *grand seigneur*, he was apt to look down on upstarts playing at statesmanship.'[116] Indeed, he soon became hostile towards the CUP, whose members refused to come into the open and to assume the role of a parliamentary party. It is ironical that Lowther, whilst never believing that the Young Turks could rule constitutionally, now expected them to come into the open. He never appreciated that their inability to govern the country was the very reason for their remaining an 'occult body'. Once he realized that the CUP would not lead the country towards a new period of constitutional regime, he sought explanations for that mystery. Unable to find any reasonable solution, he swallowed whole the nonsense supplied to him by his 'alter ego', Fitzmaurice. Lowther's own ignorance as to both the nature of Freemasonry and Ottoman Jewry further facilitated his acceptance of a theory which was facile but entirely erroneous. Moreover, his belief – that since the Jews hated Russia, they must also have been anti-British and accessories to Germany's policy to destroy the Entente – can only be described as pure fantasy.[117]

However misguided Lowther's views on the nature of the CUP, he was at least proved right as far as their attitudes towards Liberty, Equality and Fraternity were concerned. Ultimately, he was also seen to have predicted correctly their lack of good leadership. Thus nothing more remained for him to do except report to the Foreign Office on the constant failure of that body, in which the extremists had gained the upper hand. As far as he was concerned, Shevket's murder ended any hope that the moderates might prevail. 'I much fear', he wrote in his last letter to Nicolson, 'that now we are in for a period when the inner circle, which is of course the violent section, will make its power and influence felt ... They will make mistakes and endless mistakes, and will probably eventually hang themselves if given enough rope ...'[118] Lowther, as an unceasing enemy of any Jacobinism, whether in Revolutionary France, China, Portugal or Young Turkey, hastened to denounce the CUP's extremists, even though the political or social views of the Young Turks bore little similarity to those of their supposed French mentors. Ultimately, Lowther's strong antipathy to the CUP had nothing to do with his so-called failure to exploit the 'great opportunity' to win over the Young Turks. No evidence whatever exists to support any argument that either the Foreign Office or Lowther (by his own initiative) seriously wanted to launch a campaign to win them over. Even in 1909 when reprimanded by the Foreign Office, he was merely asked to be more sympathetic; and the fact that such an Anglophile as Kiamil did not obtain the support he had expected in 1908-9 and in 1912-3 was not Lowther's fault. Kiamil was not being realistic when early in 1913 he – in bitterness and frustration – exclaimed: 'Alas, where is White, where is Currie?'[119] Lowther certainly could not be blamed for the high policy considerations which decided in favour of Britain's anti-Ottoman attitude, and it is difficult to avoid the conclusion that when he left Constantinople he was simply made a scapegoat. The Foreign Office was ready to listen to Lowther's stories about the Freemason-Jewish plot, but also had good reasons not to support the Porte, whether the Government in power was Liberal or Young Turk. No doubt Lowther's antipathy contributed to the estrangement between the two countries, but on the real issues which stood between them there was no difference between Whitehall and the Embassy. Lowther merely articulated and repre-sented the Foreign Office's policies on the main problems, ranging from Pan-Islam and Christian equality to concessions and interests in Mesopotamia and the Gulf.[120] As his successor was soon to learn, Britain's policy towards the Porte was not a matter of the sympathy or antipathy of one Ambassador or another, but rather a question of high policy of an international and Imperial nature.

6

MALLET AT CONSTANTINOPLE –
THE FIRST PHASE

October 1913 – July 1914

The Beginnings

Towards the end of his career in Constantinople, Lowther knew very well that (in his wife's words) he was facing 'extinction'. In the Foreign Office he was certainly regarded as a failure; and that view was shared by Hardinge. A change in the Constantinople Embassy, he wrote to Parker (among others), was 'badly' needed. 'Had I remained at the Foreign Office, I am sure that I should have cut [Lowther's Embassy] short earlier. From what I hear the whole staff ought to be changed, as they are known to have an anti-Turkish bias, which they do not attempt to conceal.' Speculation was now rife as to the new Ambassador. Hardinge felt it might be Townley, the Minister in Tehran; Fitzmaurice would not have minded de Bunsen or Townley, but would have neither Bax-Ironside nor Sir Arthur Hardinge, the Minister in Lisbon; even Nicolson and Kitchener had been mentioned in Embassy circles. Mallet's appointment came, so Nicolson said, as a 'great surprise', but was nevertheless considered to be a 'very good one'.[1]

Constantinople was Mallet's first important mission abroad after thirteen years in London. As such, it was a real test. His own feelings were mixed. As head of the Eastern Department since 1907, he had amassed a wealth of knowledge on the affairs of the area; but he had also hoped for a higher appointment within the Foreign Office. However, he seems to have become reconciled to not succeeding Nicolson (principally in view of Crowe's aspirations and Tyrrell's attitude), and was therefore not sorry to leave for Constantinople. But with unusual prescience he added: 'I do not look forward with

much confidence to being able to accomplish anything at Constantinople, and suppose that I shall be classed as a failure like every other
Ambassador since Lord Stratford de Redcliffe. However, it will no
doubt be very interesting.' Stale as he was of being Assistant Under-
Secretary of State, he was perplexed as to the kind of policy Britain
wished to follow towards the Porte:

> I wish I were clearer as to the policy of H.M.G. in regard to
> Turkey [he wrote to Hardinge in August 1913]. To judge by the
> Prime Minister's speech when the Turks returned to Adrianople
> and by the leaders in the *Times* one would think that the re-
> occupation of that town was a grave British misfortune, but I
> confess I can't see why we should take the lead against the Turks.
> Both politically and commercially it is to our interests that the
> Turks should hold Adrianople and remain a fairly strong power.
> The longer we can postpone the break-up of Turkey, the better. I
> have strongly urged these views and your [Harding's] telegram
> about Mussulman feeling had a great effect, but there is no
> consistency in our policy ... We alone shall suffer for our foolish
> words. You can really exercise more influence than anyone in the
> formation of a policy towards Turkey. If the break-up of the
> Asiatic dominion of Turkey is something to be avoided, and I
> imagine that it would be a great misfortune for India to see
> Russia in the six Vilayets, Germany in Asia Minor and France in
> Syria, a consistent policy of maintaining and strengthening the
> Ottoman Empire (coupled with reforms) should be pursued and
> might be insisted on by India ...[2]

Hardinge agreed, but Mallet was not provided with firm guidelines by the Foreign Office. As much was apparent from the
very inception of his mission. Crowe recommended that the new
Ambassador should proceed to Constantinople in a British cruiser.

> ... It would both impress and gratify the Turks. We are at the
> present moment concluding a number of important conventions
> and arrangements which we hope will lead to a general good
> understanding with Turkey. There has been an unfortunate
> impression at Constantinople that our late Ambassador was too
> much identified with the anti-Committee parties. As a quiet
> demonstration of respect to the Turkish Government, the arrival
> of the new ambassador in one of HM ships would, I am sure, be
> welcomed by them.[3]

Nicolson, however, objected: the arrival of the Ambassador with 'exceptional pomp' constituted, he thought, an 'entirely new departure'. He was also unsure whether the Porte would view it as a compliment. But his main reservation was the danger that it might give the impression that Mallet was to inaugurate 'some new policy' and was invested with 'some special mission'. Ultimately, Grey (who had sought a compromise) decided, in view of Ottoman-Greek tension, that it would be better if the cruiser sailed only to the Dardanelles.[4]

To judge from certain sections of the Ottoman press, Nicolson's suspicions were well-founded. The 'Tasvir-i-Efkiar' wrote that the restoration of the old friendship between the Porte and Great Britain was imminent, and would coincide with the fading of the Entente with Russia and Britain's desire to appear as the protector of the Indian Moslems.[5] The 'Tanin' was even more enthusiastic. The fact that Mallet's appointment came shortly after the successful negotiations with Hakki and the Ottoman application for British inspectors for the Eastern vilayets was seen by Jahid as the beginning of 'a fresh chapter of cordiality' between the two countries.[6] Moreover, according to Mallet the Porte was also 'determined' to consider his appointment as an act of friendship on the part of the British Government. Full of optimism and enthusiasm to open a new era in Anglo-Ottoman relations, the Ambassador promised Grey, to whom he wrote with more eagerness than to Nicolson, that he would take 'what advantage I can' of the Porte's attitude. He even suggested to Grey: 'We are likely to get more done by suggestions and indirect methods than by collective notes and threats which the Powers are not prepared to back by force.'

Only time would tell whether Mallet could successfully implement this formula. Meanwhile he could not do without Fitzmaurice, described only a few days after his arrival as his 'right hand'. His suggestions for a new policy should therefore be seen in the light of his recognition of Fitzmaurice's invaluable service:

> It is becoming every day clearer to me [he wrote to Grey eleven days after his arrival] that I shall not be able to do without him. His knowledge is so extensive and his means of getting it so varied that he is indispensable. I do not believe that his presence here will injure any chance of getting good relations with the Young Turks. On the contrary it is more likely to help me.[7]

Mallet was probably relieved when Grey informed him that he 'certainly' could have Fitzmaurice if he wished. Fitzmaurice, however, left Constantinople on the advice of the Embassy doctor on 26 February 1914. He was suffering from a 'severe nervous breakdown'.[8]

Mallet and the Young Turks

Mallet was embarrassed by the CUP's misunderstanding of his functions as Ambassador. Their high expectations, he admitted, presented 'great' difficulties. He did demonstrate his pro-CUP views. He was strongly impressed by the 'complimentary character' of the dinners to which he was invited and was absolutely sure that the Porte was sincerely working for reform not only in civil administration but in the army and navy too. Altogether, Mallet added, the present Government was 'certainly more efficient' than any Ottoman administration had been for some years. Nevertheless, although Mallet told the Young Turks that he had been impressed by their goodwill towards Britain, he also warned that his views were not necessarily shared by his government. In fact, within a few days Crowe was to minute:

> If the Turkish Government were so genuinely friendly to us, they would not continue to organize anti-British agitation in India by their secret emissaries. Their professions must not be taken too seriously. Their policy, like that of most countries, is inspired not by national professions, but by calculated self-interest. They will use us when it suits them, and play us off against the other Powers at all times.[9]

By early 1914 the rise to prominence of Enver and Jemal had aroused British interest. Mallet's attitude was typical. He knew that Enver would be more 'agreeable' to Germany, yet did not see any reason to take an alarmist view of his appointment to the Ministry of War.[10] For Jemal, too, he had praise as well as criticism. He admitted that Jemal's 'somewhat uncompromising bent of mind and his want of experience and knowledge might prove a source of difficulty in the relations of the Government with Foreign Powers.'

He also warned that were he to become Minister of Marine he might embarrass Britain. Nevertheless, he had been favourably impressed by his three meetings with the man. Jemal's term as Vali of Adana and Baghdad had given him experience in provincial adminstration, and he seemed to be 'thoroughly honest and self-sacrificing, possessed of exceptional determination and not wanting in breadth of view in dealing with the non-Turkish elements'.[11] But Mallet's views were questioned in the Foreign Office. From the first, Nicolson felt that Enver's appointment was particularly ominous. This 'ambitious and forcible' person, he claimed, would certainly consider it necessary to demonstrate to his countrymen that he was the 'champion' of their rights and interests. He understood that Enver considered himself the 'future Napoleon' of the Ottoman Empire, 'who, though perhaps not a man of action is, I am told, an exceedingly astute and able politician'. Nicolson's conclusion was that the recent reshuffle in the CUP Government would bring with it 'some rather startling developments'.[12]

Unlike his predecessor, Mallet had very little to do with the question of Parliamentary rule in the Ottoman Empire. This could be explained on two grounds: Mallet's admiration for the CUP's leadership, notwithstanding its undemocratic methods; and the lack of interest which the Foreign Office displayed in the issue during this period. But the matter did command some attention after the elections of early 1914 and the opening of Parliament on 14 May. Although the elections had been a caricature of the democratic system, Mallet predicted that the CUP might hope for 'a long lease of life'. After all, the elections did show the strength of the CUP Government's grip on the country at large. Recent historical judgment has tended to be critical of such declarations. They have been adduced to show that Mallet was, on the one hand, insensitive to the influences of European diplomacy on the fate of the Ottoman Empire, and – on the other hand – 'cynical' or 'over-confident' in his attitude towards the parliamentary practices of the Young Turks.[13] These charges would seem unfair. No more than anyone else could Mallet foresee the forthcoming events which were to lead to the destruction of the Ottoman Empire. In the given political situation of May 1914, Mallet was right in claiming that only a 'convulsion', of the sort which had driven the CUP from power in July 1912, could bring an end to its rule. Neither was Mallet's regard for the CUP's 'outward respect' for constitutionalism misplaced. Rather, he regarded the Young Turks as practical and pragmatic rulers, who 'have chosen to reconcile constitutional forms with the only kind of Government suited to an Oriental country, and especially one composed of mixed elements, i.e., a more or less intelligent despotism ...'[14]

What is true is that the Embassy at Constantinople was decidedly optimistic. As late as the eve of the War, Mallet and Beaumont, his Counsellor, were quite sure that relations with the Porte had much improved since their arrival. They denied that the Young Turk regime was bound 'hand and foot' to Germany or that Kiamil's overthrow had dealt a 'serious blow' to British influence. On the contrary, the accusation that the Young Turks were hostile to Britain had been 'disproved over and over again'. As much as was apparent from the fact that the first appeal for the introduction of the Armenian reform had been addressed to Britain, and that Crawford and Admiral Limpus had always been offered 'cordial' help. What is more, and 'most striking' of all was the conclusion in December of the docks contract: 'No such contract has even been made in any country and it was secured without payment of a penny of backsheesh in the face of formidable competition by the Krupp and Orlando Works ...'[15] If anything, British capitalists were to be criticized for holding aloof from participating in Ottoman economic development. On this aspect of Anglo-Turkish relations, Mallet and Beaumont sympathized with the complaints voiced by Ottoman statesmen. They also believed that Germany aimed to maintain the integrity of the Ottoman Empire. As proof they cited her readiness to reorganize the Ottoman army and the friendship of Kaiser Wilhelm, the declared champion of Islam.[16]

This optimistic evaluation of the situation, which was shortly to be brutally shattered, has to be explained in the context of the admiration felt by Mallet and Beaumont for the Young Turk leadership, and chiefly for Talaat and Enver. Talaat was regarded as 'the most striking' personality of the CUP, a man of 'high capacity' and 'great energy'. They did add some notes of caution. As to Talaat 'there is some danger that he may be carried further [in his patriotism] than he wishes by his more violent and chauvinist associates'. The analogy between Enver and Napoleon was also not overlooked.

In boldness of conception, but not in importance of immediate results, the *coup d'état* of 23rd January might be compared to the more famous one of the 9th November 1799 ... and his recent marriage with a Princess of the Imperial family may possibly help his career in the same way as Madame de Beauharnais helped that of Napoleon.[17]

But, on the whole, the evaluation was favourable. How little the Embassy knew about the Young Turks' plans and how inadequate was the Foreign Office's knowledge, only later events would show.

The Armenian Question: Second Phase

Though Mallet stated that Fitzmaurice would be indispensable to him, he preferred not to accept the former line of opposition to the CUP advocated by Lowther and Fitzmaurice. This was fully demonstrated by his attitude towards the Armenian question, which contradicted that of his predecessor. Mallet could not of course ignore the Consuls' reports regarding tension in the area, but he greatly differed from them as to the sort of 'radical treatment' necessary. This resulted from Mallet's belief and confidence in the leadership of the Young Turks, especially Talaat and Jemal. Mallet wrote as if their personalities and politics had undergone an entire change, which was not the case. Hence his view that Talaat had recently shown himself 'thoroughly alive' to the Armenians' lot, and that he and Jemal had exhibited a 'markedly friendly disposition' by their presence at the 'national' celebration of the 1,500th anniversary of the invention of the Armenian alphabet. Both of them, Mallet wrote enthusiastically, had professed their 'firm' wish to work 'hand in hand' with the Armenian element for the constitutional regeneration of the Ottoman Empire, though he admitted the possibility that the Young Turks could be motivated by the hope of evading the reforms imposed on them by the Powers.

Britain was again in danger of being directly involved in the Armenian question when the Porte suggested to Crawford that he be the president of the 'informal' commission established to advise the Ottomans about their own reform scheme. Mallet waxed enthusiastic over this 'excellent' scheme, since the Porte had 'complete' confidence in Crawford and would accept his recommendations. Crowe, much less optimistic than Mallet as to the future survival of the Ottoman Empire, clarified the Foreign Office's position: Crawford's appointment for such a commission could be approved only if the Porte adopted the Russo-German scheme. Since Crawford's appointment might be interpreted as a unilateral act on Britain's part, it was rejected out of hand.[18] Thus, Mallet, despite his concern with the Porte's attitude, had to shelve his own pro-Ottoman views and adopt those of the Foreign Office when he spoke to the Porte. Indeed, for the first time, Mallet spoke strongly to an Ottoman statesman. On 11 November 1913, he told the Grand Vizier that the failure of the new regime to introduce reforms caused 'distrust' in England as to the future. Nevertheless, Mallet did remain hopeful. He was confident that Talaat's visit to the Eastern Vilayets would 'doubtless' be followed by good results, even though he admitted that it was a matter of 'grave doubt' whether the reforms would last long. He therefore suggested that no irritating steps should be taken which might force the Porte to adopt an extreme policy.[19]

Mallet soon realized that matters were more difficult than he had imagined. One cause was the 'weakness' of the Powers, and their failure to exert 'real' pressure on the Porte. Another was the inherent confusion of the case. In this complicated situation Mallet was grateful that Grey and Nicolson allowed him to retain Fitzmaurice who, he again stressed, was 'unrivalled in our line and has an extraordinary posture here.' But despite Fitzmaurice's help, Mallet was still confused: 'It is very difficult to know what to report to you, as this place is a sort of whispering gallery and everyone who comes to tell me tells me a different story.' Doubtless bewildered by the intricacies and intrigues of the political and diplomatic realities of the Ottoman capital, it is perhaps not surprising that Mallet was also disappointed with the standard of his colleagues; 'compared to the diplomats in London, they are not an interesting collection and rather *boutonné*'.[20]

Throughout the subsequent negotiations concerning the exact stations of the European inspectors, Mallet strongly advised against any move which might be implied as a threat. Rather he pressed the advantages of retaining Ottoman good will, and took seriously Ottoman warnings that European control would transform the Eastern Vilayets into a 'volcano'.[21] Optimistically, he hoped to solve the Armenian question by opening up the country by new railways,[22] and further believed that harmonious relations were possible between the Porte and the Armenians. Hence his confidence that friendship and ceremonies should be counted as a manifestation of policy, and the enthusiasm with which he reported the special courtesy with which the Porte had behaved towards M. Zaven, the new Armenian Patriarch.[23] Mallet believed the Patriarch's assurances that the Armenians were not seeking independence, and he tried to persuade the Grand Vizier to believe this too.

Mallet's optimism, however, suffered another rebuff. He reported that 'suddenly' the whole question had taken a bad turn, as the 'more chauvinistic' members of the CUP had obtained the upper hand. Now he was more familiar with the realities of the Armenian question as violent anti-Armenian activities had taken place. He suggested to the Foreign Office that, if the Russian proposals were rejected, Britain should take no responsibility and let the Porte work out 'their own salvation in the Eastern Vilayets – or the reverse'. In the Foreign Office, Mallet's attitude was approved; there was no alternative policy. Crowe was in favour of 'threatening definite hostile action' in the event of the Porte's refusal. But he knew very well that this was not possible in view, as Grey put it, of the division amongst the Powers over the Liman von Sanders and the Aegean Islands questions. Crowe added:

> It will not be to the interests of G. Britain to put herself conspicuously forward in leading the assault on the Turkish Government, unless HMG are prepared to risk the loss of our whole position in Turkey and the spread of grave commotion in India and possibly in Egypt.

Grey concluded that there was no alternative but to come nearer to the Porte's view. Mallet's attitude, therefore, prevailed and was regarded as 'very judicious'.[24] The Foreign Office refused to be influenced by the contrary advice emanating from the supporters of the Armenian cause in England.[25]

Even earlier, Grey and Nicolson had encouraged Mallet to believe that he had made 'a very good start'. Perhaps he needed encouragement not only in face of the complicated situation but owing to his discovery by early December that Fitzmaurice, though being 'the most interesting member of the Embassy and the most useful', was also 'certainly too prejudiced against the present regime and has not much constructive ability.' He admitted that his post was 'a very difficult one to fill properly unless one has been here for some time.' He made, moreover, the following confession to Grey: 'I am the prey of every rumour and sometimes I really feel as if I was living in a totally different world from London.'[26]

Throughout the winter of 1913-14, Mallet was inclined to sympathize with the Porte's attitude. He justified the Young Turks' refusal to allow free elections on the grounds that this was perhaps a 'natural instinct of self-preservation'. The Turks, after all, were in a minority in the Empire and inferior in intelligence and business capacity to the Arabs, Greeks, Armenians and Jews.[27] He was also pleased when, in the last days of 1913, the Porte eventually agreed to appoint two foreign Inspectors for Armenia, as recommended by the Powers. Mallet felt that this concession would produce 'good results'. Although he was somewhat sceptical as to the Inspectors' ability to perform their difficult duties over such a vast area he was able to persuade the Foreign Office that 'much' would depend upon the men selected for the post. He trusted that 'they would be able to insist on the punishment of crime and outrage brought to their knowledge'[28] and played down the Russian warning of disturbances in Erzeroum.[29] He even managed to persuade the Foreign Office that his optimism was well-grounded. There was, indeed, general agreement with Vice-Consul Smith's suggestion (from Van) that the aspirations of the majority of Armenians were economic rather than political, since the Armenians were 'above all' a commercial race. If the Porte constructed roads, placed a few motor boats on Lake Van and hurried the building of a railway, the country would then become 'prosperous' and 'the so-called Armenian question at least with regard to this vilayet, would to a great extent cease to exist with the advent of increased trade and prosperity'.[30]

Ultimately, both the Embassy and the Foreign Office were relieved and optimistic when a reform project was signed on 8 February 1914. Nicolson attributed much of the credit to Russia, and hoped that the plan would work: 'though it is one of a long series of such admirable schemes which have all hitherto been absolutely barren in their results.'[31] Thereafter, however, the Foreign Office rapidly lost interest in the problem. Not even the reports emanating from Van that land disputes between Kurds and Armenians constituted a 'vital' problem changed this attitude. The Foreign Office merely decided that the question should be dealt with by the Inspectors-General, who should contact the Consul.[32] The consequent fighting between the Ottoman Government and the Kurds also aroused little interest in the Foreign Office; even when it was reported that it had caused ill-feeling between the

Young Turks and the Armenians 'we ought not to be troubled at all', wrote Crowe impatiently.[33]

The British Government, however, was insulted when the Russians treated the question of the selection of the Inspectors as a 'purely' Russian concern, and Crowe felt that the British Government was thus put in a 'most undignified' position. The Porte had finally chosen Major Hoff, a Norwegian, and M. Westenenk of the Dutch East Indian Administration, out of the five candidates offered. In May, the new Inspectors signed their contracts with the Porte and were expected to start work early in July. Said Halim spoke with contempt about their 'rapacity' concerning their salary, and expressed pessimism as to their possible success. Mallet too felt they would not get 'cordial support' from the Porte.[34] The outbreak of the European war finally caused the practical abandonment of the Armenian reform scheme. Westenenk never proceeded to the Armenian Vilayets; Hoff did, but was recalled by the Porte because of the difficulties in accomplishing his task owing to the mobilization of the Ottoman army. Between August and October 1914, the British Government received little information about the actual situation in the Eastern Vilayets. The information on the precarious situation which had been obtained by Aneurin Williams, MP, Chairman of the British Armenian Committee, could not be verified through official channels. In any case, Grey stated that Britain had done all in her power to induce the Porte to preserve peace, and there was nothing more which he could do.[35] But in late September, Mallet reported in pessimistic tones about the unhappy relations between the Young Turks and the Armenians. Now he seemed to realize – for the first time – that the situation was explosive, but was still naïvely convinced that, were the Inspectors-General to fulfil the reform scheme under peaceful conditions, 'some substantial improvement might have been effected and the position of the Government really consolidated'.[36]

The Liman von Sanders Question

A few days after Mallet's arrival in Constantinople, Britain was faced with a crisis which threatened to cause international repercussions similar to those resulting from the Armenian issue. On 28 October 1913, General Liman von Sanders was appointed to command both the First Army Corps at Constantinople, and the German military mission in Turkey.[37] The Germans attempted to play down the incident; the appointment, they claimed, was merely part of the programme to extend their existing military mission from 12 to 42 officers. But this was not the entire story. For one thing, as the British Military Attaché in Berlin reported, von Sanders and his officers would possess 'unlimited' powers to help the Porte reorganize its entire army.[38] For another, the appointment inevitably impinged upon the delicate interplay of Great Power influence in the Ottoman Empire. Nicolson immediately grasped the implications; the Germans seemed to be challenging the Russian claim that Constantinople, as well as the Armenian provinces, came within the Russian 'sphere of influence'.[39]

Personally, Nicolson supported the Russian point of view; but it was difficult to give such sympathy practical effect. Sazonov's suggested counter-measures (the removal of German headquarters to Smyrna or the appointment of a Russian General to command Ottoman troops at Bayazid), were dismissed as impractical – if not suspicious.[40] They raised the spectre of an imminent partition of the Empire. This was Grey's line:

> The German Government could not with justice object to other Powers demanding similar advantages from the Turkish Government to compensate and safeguard their own interests, but it is difficult to see what advantages consistent with the maintenance of Turkish independence could be obtained by other Powers which would be adequate compensation and safeguard for their interests.[41]

What did concern Britain was precisely the form which such demands for compensation might take. As Vansittart put it, the Liman von Sanders affair presented Britain not with just another crisis which threatened to strengthen German influence in the Ottoman Empire, but also with the need to restrain the scramble for 'equivalents' which Russia and France had too lightly joined.[42]

Initially, Sazonov wished the British to accept his view that the Liman von Sanders affair be treated as a 'test of the value' of the Triple Entente. Germany should be made aware, he demanded, of Britain's readiness to use her fleet if necessary. Grey refused. At most he was prepared to see the Entente ambassadors present an identical (but not collective) note to the Porte, pointing out that the exclusive powers given to the Germans would give them influence over the *corps diplomatique*, the Straits, and even the Sultan's sovereignty.[43] Otherwise, however, the Foreign Office considered that Britain's interests would best be served by minimizing the importance of Liman von Sanders' appointment. One reason was the feeling, expressed even by Nicolson, that the intrinsic threat which the post posed was 'more apparent than real'; it certainly did not warrant a British effort to 'pull the chestnuts out of the fire for Russia'. A second, also noted by Nicolson, was that Sazonov himself could not really be trusted to stick to his guns. It was difficult to believe that the Russians were sincerely looking forward to a crisis with Germany, and Britain would look 'rather foolish' were she to take up the question 'warmly' and then be deserted by Sazonov.[44]

Mallet advanced a third, and equally telling argument for British moderation. The demand for compensation, he pointed out, could become two-edged; it might involve such questions as a Russian demand to open up the Straits, Limpus' command of the Ottoman navy,[45] and the monopoly given by the Porte to Vickers and Armstrong to build arsenals and dockyards anywhere in the Ottoman Empire other than the Persian Gulf and the Red Sea. Besides, Mallet was anxious not only that the Ottoman navy should remain under British control, but also that the Ottoman Government should not be weakened by the question of compensation:

> in my opinion [he wrote to Grey] they deserve encouragement and what sympathy we can give them. I think it remarkable that they should have come out as well as they have considering what they have gone through the last 2 years. The mere work which they do is colossal ...[46]

The Foreign Office could not accept that either Limpus' command or the Vickers-Armstrong concession was on the same footing as Liman's command; but it did appreciate the force of Mallet's arguments. Indeed, the possibility that the Porte or the Germans might use Limpus' command as an argument caused Grey to go 'very carefully', and to pay less attention than Russia and France to the new information that Liman von Sanders would also be Vice-President of the Supreme Ottoman Military Council.[47] Sazonov did again try to push Britain to agree to extreme measures against the Porte; financial pressure, refusal of the 4 per cent increase, the rupture of diplomatic relations, and if necessary the occupation of Ottoman ports in the Mediterranean and Black Sea by the Entente. But the Foreign Office was adamant. Such moves, Crowe explained, could 'entirely' upset the 'general line' of British policy towards the Ottoman Empire.[48] Mallet was more specific. Demands for compensation, he reiterated, could only be counter-productive:

> It must be remembered that all the other Powers are busy pegging out claims, and the best justification of our attitude of aloofness would be the maintenance of the integrity of the Ottoman Dominions. If we can do anything to help that, all the better.[49]

But once Limpus' command was associated with Liman's, even Mallet was forced to agree that Britain might soon face a dilemma between reform and her own interests. He felt that hitherto Limpus' command had been clearly classified as a reform measure, but the Liman affair now made it appear to serve purely British interests, and denied Britain the role of 'the only Power which really desires the reform and the integrity of the Empire'. Perhaps Limpus had better relinquish the title of naval commander, while retaining the real power.[50]

By this time, the Foreign Office appears to have been less sincere than Mallet in its concern for Ottoman integrity and reform. Nevertheless, the line it pursued on the Liman von Sanders question came under fire from two sources. One was Sazonov, who was 'deeply disappointed and upset' by Britain's refusal to go beyond a verbal enquiry to the Porte, and even threatened to reconsider the value of the Entente.[51] Although Nicolson was a 'little nervous' lest Britain's refusal to support Russian policy in this question would adversely affect their 'intimate friendship',[52] the Foreign Office really wanted the Liman von Sanders affair to be settled directly between Germany and Russia without involving a British concession over Limpus' command. To serve that end, Grey was ready to accept a Russian suggestion that Limpus' command and residence should be transferred to Ismid (provided this was practicable and consistent with 'performance of his duties' and the Porte agreed).[53] Said Halim, on the other hand, was 'upset and agitated' by the verbal enquiry. He had not, he told Mallet, expected Britain to place him in the embarrassing position of questioning the independence of the Ottoman Government, namely its undoubted authority over the German General. Pointedly, he also asked whether Limpus or any of his predecessors, who had (in his opinion) exercised a similar if not a more extensive command, had ever controlled the Porte.[54] The Ambassador, significantly, was concerned. He again supported the 'nominal' change in Limpus' status to that of Adviser, warned that the Porte might apply to Germany for even more help, and cautioned against any action which might intensify Ottoman ill-feeling.[55]

Eventually, albeit reluctantly, the Foreign Office began to respond to such pressures. Despite Limpus' own pleas that his status should not be diminished, Grey was prepared to make this concession in order that the Liman von Sanders issue could be solved.[56] The Germans soon supplied the *quid pro quo*. On 30 December 1913, they declared their readiness to rescind his command over the First Army Corps and to appoint him Inspector-General without special command. At the same time, Jagow, the German Secretary for Foreign Affairs, assured Goschen that German officers would in no way become involved in Ottoman internal politics.[57] Officials at the British Foreign Office were eager to accept this assurance at its face value. They did not entirely ignore the possible effects of Liman von Sanders' appointment (however reduced his capacity) on German influence at Constantinople. Neither was Nicolson, in particular, insensitive to the possible impact of the affair on Anglo-Russian relations.[58] Nevertheless, the Foreign Office did refuse to regard the issue (as did the Russians) as one on which the Triple Entente ought to place itself squarely against the Triple Alliance. Such a policy would have been fraught with dangers for both the integrity of the Ottoman Empire and the peace of Europe.[59]

Thus, Sazonov was again unsuccessful in his attempts to persuade Britain to subscribe to his policy. The Foreign Office refused to jeopardize her new agreements with the Porte by using the 4 per cent customs increase as a weapon in the Liman von Sanders question. The French, too, were very reluctant to sacrifice their considerable financial investments in the Ottoman Empire for the sake of the Russian interests.[60] In mid-January, Nicolson became convinced that the Czar, who was after all the ultimate authority in foreign affairs, would never allow the Entente to be affected by such a question. He was no longer frightened by Sazonov whom he found 'tiresome' and 'somewhat excitable, and like many weak men occasionally irritable and fractious. Too great weight need not be attached to his opinions.' In any case, Russia was unable to wage war against the Porte.[61]

Ultimately, a solution was found whereby Liman von Sanders was promoted to the rank of Marshal in the Ottoman army and thus became too senior to command the First Army Corps; instead he was appointed Inspector-General of the Army.[62] The British were considerably relieved that the affair was thus settled. Nicolson did feel that Liman's new position would be 'equally, if not more, influential' than that originally suggested. But Grey thought that the 'intrinsic' importance of the German General's command had always been 'very much' exaggerated.[63] Once the Russo-German conflict over the issue was settled, the British Government took little notice of Liman von Sanders' activities. That the Germans might use the Military Mission to increase their political grip on the Ottoman Empire was not considered. In March 1914, the British Military Attaché at Constantinople did warn that at least 47 officers were known to be serving in the German Military Mission. Many of their positions, he cautioned, were of considerable importance; they were given 'executive functions' not only around the capital but also in different regions of the Empire. But the Foreign Office was interested only in the discrepancies between the numbers of officers given by the Military Attachés in Berlin and Constantinople.[64]

The Aegean Islands, the Ottoman Navy and the Entente

From Britain's point of view, the future disposition of the Aegean Islands appeared to be a far more complicated and troublesome question during this period. The problem had first arisen in April 1912 when Italy occupied Stampalia; there followed (in May) the occupation of Rhodes and the rest of the Dodecanese and (late in November 1912) the Greek occupation of Mitylene, Chios and the rest of the Aegean Islands. The British, who had sympathized with the Greeks from the outbreak of the Balkan War, still held that the only way to avoid a repetition of the Cretan question was for Greece to hold all the Islands other than Tenedos and Imbros. Should the Porte reoccupy Chios and Mitylene, Britain would expect all the Powers to take common action against the Ottomans.[65]

For Mallet, the question of the Islands was of particular importance since it threatened to endanger his plan of opening a new era in Britain's relations with the Ottoman Government. Said Halim soon made it clear that the Ottomans would fight unless the Powers decided in their favour, and would not hear of autonomy. Mallet took the Grand Vizier's threats seriously, and therefore cautioned against the adoption of a hostile British attitude: 'That ... would really be the last straw so far as our influence here is concerned.'[66] By mid-December, Mallet did realize that 'all the Powers including ourselves, are trying hard to get what they can out of Turkey. They all profess to wish the maintenance of Turkey's integrity but no one ever thinks of this in practice.' Nevertheless, he continued to argue that Britain should help the Ottomans in every way possible and not starve them financially. He even reminded Grey of his earlier personal promise not to take any initiative in the question of the Islands.

> I shall feel very uncomfortable with the Grand Vizier and Talaat, who have confidence in my good will, and whom I have been endeavouring to persuade of British sincerity and friendship if HMG have made proposals unfavourable to Turkey.[67]

In fact, however, the Foreign Office rejected Mallet's advice. Officials in London dismissed his warnings of the Porte's threat to go to war, which they thought might be avoided by a suspension of all loans by France.[68] They even attempted to keep their pro-Greek attitude a secret from the Ambassador.[69] Grey, it is true, did feel it necessary to appease Mallet's injured feelings. He explained that he had initially not intended to initiate a transfer of the Islands from the Porte to Greece, but this now seemed 'the only chance' of avoiding 'catastrophe' over South Albania. Greece, he maintained, had to be compensated for her loss of Korytza and Stylos (in the same area) by obtaining the Islands:

> I am full of compunction at not having told you and explained it all to you beforehand and I realize what this may have added to your difficulties, and if the results are untoward at Constantinople they shall go to my account, and not to yours.

He promised Mallet that Britain had introduced a condition that the Powers should pledge to the Porte that Greece would not sanction smuggling and that Italy should return the Islands she had occupied.[70]

But if Mallet was easily appeased, this was not the case with

the Porte, which regarded Mitylene and Chios as part of the mainland and therefore strategically vital. Said Halim refused to accept
the British explanations; he was convinced that, as in the case of
Adrianople, Britain had once more decided on a hostile policy.[71]
The Ottoman resolve was strengthened, as London well realized,
by the prospect of its growing naval strength. As early as December
1912, the Admiralty had warned that were the Germans somehow
to gain command of the battleship *Mahmud Reshad V* (then being
built in Britain, and whose expense Grey had long deplored),
Britain's naval position would be 'seriously' affected.[72] To this was
now added the more immediate fear that the possession of large
vessels (the Ottomans were also rumoured to be negotiating for the
Rio de Janeiro – subsequently *Sultan Osman* – in Brazil) would
constitute an inducement to seize Chios and Mitylene.[73] Britain's
fears on this score were not pacified by either Admiral Limpus'
argument that the Ottoman fleet-building programme was perfectly
rational ('If the Greeks had super-Dreadnoughts the Turks must
keep ahead of them. It is apparently a case of two keels to one ...'[74]),
or by Jemal's assurance that the Turkish navy would always fight on
Britain's side and help to maintain the balance of power in the
Mediterranean against the growing power of Italy.[75]

Appreciating the gravity of the situation, Mallet expected 'a crisis
every morning ... almost as regularly as my boiled egg'. The British
Government, he felt, had to allow the Porte to go its own way. 'If we
don't some other Powers will step into our shoes.'[76] The Foreign
Office, however, did not show the slightest readiness to change its
policy on the disposition of the Islands. Crowe got Tewfik to admit
that the Porte had already unconditionally accepted the principle
that the Powers would decide the fate of the Islands, which was
bound up with that of South Albania and the islands occupied by
Italy.[77] He also rejected the Porte's argument that Greek rule in the
Islands was bound to promote irredentist propaganda on the mainland; he could not believe that the Greek Government had any
territorial ambitions on the Ottoman mainland, and considered
those Greeks living in the Ottoman Empire to be business-minded
rather than nationalists. As far as he was concerned, the Porte was
the true danger-point. Once they had won a naval victory, the Turks
would not be satisfied with the Islands alone.[78] He was, therefore,
even prepared to send a fleet to the area – provided the six Powers
were willing to act together.[79]

At this stage the possibility that Britain might employ force (in one form or another) against the Ottoman Empire did indeed become a common *motif* in the correspondence between Mallet and the Foreign Office. More especially was this so once the Ambassador began to despatch frequent rumours of Ottoman-Bulgarian collusion, which seemed further to threaten Greece. Mallet, it is true, thought principally in terms of financial pressure and deprecated anything in the nature of threats '*unless we are prepared to go far*' [sic]. But even he thought that the occupation of Dedeagatch could be effective.[80] The tone at the Foreign Office became even more ominous. The general feeling in London was that the Triple Alliance had 'coached' the Porte to adopt an attitude hostile towards the Triple Entente,[81] and Crowe (not uncharacteristically) considered the Germans to be cynically intriguing in an attempt to undermine the interests of the Concert and preserve her own.[82] Hardinge, in India, was concerned when the Italian Foreign Minister raised the spectre of Moslem sentiment in the sub-continent over the Islands question.[83] But Crowe was unperturbed.

> ... we are dealing with people who are incapable of straightforwardness. We should be careful not to play into their hands. Every friendly act or concession to them on our part will be turned into a further weapon of offence against us. We ought in regard to Italy to stand strictly on the principle 'do ut des', and do nothing without proper return.[84]

Grey himself made it clear that the Islands question had brought with it again another anti-Ottoman turn in Britain's policy: 'It seems madness', he warned, 'for the Turks in their present financial situation, to boycott and suppress Greek traders in Turkey; and a chauvinist policy will bring Turkey down again.'[85] Typical of the new attitude was the brusque manner in which the Foreign Office dismissed Crawford's urgent appeal to avoid a financial crash. Indeed, according to Parker, 'Financial pressure is all to the good as it will make the Turks less inclined to an adventurous foreign policy.'[86]

Mallet sensed the deterioration in Anglo-Ottoman relations and was himself less inclined than formerly to believe in the Young Turks' promises. Nevertheless, on the whole he continued to retain his initial belief that the existing Ottoman Government was 'the best' possible, and reported to London on a 'strong' tendency for peace and reform. Time and again he repeated how impressed he was with the 'ability', 'character' and 'honesty' of such Young Turks as Talaat and Jemal.[87] Assessments of that sort prompt the conclusion that Mallet was not a reliable judge of the Ottoman political scene. Even more surprising was his total failure to understand the causes for Germany's predominant position in the Ottoman capital and for Russia's difficulties there. The former he largely attributed to:

> clever handling and flattery on the part of German agents ... if the Russians would change their tactics and treat the Turks as M. Gulkevitch, the Russian Chargé d'Affaires treats them, with sympathy, they would soon acquire as much influence as Germany and our position would be much easier ...[88]

An ambassador who had served as the Head of the Eastern Department from the genesis of the Young Turk Revolution and yet who failed to perceive the enormous influence which the Germans acquired in the Ottoman army and – thereby – in the leading circles of the CUP, and who believed that good relations were dependent on sympathy alone, could not be successful for very long. Mallet overrated the importance of the ambassador's role with regard to himself, Giers and Bompard, and underrated the long-term interests and policies of such Powers as Germany and Russia in the Ottoman Empire. Rather, he thought that sympathy and money and a less irritating attitude on Russia's part could accomplish 'a great deal', provided the Entente worked together for Ottoman integrity and improvement of the administration. Thus, he very strongly urged the Foreign Office to persuade the French Government to move forward the date of the first instalment of the planned loan to the Ottoman Empire.[89]

This is not to deny that Mallet had clearly changed his tone towards the Young Turks since his arrival. The Islands question had taught him one lesson; the prospect that the Turks faced financial 'ruin' provided another. He was not now prepared to accept as easily as before the Ottoman claim that a large army was vital to the Empire's existence. He told the Young Turks that a small army would be enough to defend them from the Balkan States, besides which the present army was simply not large enough to fight Russia. He advised them to take the smaller risk and not to move 'to certain ruin financially'. Yet he remained basically optimistic that if only the Foreign Office would follow his advice, the situation would change entirely:

> As it is our policy to maintain the integrity of the Turkish Asiatic dominions [he wrote to Grey on 10 March] and if we want to prevent the Turks from joining ... the Triple Alliance, it will not be enough to sit still. The Turks are favourably disposed and they will respond to friendly overtures from us. We can do much by adopting a sympathetic attitude and by avoiding harsh and provocative criticism in which *The Times* and English Press indulges. If it were possible for you to induce British Financiers or capitalists to take a share in the big loan ... supposing the French desired it, an immense effect would be produced here and if we could help in a compromise between Greece and Turkey it would advance our interests incalculably. I venture to think that it is worth making this effort and that we now have a position which we had 6 years ago.[90]

Although Grey was prepared to make a somewhat pro-Ottoman statement to the House of Commons on 18 March, he was unable to fulfil Mallet's wishes. He could not influence British financiers to invest in the Ottoman Empire, especially after Sir Ernest Cassel's failure in the area.[91] Nevertheless, Mallet, who thought that Grey's speech was 'very helpful' and 'much appreciated',[92] still tried to induce the Foreign Secretary to sound Rothschild on taking up the new loan and thus participating in the outstanding bills for the two Dreadnoughts, *Sultan Osman* and *Reshadieh*, which Armstrong were in the process of constructing. This was an essential part, Mallet was convinced, of any attempt to preserve the integrity of the Ottoman Empire, which he felt should be the 'main object' of Britain's policy, even if it might entail 'temporary' sacrifices.

> The most obvious way of helping at present is by giving our moral support to the Turkish Government which is on the whole justifiable in the present circumstances, by avoiding all action which might weaken their authority, all small causes of irritation and all suspicion that our ends are entirely selfish and regardless of Turkey's interests ...[93]

How could Britain fulfil Mallet's wishes when the struggle for spheres of influence was so obviously mounting? Here, too, Mallet had an answer. He suggested that the 'more we obtain concessions in each other's so-called spheres, the easier it will be to avert a division of Turkey.' More specifically, Britain should apply for oil concessions in Anatolia, and object to any irrigation arrangement with the Germans in Mesopotamia without an agreement to share in the Konia irrigation.[94]

In the Foreign Office there was less optimism. Admittedly, Mallet's views were respected; and even his estimate of the characters of the CUP's leaders was accepted. Grey and Nicolson both lavished praise on the Ambassador, whom they thought was doing 'exceedingly well'.[95] But they could not agree with his analysis of the means whereby Ottoman integrity might best be preserved. In particular, they questioned his advice that Britain adopt a policy of impartiality on Ottoman questions between the Triple and Dual Alliances. Nicolson, as is well known, was – on the contrary – adamant that Britain strengthen her ties with Russia. Replying to Mallet's suggestion that the Foreign Office should not 'lean too much on either grouping of Powers', he stressed that his own ambition was in fact to convert the existing Entente into an alliance. The reasons, as he confided to Townley, were global in scope.

> The maintenance of our understanding with Russia is of the very greatest importance to us both in Europe and in regard to India and our position generally in the Mid and Far East ... She can hit us if she becomes unfriendly ... The understanding with Russia is in reality of far more importance to us than it is to her, and I am continually haunted by the fear that something may occur which may seriously impair that understanding ...[96]

The augmentation of Ottoman naval strength at this time clearly illustrated the difficulties inherent in an attempt to pursue Mallet's policy of an independent attitude towards the Porte. The issue arose in May 1914, when the Russian Government notified Britain of its apprehensions with regard to Turkish naval development. The Russians also intimated (Russell warned) that they might expect the British authorities to use their influence either to reduce the pace of the Ottoman programme or to prevent the Turks buying ships in British dockyards.[97] The British were themselves not insensitive to the possible danger in Ottoman possession of Dreadnoughts (due to be delivered in October 1914). It had long been appreciated that with 'people like Djavid, Talaat and Enver in the Cabinet, a negligible Sultan and a weak Grand Vizier, any military adventure is to be expected';[98] and the sharp rise in Graeco-Turkish tension during the spring as a result of alleged Ottoman brutalities in Asia Minor, seemed very much to increase the danger of hostilities. Nevertheless, in purely military terms, as Nicolson had always maintained, the Russians could have little to fear: the Ottoman navy was unlikely to become 'an important or efficient factor'.[99] Its real importance lay in its possible political effect. Therein, however, was Britain's difficulty. Nicolson suspected, as did Mallet, that the Russian protest was really a preliminary to an unwelcome diplomatic initiative on the Straits question. His difficulties, therefore, were dual: he had to reassure Russia that neither she nor Greece (where Britain maintained a naval mission) had anything to fear from the Ottoman fleet. At the same time, however, he had to be careful not to give offence to the Porte (and Mallet) by refusing to renew Admiral Limpus' contract.[100]

Ultimately, the Foreign Office neatly side-stepped the question. First, Britain promised Russia that were the danger of a Graeco-Ottoman war to become acute, she would enter into an exchange of views with the Russian Government. Then, she advised that Limpus' contract be renewed – not least (so the Russians were informed) in order to prevent the Ottoman navy falling under German influence, as the army had done. Finally, Britain cited the latest evidence of a rapprochement between the Turks and the Russians themselves (notably Talaat's 'complimentary' visit to the Czar at Livadia on 17 May 1914) as proof of the fact that Ottoman naval development was not anti-Russian in intent.[101]

Such diplomacy, successful though it was, did not solve the question of the Greek Islands – which, in fact, remained troublesome until the outbreak of war. It did, however, strengthen Mallet's personal belief that his opportunity to effect a substantial improvement in Anglo-Ottoman relations had finally arrived. The Russo-Ottoman rapprochment, he believed, would remove an important cause of distrust between Britain and the Porte and facilitate Anglo-Russian cooperation in pursuit of their 'common desire to maintain the integrity and independence of the Ottoman dominions in Asia'. Furthermore, he reiterated:

> The present situation, though it requires delicate handling, seems to be rather favourable than the reverse to British interests, which will be best served by maintaining the general lines of

cooperation with the Triple Entente without leaning too ostentatiously towards either group of powers.[102]

But the Foreign Office was far more sceptical and in fact regarded this advice as both curious and impractical. As early as January 1914, Nicolson had expressed the hope that members of the British Embassy Staff at Constantinople would not apply for membership in a newly formed Anglo-Ottoman Association.[103] Not even the signs of an improvement in Russo-Ottoman relations (first portended by the formation of a similar committee between nationals of these two countries in March), brought about a change in the atmosphere. The Foreign Office was pleased to hear of the amicable conversation between Sazonov and Talaat at Livadia,[104] but nevertheless resisted Mallet's appeals that it seize the opportunity to pursue a policy of neutrality in Ottoman questions. Eurocentric factors precluded that possibility.

Britain and Italy's Ambitions

Meanwhile, a related complication had arisen in the shape of the emergence of Italian claims to a sphere of influence in Asia Minor. The British were concerned on three counts. First, the Italian negotiations (initiated in February 1913) for a railway from Adalia to Selefke on the Anatolian mainland threatened to impinge upon the British Smyrna-Aidin line, a concession for which had been obtained in October 1906 and whose prolongation was now being negotiated with Hakki. Secondly – and as the Admiralty warned – Italy's claims that she (and not Greece) was to control the Aegean Islands threatened adversely to affect Britain's strategic position in the Mediterranean. As Vansittart pointed out, the danger of a permanent Italian presence in the Dodecanese was 'more important to us than the question whether Turkey or Greece gets the Islands further north.'[105] Finally, and at a different level, Italian ambitions in general appeared to presage an era of growing cooperation between Germany and Italy in the destruction of Ottoman integrity. Brushing aside the frequent (and not unjustified) Italian protests that the British had themselves carved out their own sphere of influence along the Persian Gulf littoral, the Foreign Office adopted an attitude of self-righteous opposition to the Italian Foreign

Minister's (San Guiliano's) argument that all Italy demanded was compensation for her investments in the islands now under Greek control. The phrase 'zones de travail' was merely a euphemism for 'sphere of influence'; altogether, the Italian demands were 'of a kind incompatible with the policy of maintaining the integrity of Asiatic Turkey' (Crowe) and 'rapacious' (Nicolson).[106] Besides,

> Quite apart from our own interests, in the shape of the British railway, we may find it politic from the point of view of our already rather difficult relations with Turkey not to support or connive at these Italian designs for the creation of a sphere of influence at Adalia.[107]

At this stage, it was Crowe who took the most serious view of the Italian ambitions, behind which he (as did the French) suspected an intrigue by the Triple Alliance: 'It would of course be in accord with their [the Triple Alliance's] views that the desired "compensation" to Italy for carrying out her pledges and treaty obligations should be made at the expense of British interests in Turkey as far as possible.'[108] Moreover, when the Italians mentioned the exchange of Chios and Mitylene against some of the Dodecanese as a possible solution, Crowe had 'no doubt' that the Italians wanted to include these regions in their proposed 'sphere of interest' in the Ottoman Empire.[109] Grey too now took a stronger attitude than previously. He told Imperiali, the Italian Ambassador in London, that during the last year or two Italy had encroached upon British interests more than any other European Power. She had aroused Moslem feeling in Egypt by the annexation of Tripoli, placed new conditions on the evacuation of the Islands, and claimed concessions injurious to British interests in the Smyrna-Aidin Railway. In the event of a break-up of Abyssinia, she also demanded Lake Tzana which Britain considered to be 'essential' for the waters of the Nile.[110]

The Porte, in this case, was more flexible. As early as January 1914, Said Halim had informed Mallet that some concessions would have to be made to the Italians. Indeed, the British – notwithstanding their protestations of support for Ottoman integrity – were hardly regarded with great favour in Constantinople. The reason was that the Porte was really more concerned about Mitylene and Chios, on which Britain adopted a pro-Greek attitude, than about Italy's ambitions in the Dodecanese or Adalia. The Ottomans were more appreciative of Italy's readiness to return Mitylene and Chios to them than impressed by Britain's opposition to Italy's ambitions. Italy, Germany and Austria, said Said Halim, had 'fortunately' saved the situation for the Porte by refusing to participate in Britain's 'hostile initiative' on the Islands.[111] Under these circumstances, the British retracted by restricting their interests to the Smyrna-Aidin line. Once there was a good prospect of the Italians coming to terms on this issue, even Crowe was ready to compromise. Grey also realized that the 'best solution' would be for the British Company to obtain the concession of the railway to Adalia and for the Italians to get the concession for the port of Adalia.[112] Mallet did recommend Jemal's suggestion for an Anglo-Italian combination on the ground that this would prevent the Makri-Mougla line from becoming Italy's 'exclusive sphere of influence'. He warned that the Marmarice Bay, which was adjacent to the much-coveted line, was a more valuable naval base than Stampalia or any Greek island. But Crowe regarded Mallet's view as one of unfounded 'alarm'. As long as the negotiations between the Italians and the Smyrna-Aidin Co. were proceeding on sound lines, the Foreign Office was not concerned.[113] Mallet alone feared that the Italians might create a strategically dangerous 'sphere of influence' in the Adalia-Marmarice area. Crowe took a more balanced view when he maintained:

> I confess I doubt whether there need be any such danger. Smyrna is not a British nor Mersina a German naval port, although a British railway starts from Smyrna, and a German from Mersina.
>
> If Turkey falls to pieces the Italians may wish to obtain possession of the ports where the Italian-built railways debouch. But except on the general Turkish collapse, there ought to be no difficulty in preventing such ports assuming the character of Italian naval ports.[114]

The excitement aroused by Italian ambitions in Asia Minor died down in May 1914, when the Smyrna-Aidin Railway Co. safeguarded its rights by an agreement which was finally signed with the Porte on 29 July. It was preceded by an agreement between the Company and the Italian syndicate. But the Porte was not in a hurry to give the concession to Italy. Neither was Grey more willing than before to help the Italians obtain this concession. He told Imperiali as late as 23 July: 'We had been pressing Turkey for concessions that we ourselves wished to have, and we could not well press

Turkey for concessions to other people.' Britain, however, secured her rights in the Smyrna-Aidin Railway, where she even obtained a concession from the Porte which precluded Ottoman directors from the Company's Board. The demand was based on the argument that the railway was purely British and not guaranteed by the Porte.[115]

The 'Arab Question' and Zionism

Judged by the overall standards of the modern history of the Middle East, the details of pre-War European squabbles for economic concessions in Asia Minor might seem to pale in importance besides the contemporary emergence of Arab nationalist sentiment. British statesmen of the period, notwithstanding their involvement in the former development, did not ignore the latter. Only a few days after his arrival in Constantinople, Mallet reported that the 'Arab question will henceforth be the important question in the Ottoman Empire'. He cited the appointment of Bekir Samy Bey as the new Vali of Beirout, consequent upon the recent agreement between the Young Turks and the Young Arabs.[116] Furthermore, he advised: 'Many Young Turks now hold the view that the Ottoman Empire should be formed into a "Turco-Arabia" on the lines of Austria-Hungary, with the Sultan-Caliph as the Crown link.' The Foreign Office, suspecting Fitzmaurice's exaggerated influence, was more sceptical, and tended to interest itself more in Bekir Samy's administrative record.[117] Like Mallet, however, officials in London did tend to consider the 'Arab question' within the context of its implications for the integrity of the Ottoman Empire. It was their concern for the latter which dictated the tone of their responses to such advances as were made to Britain on the subject.

One test case occurred in February 1914, when the Governor of Cairo asked that Mallet make friendly and unofficial enquiries to the Porte on behalf of his brother-in-law, Aziz Ali al-Misri, an officer in the Ottoman army who had been placed under arrest. Aware that Aziz Ali was a 'leading spirit' amongst the anti-CUP 'Young Arabs' (a group to whom he did not attach much importance), Mallet was cautious. Indeed, as a supporter of Ottoman integrity, he refused to have anything to do with the Young Arab plan to combine with local notables (including the Sheikh of Koweit), and liberate the region from the Persian Gulf to Mosul and 'compel' British intervention on their behalf. Britain, he said, would not support an adventurous policy which could only cause damage to her economic interests in Mesopotamia. The Foreign Office agreed. The Mesopotamian 'conspiracy' was regarded as a 'delicate' matter and 'probably all very abortive'. It was decided not to exhibit any local interest in the plot, and in the matter of Aziz Ali to make further intervention only on humanitarian grounds.[118]

As is well known, no more encouragement was given to Abdullah, son of the Grand Sherif of Mecca and a deputy in the Ottoman Chamber. In February 1914, he requested Britain's intervention at the Porte in the event of his father's deposition, on the grounds that he had always been helpful to the Moslem pilgrims from India. He added that the tribes of the Hedjaz would fight the Porte in such a case, and hoped that Britain would not allow the passage of Ottoman reinforcements. Kitchener, to whom this 'very secret' message was delivered, was no more inclined than Mallet to support any such separatist movement. He told Abdullah that it would be improper for the British Government to send the Grand Sherif any message.[119]

A third example of the manner in which the Foreign Office manifested its opposition to any anti-Ottoman, and practically to any anti-CUP movement, was provided by its attitude towards Ibn Saud's rising power.[120] Early in March 1914, the Porte complained that Britain had entered into 'direct' relations with Ibn Saud, citing the conversations held the previous December between Ibn Saud and the British Political Agents in Bahrein and Koweit. Hakki maintained that these contacts had created a 'very' painful impression at Constantinople, since they were contrary to the Convention agreed upon on 29 July 1913. He reminded Parker that the Ottoman Government would soon have to justify to the Ottoman Parliament the concession which had been made to Britain with regard to El Katr, the Aden delimitation and the Persian frontier. British hesitation to recognize Nejd as an Ottoman sphere would make the other agreements 'most unpopular'. Parker was able to cite in defence of Britain's action the danger that Ibn Saud, if treated 'coldly', might retaliate against the protected tribes on the Trucial Coast. Moreover, the interests of British merchants could be damaged by exclusion from El-Katif. Nevertheless, the Foreign Office immediately appreciated the need to dispel the 'erroneous impression' which had been created at the Porte. The India Office was informed that the conversations which had taken place with Ibn Saud under the auspices of the Government of India had created the feeling that Britain's policy was 'inconsistent with that of upholding the integrity of the Ottoman Empire'.[121]

Grey also rejected the India Office's suggestion that Britain attempt to control the current negotiations between the Porte and Ibn Saud, and be prepared to send a ship to the waters of Bahrein in the event that they were violated by the Porte in an action against Ibn Saud.[122] Given the existing suspicious state of mind at the Porte, such intervention would have 'a very bad effect' on Anglo-Ottoman relations. Ibn Saud 'must be dealt with as a Turkish official or not at all ...'[123]

Mallet agreed with this policy. He understood that it was designed not only to secure free access and proper treatment of British subjects in Nejd and the prevention of any disturbance of the Pax Britannica in the Gulf, but also 'to prevent, or at least postpone, anything which might lead to a general Arab outbreak, and so endanger the integrity of the Turkish dominions in Asia'. Britain should therefore allow the Porte to control Ibn Saud and only intervene in the unlikely event that the Porte resorted to force; otherwise 'the chances of an upheaval might be increased rather than diminished if an influential and centrally placed chief like Ibn Saud were to consolidate his power and extend it permanently to the seaboard'.[124]

Nevertheless, Mallet had always taken the 'Arab Question' more seriously than did the Foreign Office. Thus he had regarded a projected congress at Koweit of 'Arab chiefs' (including the Grand Sherif of Mecca, Ibn Saud, Ibn Rashid of Jebel Shammar, Ajeymi Sheikh of Muntefik and Seyyid Talib of Basra) as 'significant' proof of the 'dissatisfaction' which prevailed amongst 'Ottoman Arabs generally'. Despite their lack of cohesion and leadership, these chiefs on the periphery of the Ottoman Empire might combine in order to 'enforce nationalist aspirations'; 'the Arab movement', he cautioned, was the 'most serious feature of the present situation.' Some of the Arab leaders, he had learned, were 'intelligent and educated men'; were they to combine in either constitutional agitation, demands for autonomy, or a separatist movement, they could 'undoubtedly cause much trouble'. In view of the consequences of British support for the Arabs, and of the likelihood that they would attempt to force British intervention by attacking British subjects (as had occurred at Basra), Mallet proposed to maintain Britain's traditional policy and not to communicate any interest in the 'Arab question' to the Ottoman leaders. His advice to the Foreign Office was to be cautious, to wait and to watch events.[125]

What is more, he foresaw great opportunities for Britain in the future, since there was no doubt in his mind that the Porte would never be able to regain influence in northern and eastern Arabia, where its influence had 'almost entirely' disappeared. As a result of the forthcoming disintegration of the Ottoman rule in that part of its Empire, Mallet felt that Britain's relations with Ibn Saud would become 'natural and inevitable' without any detriment to British interests in the Ottoman Empire.[126] But the Foreign Office, altogether more sceptical of the Arab movement than was the Ambassador, now even refused to entertain the idea of a British officer to be employed in the Yemen, since to do so might add 'fresh fuel' to Ottoman suspicion of British influence with the Arabs which had now become acute because of Ibn Saud.[127]

By June 1914, negotiations between the Porte and Ibn Saud had come to a successful conclusion. Ibn Saud accepted the position of a Vali and commander of the whole of Nejd directly dependent on Constantinople, and acknowledged that he was an Ottoman subject. The Porte was not to accept any tribute from him, but it was agreed that Ottoman garrisons would be stationed in Ojair and Katif. Moreover, although he was allowed to create his own militia, Ibn Saud was to have no right to conclude treaties with foreign states.[128] As far as British policy was concerned, the principle of Ottoman integrity still prevailed. Britain was prepared to accept independent chiefs, of the type of Ibn Saud, provided they remained loyal to Ottoman rule. As subsequent events were to show, however, the issue had been shelved, rather than solved.

Zionism presented fewer difficulties. In May 1913, Fitzmaurice predicted that the Jews would obtain Palestine and the land of Midian.[129] But Britain displayed very little interest in Jewish national aspirations. Some attention was given to the matter in December 1913, when the Porte abolished the 'red passport', which had restricted non-Ottoman Jews to staying in Palestine for only three months. Mallet regarded this as an important concession; it granted the Zionists unrestricted immigration to Palestine. He also attributed a certain importance to the revival of the Hebrew language by the Zionists, whose aspiration was that it should be recognized by the Porte as soon as Jews formed the majority of the population in Jerusalem and Palestine, 'so that it may one day be possible to have a Jewish Governor of Jerusalem'. In the Foreign Office some interest was shown in the possibility of Jewish immigration, but Russell thought Mallet confused Hebrew, which he regarded as a dead language, with Yiddish. Crowe's remarks were more barbed: 'Modern Jews are not likely to take to talking Hebrew, whether at Jerusalem or elsewhere, however much it may be taught in schools. The attempt to galvanise dead languages into spoken ones is a fad of modern nationalism.'[130] Meanwhile, neither Mallet nor the Foreign Office paid any serious attention to reports from the Consul-General at Jerusalem on the 'growing resentment' amongst Arabs against Zionism and what he called the 'threatening economic preponderance' of the Jewish element. Such was also their reaction to the Vice-Consul's report from Jaffa that while natives were 'streaming out' of the country, 'the Zionists are coming in'.[131] When, in July 1914, Nahum Sokolow, the Zionist leader, attempted to enlist the Foreign Office's support for Zionist colonization in Syria and Palestine, he was regarded as a nuisance. So much so, that neither Russell nor Clerk wished to see him.[132]

On 26 June 1914, the *Inflexible*, the flagship of Admiral Sir Berkeley Milne, C.-in-C. Mediterranean, arrived at Constantinople. Jemal, according to Limpus, was 'immensely' impressed by what he had seen of the *Inflexible* and was especially struck by her superiority 'in every way' to the *Goeben* which, so Jemal said, 'bore all the marks of the Parvenu in comparison with the real article.' During the banquet given at the Yildiz Kiosk in honour of the British Admiral, and in the presence of all the members of the Ottoman Cabinet, news arrived of the assassination at Sarajevo. Mallet, always a great believer in ceremonial punctilio, had to cancel his dinner party, ball and reception, but was still satisfied that a good impression had been made.[133] But the Foreign Office was immovable in its attitude towards the Porte. On 19 July, one day after secret discussions for an alliance with Germany had commenced, Talaat, the Minister for the Interior, made a promising speech in the Ottoman Chamber, claiming that relations with the Powers were as 'cordial as in the past' and that the present Government would endeavour to achieve 'peace and tranquillity'.

However, the Foreign Office's reaction was: 'It sounds well, and there may be some practical good among what is probably mostly "eyewash".'[134]

Nevertheless, by 16 July, when Mallet went to England on home leave, Anglo-Ottoman relations seemed relatively relaxed. The Foreign Office was glad that the Gulf and Mesopotamian agreements were signed. Although the conflict with Greece was not yet solved, Ottoman problems became less prominent in Britain's foreign policy during the last few weeks before the outbreak of war in Europe. Nicolson, who initially refused to believe that the assassination at Sarajevo would lead to war, was on the 28th quite sure that Britain ought to fight on behalf of her friends.[135] But nobody could have imagined that the Ottoman Empire would also shortly take sides.

7

THE LAST PHASE

The Outbreak of War[1]

Despite the outbreak of hostilities between Britain and Turkey in late-October 1914, Mallet's contemporaries (both inside and outside the Foreign Office) did not consider him to have been a failure in his post before July of that year. This judgment has been shared by historians.[2] It is generally agreed that he was not personally responsible for the earlier tension in Anglo-Ottoman relations, since Britain's support for Greece (which was principally responsible for that tension) had been decided upon in London. If Mallet can be faulted, it is for his inability to persuade the Foreign Office to initiate a more conciliatory policy towards the Porte. Here too, however, Mallet is not altogether blameworthy. For almost nine months (since October 1913), he had assiduously courted the Young Turks. But officials in London, whilst always encouraging him to continue his policy of flattery, had themselves persistently refused his appeals to adopt a similarly conciliatory tone.

By contrast, Mallet has been severely condemned by both his contemporaries (other than in the Foreign Office) and by historians for his actions between August and October 1914. The brunt of the criticism relates to his ignorance of the Ottoman-German Treaty which was signed during his absence from Constantinople on 2 August. But that charge would appear to raise several questions. One is whether it justifies the accusation that Mallet had misled the British Government into believing that the 'moderates' inside the Young Turk Cabinet could be encouraged. Another is whether Kitchener or Stratford Canning would have 'for sure' defeated the pro-German faction at the Porte – given, of course, that the Foreign Office would have given them the backing necessary to do so. In fact, whilst on the evidence one may justify some criticism of Mallet for his pre-War Embassy at Constantinople, it would appear unjust to blame the Ambassador, rather than the entire Foreign Office, for Britain's failures between August and October 1914. By concentrating, furthermore, entirely on Mallet they overlook the fact that the Ambassador did not act independently. Both before and after July 1914, he acted with the full knowledge of officials in the Foreign Office, and without being in any way discouraged by them. That, perhaps, is why Grey and Lord Robert Cecil publicly and repeatedly defended Mallet's Embassy between August and October.[3] The simple but crucial fact was that the Foreign Office doubted whether it could prevent the Porte's entry into the war on Germany's side once the *Goeben* and the *Breslau* entered the Dardanelles on 10 August (at which time Mallet was absent from Constantinople). British efforts were really concentrated on keeping the Porte neutral for as long as possible and by any means. Hence, their exhaustive efforts to persuade the Porte to send the German crews away.

The balance of forces within Constantinople exacerbated the difficulties of pursuing such a policy. It is, therefore, difficult to accept the view that the 'progress of diplomacy' which 'played into the hands of Enver', was the overriding influence in bringing the Porte into the war on Germany's side. Talaat's failure to achieve a Russian alliance in May and Jemal's failure to achieve an alliance with France in July 1914, doubtless contributed to the triumph of Enver's pro-German party. Significantly, the Ottomans had not proposed any such alliance to Britain since June 1913. Besides, little could be expected from Britain in view of her pro-Balkan and pro-Russian policy. Both the military and diplomatic predominance of Germany and the strength of the pro-German faction, represented mainly by Enver, seem to have been crucial factors in bringing the Porte on to Germany's side.[4] Serious negotiations towards an Ottoman-German alliance had begun on 18 July. The Treaty itself was signed on 2 August by Said Halim and Wangenheim, and was immediately followed by the mobilization of the Ottoman army. With Ottoman intervention on Germany's side in the war with Russia, Liman's position was further consolidated and Germany promised to help the Porte to preserve its integrity and to help recover lost territories in Europe and the Aegean Islands.

I

While these dramatic events were taking place, Mallet was on leave
and the Embassy was in the charge of Henry Beaumont, until
recently Counsellor at Athens.[5] But the first important step was
taken in London, where the Admiralty decided not to deliver the
recently completed battleships *Sultan Osman* and *Reshadieh* to the
Ottoman navy.[6] The news of this embargo undoubtedly contributed
to Enver's ultimate victory, and came as a 'shock' to the Porte. Said
Halim, Talaat and Jemal all rejected Grey's proffered explanations
and assurances to consider financial compensation; they continued
to insist that the embargo constituted an unfriendly act.[7] Beaumont
himself was not frightened by the 'very bad temper' of Jemal or
the other Ministers. He did advise that Limpus and his staff would
now be 'doubly anxious to leave because they were placed in an
extremely difficult position.'[8] But he believed that Britain's declaration of war on Germany (on August 4) had already calmed the
pro-German ardour, 'artificially created and unscrupulously encouraged' by Wangenheim.[9]

On the evening of 10 August, the *Goeben* and *Breslau* arrived
in Constantinople – the result, it has been said, of 'A Tragedy
of Errors'.[10] In the Foreign Office, Clerk suggested linking the
question of the Ottoman ships with the *Goeben* affair. Were the
Porte to maintain strict neutrality in the matter of the *Goeben*,
Britain should 'at once' undertake to pay the cost of the *Sultan
Osman* and *Reshadieh* and guarantee their immediate delivery after
the war.[11] But the Foreign Office refused the Ottoman suggestion
that Britain also arrange an Entente guarantee to keep the Porte
'absolutely' neutral. Nicolson, especially, was most uncompromising; overriding his subordinates, he doubted the utility of such a
'bait' at a time when the Porte was thinking about the extension of
its territories.[12]

A subsequent declaration of Ottoman neutrality was regarded as
'very satisfactory' in London;[13] but the position was nevertheless
becoming increasingly critical. In early August, the Germans and
Turks effected a nominal sale of the *Goeben* and *Breslau*; on the
15th, Limpus and his staff were suddenly withdrawn from the
Ottoman fleet and ordered to continue work at the Ministry of

Marine. Beaumont admitted that he was 'at a loss' to understand the significance of the move. He appreciated both the danger which faced Russia as a probable result of the presence of German technical experts in Constantinople, who would stay even if the crews withdrew, and the 'very prevalent' anxiety felt by the Ottomans as to Russia's intentions. He felt that an Anglo-French guarantee of Ottoman integrity could clarify the situation (unless the Porte had already been 'too deeply compromised by mischievous intrigues'), and might even 'finally detach Turkey from the side of Germany and Austria'.[14] Surprisingly, the continued Ottoman mobilization convinced him that the activities of Enver and the pro-German faction were a 'blunder'.[15]

But the British Government, although deprived of exact information, was not misled by Beaumont. For London, the presence of the *Goeben* and the *Breslau* was too conspicuous a proof that the scales had already turned against the Entente. Thus on 15 August Churchill sent a personal and confidential telegram to Enver in which he warned him in a friendly way to keep strict neutrality:

> I hope you are not going to make a mistake which will undo all the services you have rendered Turkey and cast away the success of the second Balkan War ... siding with Germany openly and secretly now must mean the greatest disaster to you, your comrades and your country. The overwhelming superiority at sea possessed by the navies of England, France, Russia and Japan over those of Austria and Germany renders it easy for the four allies to transport troops in almost unlimited numbers from any quarter of the globe and if they were forced into a quarrel by Turkey their blow could be delivered at the heart. On the other hand I know that Sir E. Grey, who had already been approached as to possible terms of peace if Germany and Austria are beaten has stated that if Turkey remains loyal to her neutrality, a solemn agreement to respect the integrity of the Turkish Empire must be a condition of any terms of peace that affect the Near East. The personal regard I have for you, Talaat and Djavid and the admiration with which I have followed your career from the first meeting at Wirzburg alone leads me to speak these words of friendship before it is too late.[16]

On the same day Grey voiced his complete despair to Benckendorff: 'Turkey's decision will not be influenced by the value of the offers made to her, but by her opinion which side will probably win and which is in a position to make the offers good.'[17]

Despite Beaumont's continued search for signs of hope, on 17 August Grey warned all British vessels in the Black Sea not to attempt the passage of the Straits. Those at sea were not to proceed to Ottoman ports and those already there should leave at once.[18]

II

Mallet, who on 16 August had returned to Constantinople, felt that the situation was not serious enough to warrant such an 'extreme' measure; he convinced Grey to rescind the orders.[19] At the same time, Grey took no action on Crowe's suggestion that Limpus and his staff be recalled at once.[20] The official policy of the Foreign Office was not to provoke any quarrel with the Ottomans but to attempt to keep them neutral.

> If she [the Porte] decided to side with Germany, of course there was no help for it; but we ought not to precipitate this. If the first great battle, which was approaching in Belgium, did not go well for the Germans, it ought not to be difficult to keep Turkey neutral ... the proper course was to make Turkey feel that, should she remain neutral, and should Germany and Austria be defeated, we would take care that the integrity of Turkish possessions as they now were would be preserved in any terms of peace affecting the Near East; but that, on the other hand, if Turkey sided with Germany and Austria and they were defeated, of course we could not answer for what might be taken from Turkey in Asia Minor.[21]

From Constantinople, Mallet attempted both to convince the Porte to remain strictly neutral, and to persuade London that she could indeed do so. Thus he complained to Said Halim that the Porte was under 'entire' German influence and that there had been a serious breach of neutrality in the case of the *Goeben* and the *Breslau*. On the other hand, he nevertheless pressed Grey to remain patient. His meetings with both Said Halim and Jemal on the day of his return to his post convinced the Ambassador that there had been a 'decided' improvement in the situation and that the pro-neutrality elements were gaining strength.[22] Despite his later denials, Mallet does appear to have been particularly impressed by Said Halim's 'absolute personal sincerity', and thought there was value in his contacts with Jemal, who still presented himself as pro-French and pro-British. The latter assured Mallet that were France and Britain to guarantee his country against Russia, German influence would immediately collapse. He also asked for a defence treaty with each of the Entente Powers, the abolition of the Capitulations, the imme-diate delivery of the seized Ottoman ships, renunciation of any interference in internal affairs and the return of Western Thrace in the event of Bulgaria joining the enemy camp. Mallet knew that Jemal's proposals might appear as 'terms imposed by a victorious enemy'. He also appreciated that it was impossible to accede to the Porte's request to abolish the Capitulations before the war was over. Nevertheless, he continued to argue that if Britain was serious in keeping the Porte neutral, she could attain this end by giving them a 'real' guarantee against Russia. Moreover, he thought that the Entente should strengthen the hands of Said Halim and Djavid, in order to enable them to stand up to the pro-German party.[23]

The Foreign Office was less sanguine, Oliphant remarked: 'Unfortunately the whole Turkish Government is not incorporated in the person of the Grand Vizier.'[24] Nicolson said that the Porte's position was 'obscure and uncertain';[25] and Grey that the balance of forces within Constantinople was not in Britain's favour.[26] But it was Crowe, more than anybody else in the Foreign Office, who questioned the Turks' true intentions. Thus the news that the Porte was fostering mobilization was for him further evidence that the Turks meant to go to war. He also expected the Porte to continue their 'game' with Britain until the boilers of the *Goeben* were repaired on 2 September.[27]

Mallet, however, was more optimistic. Admittedly, he did begin to regard Ottoman assurances of neutrality with more suspicion than before. Nevertheless, he still felt 'fairly confident that unless allies suffered serious and continued reverses, Turkey would remain quiet'.[28] At this stage, he argued, a written declaration on Ottoman integrity and independence was 'most important'; so too was an undertaking that Britain was ready to negotiate at once, 'in a sympathetic spirit', a special convention to narrow the scope of the Capitulations.[29] On 25 August he also started to press the Foreign Office for a written guarantee to uphold Ottoman integrity and independence and also to allow the Turks economic freedom.

These moves (to which the Foreign Office agreed), were necessary in order to preserve the Porte's strict neutrality by helping the 'moderates'.[30] This is not to suggest that Mallet entirely closed his eyes to the worsening situation. He reported the arrival of German sailors via Sofia, the German urge to close the Straits, the feverish mobilization in both army and navy, and the story that Germany was inducing the Porte to join the war ten days after France was defeated. He also advised the Foreign Office that if the British Government was thinking of forcing the Dardanelles, a 'rapid and complete success would alone justify attempt, as failure would mean disaster here, and have most serious effect everywhere'. He admitted that the situation was 'most unsatisfactory, though not actually desperate'.[31] In fact, he realized that 'so long as German crews remained, Grand Vizier was not master of his house, but at the mercy of Germans, who had practically occupied Constantinople'.[32] At the end of August, he maintained that the administration was so entirely in German hands that the position of the Naval Mission and the five British advisers would at any moment become 'very' embarrassing. 'There are many reasons for withdrawing them at once', he wrote, 'but I should be reluctant to relinquish the struggle until the last possible moment unless I am instructed by HMG to announce their recall to the Ottoman Government.'[33]

The differences between the Foreign Office and the Ambassador were thus concerned with both emphasis and substance. Mallet stubbornly – indeed strangely – insisted that all hope of Ottoman neutrality was not yet lost. The Foreign Office, by contrast, had reached the conclusion that 'Turkey's neutrality is demonstratively non-existent'. Grey felt that it would be well to prepare the 'India mind' for a rupture between Britain and the Porte.[34] Clerk concluded that the only way to save the situation might be to rush the Dardanelles, 'desperate though such a solution may seem'. Crowe reiterated what he had felt for 'a long time', that the Porte was 'merely trying to gain the time necessary for the preparation of the contemplated hostile action'. The Foreign Office was now concerned with one question alone: how to withdraw safely all British subjects in the Ottoman service, the Naval Mission and the Consular and Embassy staff.[35] Moreover, Grey instructed Mallet to point out to the Porte the 'very serious' consequences of a turn against Britain. On this occasion (29 August) the Foreign Secretary also warned that, if necessary, Britain would consider her position in Egypt, and might feel free to support the Arabs against the Porte, and another Moslem authority for Arabia and control of the Holy places.[36] By the end of August, so convinced was the Foreign Office of the inevitability of the Porte's entry into the war, that Grey cabled to Washington asking that in the event of a pro-German *coup d'état*, the United States Ambassador should take over British interests. The decision of when to leave Constantinople had already been left to Mallet's judgment on 16 August.[37]

Even now, Mallet continued his attempt to follow a dual policy, of which he kept the Foreign Office informed. He did advise London to guard against possible Ottoman initiatives by considering a 'swift and certain' operation.[38] Yet he also told the Foreign Office that he had enough cards in his hands with the declaration of support for Ottoman integrity and independence and the status of Egypt; there was no need to mention the Arabs and the Holy places. Indeed, to do so, he feared, might give Germany a handle and endanger the efficacy of any movement in Arabia.[39] At the same time, he did his best to extract daily assurances from Ottoman statesmen that they would not go to war. Although he did not fail to inform the Foreign Office that the Dardanelles were being rapidly fortified and manned by Germans, he nevertheless remained convinced that 'a current has set in against adventurous policy'. In order to justify his view he claimed that the country was being ruined by the mobilization and that the people were frightened. He also stated that Giers, Block and 'many' others shared his view that the Porte meant to stay neutral, though he admitted that they had not given any 'concrete proof'.[40]

The Foreign Office, however, went its own way on the Arab question. Grey and Nicolson disregarded both Mallet's advice, and even Hirtzel's warning that 'in the long run' the Arabs might 'be more dangerous propagandists of Pan-Islam than the Turks'. They went as far as to state that once the Porte joined the war, the Arabs should be given every support to seize Arabia and that all preparations should be made at short notice.[41] Similarly, early in September Grey rejected Mallet's suggestion that the British fleet would be withdrawn from the Dardanelles if the German crews left, British trade remained undisturbed and the Porte stayed neutral during the war.[42]

III

On 1 September the Entente ambassadors presented Said Halim with a draft declaration on integrity and independence. Mallet 'hardly' expected the Germans to allow the Porte to accept the document, and was discouraged to hear from Morgenthau, the American Ambassador, that the Turks would not bind themselves by any agreement on neutrality.[43] This setback, however, did not change the basic course which Mallet had adopted, in which (it must be noted) the Foreign Office acquiesced.

Thus, within two days he could advocate completely contradictory actions. On 4 September he suggested that if war with the Porte was inevitable one of the 'most effective' weapons would be an 'Arab movement', directed by Ibn Saud, the Sheikh of Koweit and other friendly Arab chiefs. Its first object should be 'to attack and hold Baghdad temporarily and await events'. British help in money and armaments would 'immediately' influence the situation in Arabia.[44] Yet, on the following day he informed London that there were 'many' indications that the situation at Constantinople had improved. Admittedly, his proofs were rather slim: the almost daily assurance that the German crews would leave and the growing discontent among 'influential' people. Nevertheless, he called upon the Foreign Office to keep the Russians calm in order to ensure success.[45] On the other hand, one day later (the 6th) he himself spoke very sharply to Talaat, warning that because of the presence of German officers, military and naval, Britain regarded the Ottoman Empire as a German protectorate and expressing surprise that the Porte attached no importance to the Entente's written declaration concerning Ottoman integrity. To Grey he confided that he was personally relieved, since 'to guarantee integrity and independence of Turkey was like guaranteeing life of man who was determined to commit suicide'. As a result of his conversation with Talaat he thought it 'extremely probable' that in the long run the Porte would fight against the Entente.[46]

It is an indication of Mallet's obstinacy that he nevertheless continued his vigorous campaign to postpone the Porte's entry into the war. Thus he strongly opposed the decision of 9 September to order Limpus to leave Constantinople and to succeed Troubridge as the Commander of the British fleet in the Dardanelles. The effect of such an appointment, he claimed, would be 'disastrous'. He did favour the withdrawal of the Naval Mission (indeed he had first suggested this move one day earlier, after learning that no genuine sale of the German ships had taken place),[47] but could see no benefit at all in appointing Limpus to the command of the fleet on the other side of the Dardanelles, which the Ottomans treated as hostile. The latter step could only strengthen Germany's position and 'ruin' the Porte's confidence in Mallet himself. 'It would be very difficult for me to remain here, *as any influence I have is due to their confidence in my good faith* [Foreign Office's italics].' One result would be the closure of the Straits; another, demonstrations against British subjects by a population in any case excited by the abolition of the Capitulations on 9 September. He laboured to explain that the Russian Ambassador was also of the opinion that war must be avoided in order to prevent any setback to Russia in her Austrian campaign; the French, Italian and American representatives had also 'constantly' asked him to 'restrain' Britain. In any case, his colleagues, Limpus, the British Advisers, Block and all those who knew the country, were unanimously of the opinion that the situation was far from desperate. Limpus, who even opposed withdrawing the Naval Mission, told him that the crews of the Ottoman fleet were 'intensely' hostile to the Germans; given time their feelings would again become pro-British.

Grey was initially 'astonished' to hear that Mallet regarded Limpus' new appointment as a new departure: 'Of course we want to avoid war, and appointment of Admiral Limpus implies no change of policy.' Ultimately, however he and Churchill[48] recognized the force of Mallet's arguments and Limpus was instead ordered to proceed to Malta.[49] Nevertheless, the Foreign Office and the Embassy continued to possess differing views of the situation, even though the former continued to assert that Mallet could not have advocated Britain's position in a better manner. On 13 September, Mallet telegraphed: 'Situation is improving daily but that danger of Minister of War under German influence sending *Goeben* with transports into the Black Sea is not diminished by the fact that his position is not so secure as it was.' But the Foreign Office was even more pessimistic. 'This telegram', commented Clerk, 'shows the Power of the extremist inner ring of the CUP, and it looks much as though our efforts will after all be in vain.' Nicolson's remark is even more revealing: 'Sir Louis Mallet is making a gallant fight, but in these cases it is usually the extremists who win the day.' It is impossible to be sure whether Mallet still believed that the military party in Constantinople could be overcome; he may merely have used this argument in order to persuade the British Government to be more compromising.[50] But he certainly took a conciliatory line when the Ottomans decided to abolish the Capitulations on 9 September, insisting – together with his French and Russian colleagues – that Britain should not break off relations with the Porte on that account and thus play into Germany's hands. Military strategy, of itself, precluded any other course. 'Pending successful developments in main theatre of war, we should not burden ourselves with Near Eastern complications and all that may arise from them.'[51]

The Foreign Office initially concurred, and showed no inclination to make the abolition of the Capitulations a *casus belli*. Yet, on other points the fundamental disagreement continued. Thus, officials in London rejected Mallet's suggestions that Britain extend her guarantee of Ottoman integrity beyond the war, and that she make fiscal and commercial concessions to the Porte.[52] The fact that these proposals were reportedly supported by Bompard and Giers could not compensate for other considerations. A guarantee as to Turkey's post-war situation, for instance, would be impolitic, minuted Clerk, 'since the possibility of the Arabs asserting their independence, and perhaps being successful, always exists, and it would be fatal if we had to intervene on the side of Turkey'.[53] In any case, the Porte already seemed 'completely' in the Germans' pockets, and would succumb to their pressure to create a diversion against the Allies, especially during their retreat beyond the Marne. There was, therefore, no point in fiscal concessions. As Clerk (again) explained:

> Either Turkey will fight against us, or the reckoning when peace comes will be so heavy that it would have been better that she should have fought and been beaten. In my humble opinion we are very near the limit of possible concession, and I am not yet convinced that even the CUP have lost all sense of prudence. ...

Grey accepted Clerk's view: concessions might be regarded as a sign of weakness by the 'Extremists' and would not really strengthen the hands of the Grand Vizier. Britain would be ready to make 'reasonable' concessions about the Capitulations, but not whilst

German officers and crews were still in the country. If the Porte could not keep peace Britain could not be responsible for any consequences.[54]

Events behind the scenes at Constantinople appear to indicate that Mallet's hopes and expectations were not entirely unjustified. A struggle was in progress between the interventionists and their opponents, and in mid-September Enver was defeated by the unanimous opposition of the Ottoman Cabinet. Consequently, he had to cancel his instruction to Admiral Souchon, dated 14 September, to attack the Russians in the Black Sea. This was a victory for the anti-war party headed by Said Halim and Djavid over the war party headed by Enver and Jemal.[55] As his reports show, Mallet did nevertheless appreciate the inherent strength of Enver's position. 'It must be remembered that so long as the army is mobilized and so long as Minister of War is generalissimo, Cabinet is not in a position to enforce its will and must temporise to some extent.'[56] However, he still pressed the Foreign Office to make unconditional concessions to the Porte. But by this time the Foreign Office was not even prepared to become involved in negotiations on that issue. Instead, and in accordance with a Cabinet decision, Grey addressed a firm – although not threatening – message to the Grand Vizier on 23 September. Britain, he pointed out, was 'very dis-satisfied' with the situation, especially over the presence of the *Goeben* and the *Breslau* and the fortification of the Dardanelles by the Germans:

> … in the hope that the peace party will get the upper hand we have not hitherto taken action, but the Grand Vizier should realize that his party must succeed soon in controlling the situation and bringing it within the limits of neutrality, or it will become clear that the real control at Constantinople is no longer Turkish, but German, and the Germans will force open hostility.[57]

Grey was still ready to give Mallet's policy another chance. ('The part you have yourself taken is very much appreciated and has brought you much credit', was his private addition to the above communication.) It was Churchill who suggested hardening the line. He remarked that 'Poor Mallet's telegrams' were character-ized by the constant belief that the peace party was both gaining strength and becoming increasingly helpless in controlling Enver and the Germans. But far from despising Mallet's policy, he sympathized 'deeply' with the 'futile and thankless task on which he is engaged'. What he did suggest was a more rigid policy, instead of one which attempted to buy off the Porte by promises and concessions at a time when Germany was penetrating ever deeper and was preparing the country for war:

> ... in our attempt to placate Turkey we are crippling our policy in the Balkans. I am not suggesting that we should take aggressive action against Turkey or declare war on her ourselves, but we ought from now to make our arrangements with the Balkan States, particularly Bulgaria, without regard to the interests or integrity of Turkey. The Bulgarians ought to regain the Turkish territory they lost in the Second Balkan war ... Turkey's conduct to us with repeated breaches of neutrality would release us from any need of considering her European interests ... I do most earnestly beg you not to be diverted from the highway of sound policy in this part of the world, both during the war and at the settlement, by wanderings into the labyrinth of Turkish duplicity and intrigue.[58]

The 'cumulative effect' of Ottoman-German preparations produced an identical feeling in the Foreign Office itself. The arrival of more than 2,000 cases of shells for the *Goeben* and the fortresses, mines for the port of Alexandretta, and the stoppage of all passenger and goods traffic on the Hedjaz Railway was regarded as 'disquieting'. The movement of troops in the direction of Akaba and El-Arish and the incitement of the Egyptian population was also causing concern. On 19 September the Porte dealt another blow to the Entente Powers by announcing that foreign post offices would be closed on 1 October. Even Mallet had by now given up hope that the peace party could dismiss the Germans from the country: at the most Said Halim might prevent the Porte from openly joining Germany. Together with Giers, Mallet did believe that it was worthwhile to 'try and pull through' by temporizing as long as possible in order to avoid war. But in the Foreign Office, the last shreds of faith in the Porte's neutrality were fast disappearing. It was generally recognized that Mallet had fought a 'good battle'. But opinion was growing that, in view of the increasing Ottoman demands, it was time that Britain showed her teeth: 'The Turks will respect nothing else.'[59]

IV

It was now Britain's turn to strike a blow against the Porte. As early as 19 September, Mallet had taken the initiative in warning each Minister separately and in writing that the Ottoman fleet would be treated as an enemy if found outside the Dardanelles. But by the 21st, Grey and Churchill thought it would be 'better and safer' to tell the Porte that as long as their fleet was under German control they must not send the ships out to sea. This amounted in fact to a British blockade against Ottoman warships.[60] Meanwhile, Britain also tightened her control in the Shatt-el-Arab region. Despite Ottoman protests, Grey insisted on the Admiralty's right to station the *Odin* and the *Lawrence* in those waters, and their use of wireless. By the end of September, Crowe, following the Indian Government, even suggested the despatch of troops to the head of the Gulf.[61]

This uncompromising attitude was also possible because Pan-Islam no longer constituted a danger as far as the Government of India and the India Office were concerned. The Viceroy explicitly reassured the British Government that even if the Sultan declared a *Jihad*, the 'vast' majority of Indian Moslems would remain loyal.[62] Little more than a week later, Kitchener was to instruct Cheetham to open secret negotiations with Abdullah, designed to determine his attitude towards Britain in case of war.[63]

At the same time, and unknown to the Embassy, General Barrow and Admiral Slade impressed upon the Foreign Office the need for action in a different theatre. In the name of the India Office and the Government of India, they voiced their serious alarm at the effect on the Arabs of Britain's 'absolute' inactivity in view of Ottoman war preparations and provocations. Captain Shakespear supported this view, saying that it would menace Britain's position not only in Arabia but also in Egypt and the Persian Gulf. He suggested therefore that they at once support Ibn Saud and the Arabs against the Porte. The Indian authorities, supported by Crowe and Kitchener, suggested to the Cabinet that part of the Poona division be diverted to the head of the Persian Gulf and landed in Mohammera, ostensibly to defend the Admiralty oil pipeline. Should this landing be carried out before the beginning of hostilities it would have a 'steadying influence' upon the Porte.[64]

Clearly, the situation was becoming increasingly critical. On 26 September, Enver ordered the closure of the Dardanelles. Said Halim attempted to make diplomatic capital out of the move by promising to re-open the Straits provided the British fleet moved 'a little further' towards Lemnos. During the course of the next few days, Mallet adduced several arguments in support of the Ottoman request: the effect on opinion within Constantinople and the impression of weakness produced by a meek acquiescence in the closing of the Straits. Grey did express 'much confidence' in Mallet, 'who is on the spot'. But opinion within the Foreign Office nevertheless ran strongly against accepting his advice. In any case, Said Halim's promise had been impractical. On 3 October Mallet reported that the Dardanelles had been closed not only by an administrative act but also by mines, placed there by Germans. The next day the British fleet was instructed to prevent the shipment of coal to the Ottoman fleet.[65]

The Foreign Office took a similar line over Shatt questions. In this region, tension was raised on 3 October, when the Vali of Basra informed the British Consul that British men-of-war had to leave the Shatt within twenty-four hours since the river from Fao to Gurna, like the Dardanelles and Smyrna, constituted inland waters, and were thus closed to foreign warships.[66] On the 6th the Porte declared the entire Shatt and the sea within six miles of shore to be Ottoman territorial waters; any men-of-war in those regions would be fired upon. The implications were clear. Britain had now either to abandon all her interests and subjects in Baghdad, Basra, Abadan and Mohammera, or to risk a collision which might start a war. The Foreign Office, strengthened by the Indian authorities who claimed that a blocked Shatt might disturb troop landings at Abadan, rejected the new Ottoman regulations. In so doing, it also rejected Mallet's repeated warnings and advice, which were again aimed at strengthening the hands of the 'Moderates' by a policy of concessions. With Grey's approval, Clerk minuted: 'Turkey will not go to war with us, or risk an incident which will lead to war, because of the presence of British men-of-war in the Shatt-el-Arab, but because she thinks it is to her interest to fight us.'

Under these circumstances, if Britain yielded to the Porte over the Shatt it would destroy her prestige with the Arabs and throw them on to the Porte's side;[67] and 'the more we give way the more the Turks will be encouraged to ask'. Nicolson, too, was convinced that Britain had made all 'reasonable' concessions and added: '... though Turkey has not yet gone to war it is probably because the Germans and Enver have not yet quite completed their preparations.' In its official reply, the British Government stated that it would only be ready to re-examine its attitude, in a 'most friendly' spirit, were the Porte properly to fulfil its neutrality obligations respecting the *Goeben* and the *Breslau*.[68] By the end of October, the *Espiègle* had been ordered to prevent any Ottoman attempt to sink a ship on the Shatt, and to remove any mines in those waters. If she was fired upon, operations could be started by despatching the expeditionary force now at Bahrein.[69]

Earlier that month, Seyyid Talib had come to see the British Consul at Basra and told him that the Porte's intention to enter the war did not 'suit' him and that he would like to enter into negotiations with Britain. He also mentioned his conversation with Kitchener three years earlier and asked whether the latter might be reminded that the time for action had arrived. Kitchener was responsive: 'This man might be useful, he has large party.' But Mallet, still far behind the Government in London, proposed that Talib should be given a 'friendly but evasive' reply. He also added a 'very confidential' comment, that although Talib might be needed in time of war, 'he has been too much in both camps to justify any confidence in him'. The British Government, however, was already committed to what was termed the necessity of securing 'Arab good-will'. Clerk, therefore, severely censured Mallet's proposed reply and, on the former's suggestion, the Foreign Office omitted a clause in its despatch referring to 'the maintenance of Turkish integrity in Asia as a British interest'. Surprisingly, however, and as suggested by Mallet, it did state that 'HMG have every sympathy with the Arabs, and they have always hoped, and indeed still hope, to see Arabs forming an integral part of the Turkish Empire under a tolerant and intelligent central Government'. If war erupted, Britain would 'remember' that she was at war with the Ottoman Government rather than with the Arabs.[70]

By now it was clear the initiative on the Arab question had been taken wholly out of Mallet's hands. Thus, in Yemen the Foreign Office (acting on the advice of the Resident) decided to approach the Imam and Idrissi 'soon', before the Porte could win them over.[71] As for other regions of Asiatic Turkey, the counsels of Fitzmaurice (who had been recommended by Ryan as an 'expert' on 'questions relating to Arabs'), carried weight. His general assumption was that in the event of war, Britain's policy should be 'to render [the Ottoman Empire] innocuous by every means at our command, regardless of such minor considerations as the future administration of parts of her present territories, or even the question of the Caliphate'. He therefore recommended that Britain exploit native opposition to Ottoman rule in Mesopotamia and, provided France and Cairo could be reconciled, especially in Syria. The Caliphate was an internal Islamic matter, but still might prove 'not an unmixed evil' for Britain since there was a probability that an Arab Caliph might replace the Ottoman one and thus remove the 'sting' from Pan-Islam which had its roots in the union of the spiritual and temporal powers in the 'Turkish Vatican of Islam' at Constantinople. Ultimately, these were the guidelines of the Foreign Office's subsequent policy. Thus, it was decided to seek French cooperation concerning Syria without delay.[72] In mid-October, enquiries were also made as to the local feeling in Syria and Lebanon on a possible war or an attack on Egypt.[73] Less than two weeks later, and with what seemed to be Cheetham's connivance, adherents of the 'Pan Arab movement' in Cairo sent 'reliable' agents to Arabia, Syria and Palestine in order to communicate Britain's message to Arab chiefs. They also were instructed to dissuade them from joining the Porte. The leaders of the movement stated that they did not for the moment expect more than a 'benevolent' attitude and moral support. But if war came and more than passive resistance was expected of them, they should be provided with arms and ammunition. Though it was felt that the arms question presented difficulties, it seemed that the Foreign Office had also agreed to support the 'Pan Arab movement'. Cheetham recommended that those agents who had been sent to Koweit should be given every assistance by the British Resident with whom they ought to work in 'unison'.[74]

Even at this late hour, Mallet was trying to persuade the Foreign Office that the Porte wanted to gain time before committing itself to Germany. Britain could therefore postpone the war for some months, and need not fear an imminent attack on Egypt.[75] He also maintained that any policy which amounted to an encouragement for Arab provinces to break away from the Ottoman Empire would precipitate events and bring war. He called for 'profound' secrecy in Britain's negotiations with the Arabs and warned against any written agreement. But in the Foreign Office nothing could convince Crowe and his colleagues that they had acted 'too soon'.[76] Together with the India Office, the Foreign Office did seem to agree with Mallet that Seyyid Talib could not be given the written guarantee which he might demand.[77] Moreover, it did not rely on the remote possibility of a 'revolt' of the Mesopotamian army, as suggested by Aziz Ali. But it did welcome the news that the Indian Expeditionary Force 'D' had arrived at Bahrein and that the Sheikh of Koweit was loyal to Britain.[78] Without notifying Mallet, Grey had no objection to the declaration Kitchener had made to Abdullah: 'It may be that an Arab of the true race will assume the Caliphate at Mecca or Medina and so good may come by the help of God out of all evil which is now occurring.'[79]

V

The Germans and their supporters in Constantinople had also been active. By 9 October, Enver had informed Wangenheim that Talaat and Halil had agreed to support his policy of war. Despite the subsequent hesitations of the latter two, on 11 October Enver and Jemal declared that Souchon would be ordered to attack the Russians as soon as the German Government deposited T£2 million in Constantinople. The money was delivered on the 16th and the 21st.[80]

Mallet was, as usual, optimistic. Misled by Rahmy, Vali of Smyrna,[81] he regarded all Britain's setbacks as 'appearances'. He consoled himself that despite the presence of the *Goeben* and the *Breslau*, the Germans had not dragged the Porte into war, which was their main object.

> I cannot give up hope [he wrote to Tyrrell on 16 October] that if we still continue to exercise patience and if we still have successes as I do not doubt, we may pull it off, and that although we are at the mercy of an incident, it is not I but Wangenheim who will have to leave first. I confess that I should hate to be beaten now by Wangenheim, who is a typically unscrupulous and contemptible form of Teuton. It must not be thought that we could have prevented the abolition of the capitulations or the Post Offices or anything else by taking a different line.

Mallet was now convinced that the success of his policy depended on Entente victories in France and Poland, and that hitherto the situation had been saved by the great Russian victory at Tannenberg. It is significant, however, that he was ready to give free passage in the Straits to Russia after the war and to dismantle the Dardanelles forts. For once, he allowed himself to slip into an anti-Ottoman style. 'It will be impossible to allow this gate on a great highway to be in the hands of a set of epileptic lunatics for ever.'[82]

By this time the Russians had relayed the news on the shipment of German gold to the Porte; Sazonov also predicted that hostilities would commence within a few days. This prophecy was regarded in the Foreign Office as 'more than probable'. Initially, Mallet continued to calm London. Relying on the Bulgarian Minister and Crawford, he reported that though the situation was 'precarious' (his own life had been threatened), there was no reason to despair unless Russia suffered a defeat or Enver launched a *coup d'état* with the Germans.[83] By the 23rd, however, he was less certain. He now called for a propaganda counter-campaign in reply to Ottoman-German rumours about alleged German success in Europe, insurrections in the Egyptian army, and general disaffection in India. Admittedly, he sought a rational reason for the arrival of German gold. 'This need not necessarily indicate immediate declaration of war, although it seems to fit in with Russian Ambassador's secret information. Country being on the brink of financial ruin money is essential to keep things going and unless Germany considered game here to be lost its supply would have been necessary.' He also used all the available evidence to prove that war was not imminent. Nevertheless, he did note the French Ambassador's claim of the existence of an Ottoman agreement to join Germany in the war and warned that although the Turks might not launch a full-scale attack on Egypt, they might make raids which could be 'equally dangerous'. As a further precaution, he also requested Grey's permission to join his French and Russian colleagues in a warning to Said Halim that an attack on one Entente Power would involve the Porte in war with the others.[84] Grey agreed and on the same day (28 October), the Foreign Office also warned the Porte that as long as the German officers remained on the *Goeben* and the *Breslau* and the Ottoman fleet under their control, Ottoman ships (in this case four gunboats on their way to Alexandretta) would be regarded as hostile and must be stopped in self-defence.[85]

Meanwhile, Enver had finally shaped the fate of the Ottoman Empire; on 25 October he gave Souchon a definite order to attack the Russian fleet on the high seas when a 'suitable opportunity' presented itself. Only Talaat and Jemal knew of the forthcoming attack. On the 27th the Ottoman fleet left for the Black Sea where Souchon changed the original plan and decided to attack Russia's coastal bases first. On the 29th at around 3.30–3.45 am, Odessa and Sebastopol were attacked, and the die was cast.[86]

Even then, Mallet desperately sought reasons for hope. Thus he cited Halil's attempt to go to Berlin, which was regarded by Giers as evidence of the Ottomans' wish to gain time: 'It is evident that great struggle is going on, but I do not think that all is lost. My Russian colleague strongly recommends patience.'[87] He called upon the Foreign Office to avoid a rupture with the Porte unless there were military reasons to the contrary. In spite of the preparations against Egypt and the Bedouin incursions, on the 29th he insisted that opposition to the Germans would grow if the Allies continued to do well. After consulting with Giers and Bompard, he also requested permission to verify whether the raid had been executed with the 'full' authority of the Porte. If not, the latter must be told to choose between rupture with the Entente and the dismissal of the German naval and military missions.[88]

The Foreign Office by contrast was not taken by surprise: 'Enver has carried out his intentions.' Britain was quite ready for war with the Porte. First concern was for the British subjects in the Ottoman Empire and their safety; the time had come for the publication of a statement to the Moslems in the British Empire, for the troops at Bahrein to embark for the Shatt-el-Arab, and for the Foreign Office to complete its Blue Book on the immediate causes of the rupture.[89] Grey also acceded to Sazonov's request that, unless the German missions were withdrawn, Mallet and Bompard should follow the lead taken by Giers and request their passports. Mallet was accordingly informed of Britain's 'utmost surprise' at the attack on Russia and reminded of the Ottomans' 'provocative' sponsorship of Bedouin incursions into Sinai.[90] In the Foreign Office's announcement to the Press, made on the 31st, the British Government made its first apologia in defence of its policy since the beginning of the European war:

It was well-known that the Turkish Minister of War was decidedly pro-German in his sympathies, but it was confidently hoped that the saner counsels of his Colleagues, who had experience of the friendship which Great Britain has always shown towards the Turkish Government, would have prevailed and prevented that Government from entering upon the very risky policy of taking part in the conflict on the side of Germany.[91]

As late as 31 October, Mallet still harboured slender hopes that the situation could be saved: 'I am, however, unwilling to leave if there is slightest chance of change in the situation during next twenty four hours.' This time he relied upon the stormy meeting of the Ottoman Grand Council of the 30th which, Djavid informed Bompard, had decided against war but was unable to implement its decision. However, he added 'very confidentially' that Morgenthau, the American Ambassador, had informed him that there was no chance of a favourable solution. Even in his last meeting with the Grand Vizier on the 31st, Mallet, though he 'gravely' doubted whether Said Halim could prevent war at this stage, was sure that the latter was sincere. This, together with the opposition of Djavid and a 'large' majority of the Cabinet, allowed Mallet to delude himself into thinking that at this late hour something could be done and he tried to persuade the Foreign Office accordingly:

> I venture to think that HMG might let it be understood that they consider the activity in Syria and the attack on Russian ports as a German plot[92] of complicity in which they do not accuse the majority of the Turkish Government. It might be said that unless we are attacked in Egypt or elsewhere we will not make war on Turkey although relations must cease until German influence is broken.

The Foreign Office, however, made it clear that the matter was not one between the Porte and Britain, but between the Porte and the Entente. Contradicting Mallet, Nicolson stated that no attention should be paid to Said Halim's 'friendly say'. 'They are', he added, 'words in the air.' By this time HMS *Savage* had bombarded Akaba and the fact that a British steamer had been sunk by the Ottomans at Novorossisk also served as proof that Mallet's hopes were ill-founded.[93]

On 1 November Mallet left for Athens and a few days later Tewfik left London. On Tewfik's pro-Entente views, Grey commented: 'If Tewfik had had control of Turkish policy there would be no war with Turkey now, any more than there would have been with Germany and Austria if Lichnowsky and Mensdorff had had control.' But Tewfik was poorly regarded by the Young Turks, as was Rifaat in Paris, and during most of October he obtained no replies to his numerous letters in which he had urged the Porte to abandon its policy, which as he had told Nicolson 'must inevitably end in disaster for the country'.[94]

VI

These were the antecedents which led to the proclamation of war by Britain on the Ottoman Empire on 5 November. Shortly afterwards Mallet sent Grey a despatch which 'summarized' the events leading to the rupture of relations between the two countries. In this apologia, Mallet placed the blame entirely on the shoulders of the Young Turks and the Germans. Not even the 'peace party', he claimed, was blameless. Said Halim, he reported, had failed to appreciate the German danger and to admit that he could not control events before, or on the 29 October.

> On this, as on every occasion of my interviews with the Grand Vizier, I was impressed with his inability to realize the facts or to disabuse himself of the conviction, in spite of his many unfortunate experiences, that he would be able, in a really serious crisis, to exact his authority with effect.

This, as the records clearly demonstrate, was hardly fair. Mallet had himself placed too much faith in Said Halim, and now seemed to have used him as a convenient scapegoat. There was really no justification for his comment that 'The crisis which I had predicted to His Highness [Said Halim] at almost every interview which I had with him since my return had actually occurred ...'

Nevertheless, Mallet is deserving of sympathy. 'However slender the chances in our favour, it was obviously my duty, in conjunction with my French and Russian colleagues, to support and encourage by all possible means those forces which were obscurely striving for the preservation of peace.' What is more, the Foreign Office had backed his policy. Not only did its officials praise the 'marked ability, patience and discretion' demonstrated by Mallet in carrying out Britain's policy, but also emphasized that he had 'rightly directed all [his] efforts to encourage those influences at Constantinople that were moderate and reasonable. To your efforts it was at any rate in some degree due that the inevitable catastrophe did not occur sooner.'[95]

As late as 24 August 1917, Mallet was publicly attacked in a leader in *The Times*. The article claimed that it seemed that Mallet had returned to Constantinople on 16 August from England 'with general instructions to work with the Turkish "Moderates" though the Turkish Government as we now know, was already committed against us. But his messages after his return, so far from correcting only confirmed the Foreign Office view.'[96] Not unexpectedly, these accusations enraged Mallet who wrote a second apologia. He hotly denied that he had misled the Foreign Office, because of his ignorance of the treaty. In addition, he claimed that he knew of its existence: 'The *Goeben* and *Breslau* passed close to my windows at Therapia every other day, the crews stripped to the waist, and all guns ready for action!' He maintained moreover that he had reported that Enver was the master of the situation and committed to Germany, that military preparations were in progress, and also on the 'rapid decrease' of Britain's influence. He did not deny that he had retained hopes of peace until the end, but this was only in order to postpone hostilities. He claimed that he personally had been cleared by Grey, who had commended him for his 'splendid rearguard action', but hinted that the blame should be laid at the door of those who had failed to prevent the escape of the German ships into the Dardanelles. The subsequent refusal to undertake an operation to force the Dardanelles had not depended on his reports but, as Kitchener subsequently told him, had been the result of London's feeling that it was important 'at all costs' to avoid war in the Near East. Moreover, Mallet indicated that the policy of postponing the war had not been initiated by the Foreign Office; it was, in fact, his own: 'I was glad to hear all this, [Kitchener's appreciation of his patience] for my own view, which I had formed independently of any instructions, was that *it was at all costs vital* [Mallet's italics] to defer, at almost any risk, the commencement of hostilities with Turkey.' He congratulated himself on the adoption of this policy in view of the military defeat in Belgium and the risks for India and Egypt. Only a 'madman' could contemplate war in such circumstances. Hence he was positive that his policy was 'the lesser of two evils'. But he still had to defend his daily interviews with Said Halim: 'I am not infallible but I should be surprised if I were not right in stating that it was not I who was taken in by the Grand Vizier, but the Grand Vizier who was taken in by Talaat and Enver.'

In effect, the reverse was true. It was Said Halim who signed the treaty with Germany; he was duped only in the question of Souchon's attack on Russia. As for Mallet, he learned about the struggle between the moderates and the interventionists from Giers, who had obtained the cypher telegrams of the Austrian Ambassador by bribing the Ottoman Post Office. To this he added his own assessment (and that of Sir Edwin Pears) of the 'Turkish character' by which he meant the Turks' love of intrigue and procrastination, and their 'volatile and unreliable' nature including 'their almost regular habit of evading at the eleventh hour, on entirely inadequate pretexts, the performance of their most solemn engagements'. It was on this sort of analysis, together with a few Austrian telegrams, that Mallet based his 'independent' policy. He also harboured 'elements of hope' of a kind which he was not ashamed to divulge:

> Supposing Enver had been murdered (for this omission I have never forgiven de Giers) – supposing the German retreat at the Marne had gone a little further – supposing Russia had done a little more – supposing Roumania had 'come in' – and one was hoping feverishly all those anxious, humiliating weeks that something of this kind *would* [Mallet's italics] happen – how differently the future might have shaped itself.[97]

Controversy over the events of August – October 1914 did not end with the First World War; the debate on the responsibilities and actions of the various parties continues. One historian[98] has commented that, considering the 'immense' issues at stake (he included free passage through the Straits and German military dominance in Ottoman Asia), the autumn of 1914 ought to have witnessed an intense campaign between Britain and Germany for the soul of the Ottoman Empire. Stratford Canning, he claimed, would have fought 'like a dragon, and in all probability with success' since in Constantinople a diplomat of 'bold temperament', equal to that possessed by Enver, could have determined the course of events. But certain as he is that Stratford Canning would have defeated the pro-Germany party, he doubts whether the British diplomats of 1914 would have been allowed to make the attempt. It does not seem that Kitchener would have been successful either, as has been suggested elsewhere. As has been seen, Mallet was allowed to try to postpone hostilities, as were the other Entente Ambassadors, and his unavailing attempts were supported by a despairing Government in London. But after 10 August 1914, what was really required to effect such a policy was the expulsion of the German naval crews as well as Liman's mission. Since this could not be done in view of Enver's complete grip on the situation, one cannot see how any Ambassador, no matter how bold, would have been able to launch a *coup d'état* behind the scenes. Furthermore, account must be taken of Ottoman apprehensions with regard to Russia and the inability, or unwillingness, of Britain and France to make any territorial concessions. The only other solution was to effect a forceful passage through the Dardanelles. Mallet was not against this course, but even had he advocated it there was no sign that the Government in London would have accepted his suggestion.[99] Given this situation, it was left to the Germans and the Young Turks to take the initiative and commence hostilities at a time of their own choosing.

Conclusions

The most striking feature of British policy towards the Ottoman Empire, during the period between the Young Turk Revolution of July 1908 and the outbreak of war in November 1914, was the change from a sympathetic attitude to one of hostility. British policy should not, however, be assessed solely by the failure explicit in the rupture of diplomatic relations. It should be placed, rather, in the context of the potentialities existing before August 1914, and judged by the extent to which the British could and did exploit those potentialities. Conversely, it would be equally fallacious to concentrate on peripheral issues: the subsidiary points of the successful negotiations concerning the Persian Gulf and Mesopotamia (which had no importance in terms of higher policy after 1912); the appointment of Orme Clarke as Inspector-General to the Ottoman Ministry of Justice; and the positions occupied by Graves and Crawford in the other Ministries. These functions clearly carried with them no political influence whatsoever. Again, no importance can be attached to the goodwill visit to Constantinople by the C.-in-C. Mediterranean on the very eve of the European War.[1] The real differences between Britain and the Porte had not been solved by August 1914. Basically, this was because those differences could not, from the British point of view, be treated in isolation. The fundamental fact of British policy towards the Ottoman Empire, and indeed towards any other country during this period, was its complete subordination to two major considerations: the agreements with France and Russia, and the welfare of the British Empire. Young Turk policy, in a number of ways, threatened both. Never, therefore, were the Ottoman suggestions for an alliance with Britain a question of practical policy for Britain, even when relations were at their peak in late 1908. That is why they were rejected out of hand.

Even before the Young Turk Revolution, the Ottoman Empire had presented major difficulties for the makers of British policy. Relations were clearly at a very low ebb and Britain was not concerned to improve them but rather to better the lot of the Christian subjects of the Sultan. The Young Turk Revolution radically changed this clear-cut policy. The manner in which Grey welcomed the Revolution is understandable; it saved him, so he thought, from the Macedonian impasse. But from the beginning, he also appreciated the potential danger it entailed as far as the Entente with Russia and the future of Egypt and India were concerned. The most serious of these potential dangers for Grey was that his friendly policy towards the Young Turks might clash with an improvement in Anglo-Russian relations. But the Young Turks had in any case failed to live up to his expectations both internally and externally by 1910 – even before the Russians had begun to question or jeopardize the kind of Anglo-Ottoman friendship Britain had originally envisaged. This failure, coupled with the Porte's claims in questions affecting Pan-Islam, the Gulf and Mesopotamia, in fact ended Britain's benevolent attitude towards the Young Turks long before it could clash with Russia's anti-Ottoman policy.

In the final analysis, it was the disastrous failure of the Young Turks in their Balkan policy that saved Britain from the greatest dilemma she could have faced. Had the active Slavophil policy of the Russians succeeded before 1910, then Britain would indeed have had to decide whether to support Balkan or Young Turk nationalism. This could have placed her in an awkward dilemma: European and Imperial interests undoubtedly demanded sympathy towards Russia's support for Balkan nationalism; nevertheless, had Young Turk rule in Europe been successful, Britain's apprehensions concerning Pan-Islam and her interests in the Gulf would have pushed her into support of the Ottoman Empire. On the other hand, however, the failure of the CUP posed other problems, for their disastrous record in the Balkans had effectively brought about the destruction of the Ottoman Empire in Europe at the end of 1912. The dangers were dual. First, the successor Balkan States did not bring peace to Europe. On the contrary, they were themselves the cause and flashpoint of further Great Power rivalry. Secondly, and because of her support to Russia's friends during the ensuing Balkan Wars, Britain irretrievably lost her position at the Porte. As much was demonstrated during the negotiations over Adrianople and the Aegean Islands. Instead, Germany strengthened her position in the Ottoman Empire – especially as her ambitions again evoked a powerful response in the Ottoman army as well as in the CUP.

It is not easy to assess the role of the British Embassy in this continuous deterioration in Britain's relations with the Ottoman Empire. It might be considered unfortunate that such critical and anti-Revolutionary diplomats as Lowther, Fitzmaurice and Marling served in the British Embassy during this period. These men aspired to a constitutional monarchy in the Ottoman Empire of the British type, but found themselves in the throes of a 'Jacobin'-like regime which detested the Entente and permitted increasing penetration by German military and economic interests. When due consideration is taken of the eventual march of events, the Embassy's apprehensions cannot be thought entirely unfounded. Neither, however, can it be denied that the vehemently anti-CUP tone which permeated the Embassy's correspondence with the Foreign Office was bound to influence London. There, officials had in any case strongly imbibed these anti-Ottoman prejudices which, enhanced by the CUP's failures, found the Foreign Office quite ready to accept the Ottoman setbacks in Tripoli and the Balkans as *faits accomplis*. At this level of analysis, it must be remembered that only once, in mid-1909, did the Foreign Office warn the Embassy of its anti-CUP attitude. Throughout the rest of the Lowther-Fitzmaurice-Marling incumbency, a period of over four years, the Foreign Office never again reproached the Embassy for its conspicuous bias. Moreover, the other British diplomatic representatives – while reflecting the attitudes of the countries to which they had been accredited – encouraged the Foreign Office in its acceptance of the views propagated by the Embassy in Constantinople.

Throughout the period, Britain was very anxious to obtain the Porte's recognition of her exclusive rule in the Persian Gulf. For this she was even ready, in mid-July 1912, to relinquish her ambitions in the Baghdad-Gulf line. This was a major sacrifice and a considerable retreat from her previous attitude. What is more, the Foreign Office refused to harden its attitude in these questions, despite the Embassy's pressure to take advantage of the crushing defeats suffered by the Ottoman Empire later in 1912. The Persian Gulf and Mesopotamia were regarded as matters with an importance quite independent of Balkan problems or the internal rule of the CUP. As had always been the case, the prime determinant of policy was the need to secure the north-east flank of India.

Pan-Islamic considerations fell into the same sort of category, albeit with different results. As far as the Embassy was concerned this was a bogey which had to be taken into serious account. But consideration for Young Turk aspirations with regard to the Moslem subjects of the British Empire influenced the Foreign Office in two different and contradictory ways. On the one hand it did strengthen the Foreign Office's belief in the mischievous and harmful character of the Young Turk regime; on the other hand, and especially when cited by the Viceroy, it acted as a restraint upon the anti-Ottoman attitudes adopted by the British Government. The net result was nonetheless an anti-Ottoman policy.

It is in the light of the crucial Lowther-Fitzmaurice-Marling period that an assessment should be made of the subsequent period dominated by Sir Louis Mallet. It is not altogether clear whether he was instructed to initiate a new and favourable period in the relations with the CUP Government by both reversing the policy of Lowther-Fitzmaurice-Marling and attempting to keep Turkey neutral. As Mallet himself appreciated, considerations of high policy really precluded radical changes. But the fact remains that Mallet did distinguish himself from his predecessor in both his extravagant flattery towards the CUP leadership and his continuous attempts to persuade the Foreign Office as to the successes (however illusory) of the Young Turks. Nevertheless, his policy did not include any systematic programme to solve the main issues at stake: Ottoman relations with Russia and Greece. The result was that Mallet really achieved nothing at all of substance. After, and as a result of, the catastrophe in the Balkans, German influence quickly predominated at Constantinople. Significantly Mallet failed, or perhaps did not even try, to court Enver as much as he did Talaat and Jemal. Consequently, the Ambassador was faced with the complete bankruptcy of his policy on his return from London on 16 August 1914.[2]

That Mallet was ruthlessly criticized for his blunders during the period between August and October 1914 can be attributed to the ignorance of *The Times* and of everyone else outside the Foreign Office, about the enormity of the blunders he had committed earlier. His attempts before July 1914 to project a new image of the CUP leadership were, indeed, groundless and, in view of the record, unjustified. He was also far too slow to begin to fight the Germans and their protégés, although it is doubtful whether any other Ambassador could have achieved more after August 1914.

But strong prejudices, like unjustified admiration, need not be given too much weight. Britain's Ottoman failure in 1914 was more a result of Britain's Entente with Russia than of blunders committed by Lowther, Fitzmaurice or Mallet. The Entente Powers could not be expected to offer the Young Turks as much as the Central Powers always did, and Britain could not launch an independent pro-Ottoman policy. The only period during which such an opportunity might have existed was in 1908-9, when the CUP had not yet shown its true colours and when it was easy to condemn the Austrian annexation of Bosnia and Herzegovina and the Bulgarian declaration of independence. But these questions were patched up with comparative ease. What really mattered was the subsequent failure of the CUP to govern their Christian citizens (which was not their fault alone in view of the unchecked growth of Balkan nationalism), and their aggressive Pan-Islamism. By comparison, their failure to establish constitutional rule, much as it shocked and disappointed the British Government, exerted a less powerful influence on Britain's policy. That much is indeed indicated by the apathetic attitude towards Kiamil's and Ghazi Moukhtar's Governments.[3]

To say that is not to absolve Britain of all responsibility for the destruction of the Ottoman Empire. Although ready to assist in its reform, she ultimately subordinated that consideration to her much more important international and Imperial interests.[4] Her main preoccupation was her friendship with Russia rather than her desire to win over the Young Turks. The latter, whatever their own 'contribution' to the destruction of the Ottoman Empire, were pawns in a cruel diplomatic game being played by Russia and Germany, and to a lesser extent by Austria and Italy too. In some measure, so was the less reckless British Government. Grey, after all, was willing time and again to give the Young Turks a chance to stay out of the European groupings before 1914. But neither he nor his subordinates could have been expected to change their overall policies in order to facilitate those changes. Together with Nicolson and Hardinge, he had to give overriding importance to the Entente, to Britain's interests in India and Egypt, and – before late-1912 – to the Gulf and Mesopotamia. The morality of their claim to stand for constitutionalism and reform in Turkey is questionable. But in reality they supported (and had to support) Britain's self-interest in the European Concert, the Empire and, to a lesser degree, in the improvement of her trade and economy.

In effect, the Ottomans, both Young Turks and their opponents, had parallel standards. But they were never ready to be satisfied with anything short of alliance. Their main mistake, not yet admitted by Turkish historians,[5] was their belief in the necessity to join one European alliance or another. Consequently, they ruled out, mainly from fear of Russia, the safer course of staying neutral. Enver and his pro-German faction were clearly responsible for this policy rather than the Entente Powers – who did not conceal their support for the Porte's enemies. Mallet's failure to discover the existence of the Ottoman-German Treaty did not really influence the issue of the Porte's entry to the war. This decision was entirely in the hands of the Ottoman rulers in 1914. They could have afforded to stay neutral; but their vanity, pro-Germanism and their ambition to recover their lost territories seem to have prompted their decision to join Germany. Their fears regarding further partition were really groundless. In 1914 the Entente's plans as to the future of Asiatic Turkey were only vague; even Russia was prepared to leave the Ottoman provinces there in Young Turk hands. But the latter instead preferred to share their fate with those whom they thought were the stronger. This was not a gamble, as some historians have claimed, but a calculated decision. The CUP claim in 1908 of attachment to England because of the so-called affinity of constitutional goals rapidly faded away and only interests and old prejudices counted for most of the period. Germany, with no Moslem subjects and with no constitutional pretensions, appeared to the Young Turks to be their ideal ally. Britain, with both Moslem subjects and constitutional pretensions, could be only an enemy to the CUP, such was the belief of Enver and his friends. It was perhaps the fact that the Young Turk rulers were soldiers rather than statesmen which led them to the abyss, and for this Britain could not be responsible.

LIST OF SOURCES

Unpublished Sources

CABINET PAPERS

Cab. 41, Asquith to the King. Reports of the Cabinet Meetings, 1908-14.
Cab. 37, Cab. Memo. 1908-14.
Cab. 38, CID Papers, 1908-14.

GENERAL CORRESPONDENCE, TURKEY

PRO; FO/371/Political (1908-14).

PRIVATE PAPERS

Bertie Papers, PRO.
Crewe Papers, Cambridge University Library.
Grey Papers, PRO
Hardinge Papers, PRO and Cambridge University Library; FO/800/192 (1906-11);
    PRO, Vols. 11-21 (1908-10); 93, Cambridge University Library.
Lowther Papers, PRO
Morley Papers, India Office Library.
Nicolson Papers, PRO.
Vambéry Papers, PRO

Published Sources

DOCUMENTS

British Documents on the Origins of the War, 1898-1914, eds. G.P. Gooch & H.
    Temperley, vols. V, VI, IX, X (London 1928-38).
Die grosse Politik der europaischen Kabinette, 1871-1914, eds. J. Lepsius, A.M.
    Bartholdy, E. Thime. Vols. XXV–XXXIX (Berlin 1925-6); a small selection
    was translated into English by E.T.S. Dugdale, *German Diplomatic Docu-
    ments*, 4 vols. (London 1930-1).
Documents diplomatiques français (1871-1914), 2ᵉ série (1901-11) T.XI–XIII
    (Paris 1950-5); 3ᵉ série (1911-14) T.I–XI (Paris 1929-36).
*Österreich – Ungarns Aussenpolitik von der Bosnischen Krise 1908 bis zum Krieg-
    ausbruch 1914*, eds. L. Bittner & H. Uebersberger, 9 vols (Wien und Leipzig
    1930).

Die Internationalen Beziehungen im Zeitalter des Imperialismus. Dokumente aus den Archiven der Zarischen und der Provisorischen Regierung (Berlin 1931-?) Ser. 1, vols. 1-4, ed. M.N. Pokrovski (Russian edition); ed. O. Hoetzsch (German edition).

MEMOIRS, ARTICLES AND BOOKS

Abbot, G.F., *Turkey in Transition* (London 1909).
Ahmad, F., 'Great Britain's Relations with the Young Turks, 1908-1914', *Middle Eastern Studies* (1966) pp.302-29.
   The Young Turks: The Committee of Union and Progress in Turkish Politics, 1908-1914 (Oxford 1969).
Albertini, L., *The Origins of the War of 1914*, vols. I–III (London 1952-7).
Anderson, M.S., *The Eastern Question, 1774-1923* (London 1966).
Anderson, Mosa, *Noel Buxton: A Life* (London 1952).
Askew, W.C. *Europe and Italy's Acquisition of Libya, 1911-1912* (Durham, N. Carolina 1942).
Blunt, W.S., *My Diaries*, vol. II (London 1919).
Bosworth, R., 'Britain and Italy's Acquisition of the Dodecanese, 1912-1915', *Historical Journal* (1970) pp.683-705.
Bridge, F.R., *Great Britain and Austria-Hungary, 1906-14: A Diplomatic History* (London 1972).
   From Sadowa to Sarajevo: The Foreign Policy of Austria-Hungary, 1866-1914 (London 1972).
   'Relations with Austria-Hungary and the Balkans, 1905-1908' in F.H. Hinsley (ed.) *British Foreign Policy Under Sir Edward Grey* (Cambridge 1977) pp.165-77.
   'Izvolsky, Aehrenthal and the End of the Austro-Russian Entente, 1906-8', *Mitteilungen des Österreichischen Staatsarchivs*, Bd. 29 (1976) pp.315-62.
Bullard, R.W., *The Camels Must Go* (London 1961).
Buchanan, G., *My Mission to Russia and other Diplomatic Memories* vol. 1 (London 1925).
Busch, B.C., *Britain and the Persian Gulf, 1894-1914* (Berkeley 1967).
Buxton, N., 'Young Turkey After Two Years', *Nineteenth Century and After* (March, 1911) pp.417-32.
   'The Russians in Armenia', *ibid*. (December, 1913) pp.1357-66.
Chapman, M.K., *Great Britain and the Bagdad Railway, 1888-1914* (Northampton, Mass 1948).
Churchill, W.S., *The World Crisis, 1911-1914* (London 1923).
Churchill, R.S., *Winston S. Churchill, Vol. II, Part 2: 1907-1911* (London 1969).
Cohen, S.A., *British Policy in Mesopotamia, 1903-1914* (London 1976).
Cooper, M.B., 'British Policy in the Balkans, 1908-9', *The Historical Journal* (1964) p.258-79.
Conwell-Evans, T.P., *Foreign Policy From a Back Bench, 1904-1918* (London 1932). This is a study based on the papers of Lord Noel Buxton.
Corrigan, H.S.W., 'German-Turkish Relations and the Outbreak of War in 1914: A Re-Assessment', *Past and Present* (1967) pp.144-52.
Crampton, R.J., 'The Balkans, 1909-1914', F.H. Hinsley (ed.), *op. cit.* pp.256-70.
Cunliffe-Owen, F. 'The Entry of Turkey into the War: The Action of H.M. Embassy', *National Review* (November, 1931) pp.611-22.

Cunningham, A., 'The Wrong Horse? – A Study of Anglo-Turkish Relations Before the First World War', *St Antony's Papers No. 17* (Oxford 1965) pp. 56-76.

Dakin, D., 'The Diplomacy of the Great Powers and the Balkans, 1907-1914', *Balkan Studies* (1962).
   The Greek Struggle in Macedonia, 1897-1913 (Salonika 1966).
   The Unification of Greece, 1770-1923 (London 1972).

David, E., ed. *Inside Asquith's Cabinet: From the Diaries of Charles Hobhouse* (London 1977).

Davison, R., 'The Armenian Crisis, 1912-1914', *American Historical Review* (1948) pp. 481-505.

Djemal Pasha, *Memories of a Turkish Statesman, 1913-1919*, (London n.d.).

Durham, M. E., *High Albania* (London 1909).

Einstein, L., *A Diplomat Looks Back* (New Haven 1968).

Eliot, C., *Turkey in Europe* (London 2nd. ed. 1908; reprinted Frank Cass, 1965).

Farhi, D., 'The Şeriat as a Political Slogan – or the Incident of the 31st Mart', *Middle Eastern Studies* (1971) pp. 275-99.

Fieldhouse, H. N., 'Noel Buxton and A.J.P Taylor's "The Trouble Makers"', M. Gilbert, ed., *A Century of Conflict, 1850-1950: Essays for A.J.P. Taylor* (London 1966).

Fischer, F., *War of Illusion: German Policies, 1911-1914* (London 1975).
   'World Policy, World Power and German War Aims', in H.W. Koch, ed., *The Origins of the First World War* (London 1972).

Gilbert, M, *Winston S. Churchill, Vol. III: 1914-1916* (London 1971).

Gooch, G. P., *Under Six Reigns* (London 1958).

Gottlieb, W. W., *Studies in Secret Diplomacy* (London 1957).

Graves, P. P., *Briton and Turk* (London 1941).

Graves, R. W., *Storm Centres of the Near East: Personal Memories, 1879-1929* (London 1933).

Grenville, J. A. S., *Salisbury's Foreign Policy* (London 1964).

Grey, Edward, *Twenty-Five Years (1892-1916)* (London 2nd. ed. 1935).

Gwinner, A. von., 'The Bagdad Railway and the Question of British Cooperation', *Nineteenth Century and After* (June, 1909) pp. 1083-91.

Halpern, P.G., *The Mediterranean Naval Situation, 1908-1914* (Cambridge, Mass. 1971).

Hardinge, Charles, *Old Diplomacy* (London 1947).

Heller, J., 'Sir Louis Mallet and the Ottoman Empire: The Road to War', *Middle Eastern Studies* (1976) pp. 3-44.
   'Britain and the Armenian Question 1912-1914 – A Study in Realpolitik', *ibid.* (1980) pp. 3-26.

Helmreich, E.C., *The Diplomacy of the Balkan Wars, 1912-1913* (Cambridge, Mass. 1938).

Herbert A., *Ben Kendim: A Record of Eastern Travel* (London 1923).

Heymann, M., *British Policy and Public Opinion on the Turkish Question, 1908-1914* (unpublished Ph.D. thesis, Cambridge 1957).
   History of the Times, Vol. IV, pt. I: 1912-1920 (London 1952).

Hohler, T. B., *Diplomatic Petrel* (London 1942).

Hovannisian, R. G., *Armenia on the Road of Independence, 1918* (Berkeley 1967).
   'The Armenian Question in the Ottoman Empire', *East European Quarterly* (1972) pp. 1-26.

Howard, H.N., *The Partition of Turkey: A Diplomatic History, 1913-1923* (Oklahoma 1931).

Jack (Kent) M., 'The Purchase of the British Government's Shares in the British Petroleum Co., 1912-1914', *Past and Present* (1968) pp. 139-68.

James, R. R. *Churchill: A Study in Failure* (London 1970).

Jefferson, M.M. 'Lord Salisbury and the Eastern Question, 1890-1898', *Slavonic and East European Review* (1960) pp. 44-60.

Johnston, H. H., 'The Final Solution of the Eastern Question', *Nineteenth Century and After* (March, 1913) pp. 536-47.

Joll, J., *Britain and Europe: Pitt to Churchill, 1793-1940* (London 1961).

Kautsky, K., *Outbreak of War: Documents Collected by* (New York 1924).

Kedourie, E., *England and the Middle East, 1914-1921: The Destruction of the Ottoman Empire* (London 1956).

'Minorities' in: *The Chatham House Version and other Middle Eastern Studies* (Frank Cass, London 1970) pp. 286-300.

'Young Turks, Freemasons and Jews', *Arabic Political Memoirs* (Frank Cass, London 1974) pp. 243-62.

In the Anglo-Arab Labyrinth: The McMahon-Husayn Correspondence and its Interpretations, 1914-1939 (Cambridge 1976).

Kelly, J. B., 'Salisbury, Curzon and the Kuweit Agreement of 1899', *Studies in International History*, eds. K. Bourne and D.C. Watt (1967) pp. 249-90.

Kent, M., *Oil and Empire: British Policy and Mesopotamian Oil, 1900-1920* (London 1976).

'Constantinople and Asiatic Turkey, 1905-1914', in F. H. Hinsley, *op. cit.* pp. 148-64.

'Asiatic Turkey, 1914-1916', *op. cit.* pp. 436-51.

'Agent of Empire: The National Bank of Turkey and British Foreign Policy', *Historical Journal* (1975) pp. 367-89.

Kerner, R.J., 'The Mission of Liman von Sanders', *Slavic Review*, 6 (1927-8) pp. 12-27, 344-63, 543-60; 7 (1928) pp. 90-112.

Knaplund, P., *Speeches on Foreign Policy, 1904-1914* (London 1931).

Knight, E.F. *The Awakening of Turkey* (London 1909).

Kühlmann, R. V., *Erinnerungen* (Heidelberg 1948).

Kurat, Y.T., 'How Turkey Drifted into World War I', *Studies in International History, op. cit.* pp. 291-315.

Lewis, B., *The Emergence of Modern Turkey* (Oxford 2nd. ed. 1968).

Liddell Hart, H. B., *T. E. Lawrence to his Biographer Liddell Hart* (London 1938).

Lowe, C.J., *The Reluctant Imperialists* (London 1967).

'Grey and the Tripoli War, 1911-1912', in F.H. Hinsley, *op. cit.* pp. 315-23.

Lowe, C.J. & M.L. Dockrill, *The Mirage of Power: British Foreign Policy, 1902-1922* (London 1972).

Lowe, C.J. & F. Marzari, *Italian Foreign Policy, 1870-1940* (London 1975).

Lumby, E. W. R. ed., *Policy and Operations in the Mediterranean: 1912-1914* (London 1970).

Lynch, H.F.B., *Armenia*, vol. I–II (London 1901).

McCullagh, F., *The Fall of Abdul Hamid* (London 1910).

Magnus, P., *Kitchener: A Portrait of an Imperialist* (London 1958).

Mandel, N., 'Turks, Arabs and Jewish Immigration to Palestine, 1882-1914', *St Antony's Papers, op. cit.* pp. 77-108.

The Arabs and Zionism Before World War I (University of California 1976).

Marder, A.J., *From the Dreadnought to Scapa Flow: The Royal Navy in the Fisher Era*, vol. II (London 1965).

Fear God and Dreadnought, vol. II: Years of Power, 1904-1914 (London 1956).

Medlicott, W.N., *The Congress of Berlin and After* (London 2nd ed. Frank Cass, 1963).

'Gladstone and the Turks', *History* (1928) pp. 136-7.

'The Gladstone Government and the Cyprus Convention, 1880-1885', *Journal of Modern History* (1940) pp. 186-208.
Bismarck, Gladstone and the European Concert (London 1956).
Monger, G., *The End of Isolation* (London 1963).
Morris, A. J. A., *Radicalism Against War, 1906-1914* (London 1972).
Nicolson, H., *Lord Carnock* (London 1930).
Ostrorog, L., *The Turkish Problem* (London 1919).
Parker, A., 'The Baghdad Railway Negotiations', *Quarterly Review* (October, 1917) pp. 487-528.
Pears, E., *Forty Years in Constantinople* (London 1915).
Platt, D.C.M. *Finance, Trade and Politics in British Foreign Policy, 1814-1914* (Oxford 1968).
Ramsaur, E.E., *The Young Turks: Prelude to the Revolution of 1908* (Princeton 1957).
Ramsay, W.M., *The Revolution in Constantinople and Turkey: A Diary* (London 1909).
Renzi, W.M., 'Great Britain, Russia and the Straits, 1914-1915', *Journal of Modern History* (1970) pp. 1-20.
Rich, N. & M.H., eds., *The Holstein Papers, vol. IV: Correspondence, 1897-1909* (Cambridge 1963).
Robbins, K., 'British Policy and Bulgaria, 1914-1915', *Slavonic and East European Review* (1971) pp. 560-85.
Sir Edward Grey (London 1971).
Ro'i, Y., 'The Zionist Attitude to the Arabs, 1908-1914', *Middle Eastern Studies* (1968) pp. 198-242.
Rustow, D.A., 'Enver Pasha', *Encyclopaedia of Islam*, new ed. Vol. II.
Ryan, A., *The Last of the Dragomans* (London 1951).
Schmitt, B.E., *The Annexation of Bosnia, 1908-1909* (Cambridge, Mass. 1937).
Skendi, S., *The Albanian National Awakening, 1878-1912* (Princeton 1967).
Smith, C.J., 'Great Britain and the 1914-1915 Straits Agreement with Russia: The British Promise of November 1914', *American Historical Review* (1965) pp. 1015-34.
Steiner, Z.S., *The Foreign Office and Foreign Policy, 1898-1914* (Cambridge 1969).
'The Foreign Office Under Sir Edward Grey, 1905-1914', in F.H. Hinsley, *op. cit.* pp. 22-69.
Britain and the Origins of the First World War (London 1977).
Stieve, F., *Isvolsky and the World War* (London 1926).
Story, S., ed., *The Memoirs of Ismail Kemal Bey* (London 1920).
Sweet, D.W., 'The Bosnia Crisis', in F.H. Hinsley, *op. cit.* pp. 178-92.
Sykes, M., *The Caliph's Last Heritage* (London 1915).
Taylor, A.J.P., *The Struggle for Mastery in Europe, 1848-1918* (Oxford 1954).
Temperley, H., 'British Policy Towards Parliamentary Rule and Constitutionalism in Turkey (1830-1914), *Cambridge Historical Journal* (1933) pp. 156-91.
Temperley, H. and Penson, L.M., *A Century of Diplomatic Blue Books, 1814-1914* (Cambridge 1938).
Thaden, E.C., 'Montenegro: Russia's Troublesome Ally, 1910-1912', *Journal of Central European Affairs* (1958) pp. 111-33.
Russia and the Balkan League of 1912 (Pennsylvania 1965).
Tilley, J.A.C., *London to Tokyo* (London 1942).
Troeller, G., *The Birth of Saudi Arabia: Britain and the Birth of the House of Saud* (London, Frank Cass, 1976).
Trumpener, U., 'Liman von Sanders and the German-Ottoman Alliance', *Journal of Contemporary History* (1966) pp. 179-92.

Germany and the Ottoman Empire, 1914-1918 (Princeton 1967).

'The Escape of the Goeben and Breslau: A Reassessment', *Canadian Journal of History* (1971).

Vansittart, R., *The Mist Procession* (London 1957).

Wank, S., 'Aehrenthal and the Sanjak of Novi-Bazar Railway Project: A Re-appraisal', *The Slavonic and East European Review* (1964) pp. 343-69.

'The Appointment of Count Berchtold as Austro-Hungarian Foreign Minister', *Journal of Central European Affairs* (1963) pp. 143-51.

Ward, W.A. and Gooch, G.P., *The Cambridge History of British Foreign Policy, vol. III: 1866-1919* (Cambridge 1923).

Waugh, T.A., Sir, *Turkey, Yesterday, Today and Tomorrow* (London 1930).

Weber, F.G., *Eagles on the Crescent: Germany, Austria and the Diplomacy of the Turkish Alliance, 1914-1918* (Cornell 1970).

Willcocks, W., *Sixty Years in the East* (London 1935).

Williamson, J.G., *Karl Helfferich, 1872-1924* (Princeton 1971).

Williamson, S.R., *The Politics of Grand Strategy: Britain and France Prepare for War, 1904-1914* (Cambridge, Mass. 1971).

Zeman, Z.A.B., *A Diplomatic History of the First World War* (London 1971).

Notes

INTRODUCTION

1. He was not, however, a Turcophobe as was conventionally thought. Cf. W.N. Medlicott, 'Gladstone and the Turks', *History* (1928), pp.136-7; *id*., 'The Gladstone Government and the Cyprus Convention, 1880-85', *Journal of Modern History* (1940), pp.186-208, *id., Bismarck, Gladstone and the European Concert* (London 1956).
2. Cf. W.N. Medlicott, *The Congress of Berlin and After* (London 2nd ed., Frank Cass, 1963).
3. H. Temperley, 'British Policy Towards Parliamentary Rule and Constitutionalism in Turkey, 1830-1914', *Cambridge Historical Journal* (1933), pp.156-91. But compare the contemporary view of a neutral American diplomat: 'A country like Turkey, notoriously in a hopeless mess, could continue its disorder providing only that the old familiar abuses went on, but it was certain to collapse as soon as any real attempt was made to introduce reforms.' L. Einstein, *A Diplomat Looks Back* (New Haven 1968), p.35.
4. C.J. Lowe, *The Reluctant Imperialists* (London 1967), pp.196-203.
5. GD, 27,II,9789, pp.253-5. On the influence of the Anglo-Russian Convention cf. O'Conor to Grey, 15.10.07. no. 652, Conf. FO/371/355.
6. Cf. G. Monger, *The End of Isolation* (London 1963), pp.137-8. On Macedonia from a Greek point of view, see D. Dakin, *The Greek Struggle in Macedonia, 1897-1913* (Salonika 1966).
7. Annual Report for Turkey for the Year 1907, in O'Conor to Grey, 13.1.08, no. 21, BD.V., p.43.
8. C.J. Lowe & Dockrill, M.L. *The Mirage of Power, British Foreign Policy, 1902-1922* (London 1972), pp.461-4; and S. Wank, 'Aehrenthal and the Sanjak of Novi-Bazar Railway Project: A Re-Appraisal'. *The Slavonic and East European Review* (1964), pp.343-69.
9. Grey to O'Conor, 22.12.05, Pte. GP 79.
10. Compare O'Conor to Grey, 12.2.08, Pte. BD.V. no. 186 and Nicolson to Grey, 18.2.08, no. 85; *ibid.* no. 188; with Grey to Lascelles, 24.2.08, no. 59; *ibid.*, no. 238 and *Hansard*, Parliamentary Debates, House of Commons, 4th Series, Vol. 184, cols. 1707-8, 25.2.08.
11. Grey to Bertie etc., 3.3.08. Turkey no. 1 (1908) A. & P. (1908) CXXV, pp.587-96.
12. Grey to Goschen, 11.2.08, Pte. BD.V. no. 191.
13. Hardinge to Barclay, 24.3.08, Pte. HP.13.
14. Block to Hardinge, 25.3.08, Pte. HP.11.
15. The same point was later raised by the First Secretary of the Embassy, Sir T.B. Hohler. See his *Diplomatic Petrel* (London 1942), p.151, and by L. Einstein, *op. cit.*, p.59. D.C.M. Platt, *Finance, Trade and Politics in British Foreign Policy, 1815-1914* (London 1968), pp.187-88 ff.

16. Fitzmaurice to Tyrrell, 12.4.08, Pte. BD.V. no. 196. Same to same 25.8.05, Pte. *ibid.* no. 210 Ed. On Fitzmaurice's important position at Constantinople see Sir R. Bullard, *The Camels Must Go* (London 1961), pp. 62-4; Sir A. Ryan, *The Last of the Dragomans* (London 1951), p 46; A. Herbert, *Ben Kendim: A Record of Eastern Travel* (London 1923), p. 268; Sir R. Vansittart, *The Mist Procession* (London 1957), p. 68-9; *The Cambridge History of British Foreign Policy*, Vol. III (Cambridge 1923), describes him as an *éminence grise* behind his chiefs in the Embassy, p. 621. GD. 27, p. 562. For a German view on Fitzmaurice, GD. 37,I,14732; Djemal Pasha, *Memoirs of a Turkish Statesman* (London n.d.), pp. 21, 24, 30, 100.
17. Hardinge to Nicolson, 13.4.08, Pte. BD.V, no. 194.
18. The Balkan Committee Resolution on Macedonia, 9.4.08. FO/371/536/12387 and the Statement signed by 107 MPs, 10.4.08, expressing their 'strong satisfaction' at Grey's recent speech, *ibid.* File no. 12491.
19. Turkey no. 3 (1908) May 1908 A. & P. CXXV (1908) pp. 607-889.
20. Grey to Barclay, 26.5.08, Pte. BD.V. no. 197.
21. Hardinge to Barclay, 19.5.08, Pte. HP. 13.
22. Hardinge to Nicolson, 17.3.08, Pte. BD.V. no. 254. Since 1907 Britain demanded, not an internationalized railway as after 1903, but rather a monopoly of the southern section, as the only guarantee for her trade. This increased Britain's interest in Mesopotamia. For a detailed account: cf. S.A. Cohen, *British Policy in Mesopotamia 1903-1914* (London 1976).
23. Block to Hardinge, 22.5.08, Pte. HP.11. Same to Same, 28.5.08. Pte. *ibid.*
24. Hardinge to Barclay, 2.6.08. Pte. HP. 13.
25. Hardinge to Buchanan, 2.6.08, Pte. *ibid.*
26. Memorandum by Hardinge, 12.6.08, BD.V. no. 195. Izvolsky to Benckendorff, 5(18).6.08. *Ibid.*, pp. 245-6, DDF. 2ᵉ ser. T.11, no. 402.
27. This understanding with Britain suited Russia as much as Britain. Izvolsky exclaimed that relations with Austria could not be the same after Aehrenthal's act in Novibazar. BD.V. pp. 245-6.
28. On the internal background to the Revolution of 1908 see: F. Ahmad, *The Young Turks* (Oxford 1969); E.E. Ramsaur, *The Young Turks* (Princeton 1957); B. Lewis, *The Emergence of Modern Turkey* (Oxford 2nd ed. 1968). For contemporary accounts: E.F. Knight, *The Awakening of Turkey* (London 1909); G. .F. Abbott, *Turkey in Transition* (London 1909). Lowther's account in his Annual Report for Turkey for the Year 1908. Encl. in: Lowther to Grey, 17.2.09. no. 105. BD.V. p. 249. cf. GD, 25, p. 577, BD.V. no. 216.
29. Same to same. 14.7.08. Pte. *ibid.*, cf. Marschall's analysis of the Revolution. GD. 25, 8910.
30. Memorandum respecting the Baghdad Railway. Foreign Office, 3.7.08 (by L. Mallet), BD.VI., no. 266. Grey to de Salis, 13.7.08, no. 176. Secret. *Ibid.*, no. 267. Note by Grey to Hardinge's minute 25.6.08. *Ibid.*, Ed. Note. p. 368.
31. Minute by Mallet. Grey to de Salis, 13.7.08, no. 176. Secret. *Ibid.*, minute by Grey.
32. Ahmed Riza was considered by the Paris Embassy as a 'very suspicious and untrustworthy character.' FO/371/346/6840. Memorandum on the CUP in: Bertie (Lister) to Grey, 28.2.07, no. 112, *ibid.*

CHAPTER 1

1. Barclay to Grey, 8.7.08. tel. no. 160. Minutes FO/371/544/23627.
2. 'This movement, if it grows, will be an important factor in the Macedonian

situation.' Minutes by H. Norman, Assistant Clerk in the Eastern Department. Same to same, 9.7.08, no. 378, *ibid*/24315.

3. Hardinge to Barclay, 14.7.08, Pte. HP,13. Hardinge to Buchanan, 14.7.08, Pte. *ibid*. However, Hardinge envisaged that Germany, Austria and Bulgaria might disturb the success of the Revolution. The Germans did not intend to fight it. GD, 25,II, p.577, *ibid*., no. 8889. Cf. D. Dakin, *The Greek Struggle in Macedonia, 1897-1913* (London 1966), p.397.

4. Barclay to Hardinge, 15.7.08, Pte. HP,11. Same to same, 18.7.08, Pte.*ibid*. Not one of the diplomats accredited to the Porte could claim any foreknowledge of the coming Revolution: Einstein, *op. cit.*, pp.64-5.

5. Barclay to Grey, 22.7.08. tel. no. 171. Minute by Hardinge, FO/371/544.

6. Fitzmaurice to Tyrrell, 25.8.08. Pte. BD.V. no. 210, Ed. Add.

7. Block to Hardinge, 25.7.08, Pte. HP,11. Block and Fitzmaurice were considered by the Germans as the prime movers of the anti-German orientation in Constantinople, GD, 27, p.562. M. Gilbert, *Winston S. Churchill: Companion*, vol. II (London 1969), p.835.

8. Grey to O'Bierne, 27.7.08. tel. no. 274. BD. *op. cit.*, no. 212.

9. *Hansard*, House of Commons, 27.7.08. 4th Series, vol. 193, cols. 966-9. The day after, Grey remained true to his parliamentary statement while talking to the Bulgarian Agent, Stancioff. Grey to Buchanan, 28.7.08. no. 40, BD.V. no. 213.

10. Barclay to Hardinge, 28.7.08. Pte. HP,11.

11. Hardinge to Buchanan, 28.7.08. HP,13. More on Hardinge's views, especially his fears of Russia repeating her 'intrigues' from 1876 against Ottoman reform, in Lowe and Dockrill, p.464.

12. Hardinge to Goschen, 28.7.08, Pte. HP,13.

13. Hardinge to de Salis, 28.7.08, Pte. *ibid*. This was only a temporary blow. For different German views on the Revolution, cf. GD,27,II, pp.560-5. J.G. Williamson, *Karl Helffrich, 1872-1924* (Princeton 1971), pp.87-90. Rich & Fisher, *The Holstein Papers*, IV, pp.546, n. 4, 547-8, 552, n. 2.

14. Hardinge to Lamb, 28.7.08, Pte. HP,13. Barclay to Grey, 28.7.08. tel no. 197. Minute by Hardinge, FO/371/544.

15. Hardinge to Bertie, 30.7.08. Pte. BP.180; Morley to Minto, 30.7.08. MSS. Eur. D.573/3. But cf. Minto's optimism: Minto to Morley, 29.7.08. Pte. MP.MSS. Eur. D.573/16. '... we have much to gain politically by our goodwill to Mussulman enlightenment. We lost a chance long ago when Ignatieff got round Lord Salisbury and threw cold water on Midhat's reforms. I have always had great belief in the ordinary Turk. It is the corruption of the Pasha class which has ruined him ...' *Ibid*.

16. 'How little we either of us foresaw, when you were appointed, the reception you would actually get!' Grey to Lowther, 31.7.08. Pte. BD.V. no. 204. Ed. Add. For a recent description of Lowther's arrival, cf. L. Einstein, *op. cit*., p.67. He was recommended to this post by Hardinge; cf. Z. Steiner, *The Foreign Office and Foreign Policy, 1898-1914* (Cambridge 1969), p.102. Grey suggested him to the Porte in a letter to Barclay on 16 May 1908. GP,79.

17. Hardinge to Block, 31.7.08. Pte. HP,13. Cf. D. Dakin, *op. cit.*, p.398. Rich & Fisher, *op. cit.*, p.584.

18. Grey to Lowther, 31.7.08. Pte. tel. FO/371/544/26664.

19. Lowther to Grey, 7.8.08. tel. no. 218. Minutes. The Germans quickly grasped the British dilemma. They foresaw a deterioration in Anglo-Russian relations, and did not believe that behind the enthusiastic reception for Lowther was any *realpolitik*. Moreover, they pointed out the contradiction between the British support for the new regime, and their unconstitutional rule in Egypt and India.

GD, *ibid.*, pp.591, 623. No. 8911. Cf. A.J. Marder, *Fear God and Dread Nought* (London 1956), II, p.187 and n. 3.

20. Lowther to Grey, 9.8.08. tel. no. 222. Minutes, FO/371/544.
21. F.O. to Admiralty, 10.8.08. Immediate and Confidential. FO/371/545/27619.
22. M. Heymann, *British Policy and Public Opinion on the Turkish Question, 1908-1914* (unpublished Ph.D. thesis, Cambridge 1957), p.68. The author relied here on the *Grosse Politik*, which depicted British policy as aggressive.
23. Lowther to Grey, 19.8.08. tel. no. 231. Minutes. GD.25.II,8887, 8889, 8906, 8910. GD.26,I, p.48, n. Rich & Fisher, p.572. Two days later, Lowther reported that the Ottoman Council of Ministers had requested the loan of a British admiral. 21.8.08, tel. 235. Minutes, FO/371/545.
24. Nicolson to Grey, 13.8.08. no. 360. Confidential, *ibid.*, BD. no. 215. Nevertheless, the apprehension as to Russia's Pan-Slavic intentions were rife at the Porte. No change occurred in Ottoman policy towards Russia, which was considered by Kiamil as a 'natural enemy' as much as England was regarded as a 'natural friend'. Lowther to Grey, 11.8.08. Pte. *ibid.*, 206, Ed. Add.
25. Ext. memo. by Hardinge, 16.8.08, BD.V. App. IV, F.R. Bridge, *Great Britain and Austria-Hungary, 1906-1914: A Diplomatic History* (London 1972), p.103.
26. E.G., Buchanan to Grey, 19.8.08, no. 72. BD.V. no. 263.
27. The Smyrna-Aidin railway was seen by Grey as an example of a fair British enterprise, because it did not involve any kilometric guarantees. Grey to Lowther, 23.8.08. Pte. *ibid.*, no. 208. Ed. Add.
28. Lowther to Grey, 21.8.08. tel. no. 235. Minutes. FO/371/545.
29. Lowther to Grey, 25.8.08. Pte. BD.V. no. 209. Ed. Add. Ryan, *The Last of the Dragomans* (London 1951), pp.70-71. Dakin, *op. cit.*, p.401, n.14.
30. Fitzmaurice to Tyrrell, 25.8.08. Pte. BD.V. no. 210. Ed. Add. Cf. Marschall's view: 'von der Ottomanischen Christen wird gegen die neue Ordnung der erste Stoss geführt werden', GD, *ibid.*, p.618.
31. Lowther to Grey, 2.9.08. Conf. no. 541. FO/371/549. Fitzmaurice to Tyrrell 14.5.10. Pte. GP.79.
32. The Foreign Office approved, as Hardinge had suggested, Lowther's attitude towards the CUP. Grey alone forwarded a warning here: 'We need not lay too much stress upon deference to the present Sultan.' 14.9.08. Minute on Lowther to Grey, 2.9.08, no. 541, FO/371/549.
33. Same to same, 7.9.08, no. 552, *ibid.* Mallet applied to Rothschild for a loan on 11.9. *Ibid.*
34. Lowther to Grey, 14.9.08. Pte. LP. Same to same, 14.9.08. no. 567, FO/371/559.
35. *Ibid.* Minute. See also: J.A.C. Tilley, *London to Tokyo* (London 1942), p.55.
36. Vambéry to Grey, 11.9.08. Pte. Minute by Asquith 'most interesting and the memo is admirable.' 21.9. VP,33.
37. Hardinge to Lowther, 21.9.08. Pte. HP,13. Cf. Dakin, *op. cit.*, p.399, n.4.
38. Hardinge to Block, 21.9.08. Pte. HP,13.
39. Hardinge to the King, 18.9.08. Pte. HP,14.
40. Lowther to Grey, 13.9.08. no. 259. Minute. FO/371/549.
41. Same to same, 15.9.08. no. 573, FO/371/550. Minute by Tilley.
42. Grey to Lowther, 20.8.08. Pte. GP,79.
43. Hardinge to Nicolson, 30.9.08. Pte. BD.V. no. 274.
44. Hardinge to Villiers (Lisbon), 30.9.08. Pte. HP,13.
45. Bertie to Grey, 3.10.08. tel. no. 49. Confidential BD.V. no. 285, Same to same, tel. no. 50. Confidential, *ibid.*, no. 286.

46. Bertie to Grey, 4.10.08. no. 380A. Confidential, *ibid*., no. 294: and Minute by Tilley, FO/371/550.
47. Grey to Lowther, 5.10.08. tel. no. 284. BD.V. no. 296.
48. Lowther to Grey, 5.10.08. tel. no. 294. FO/371/550.
49. Grey to Nicolson, 5.10.08. tel. no. 432. BD.V. no. 301. GD.26,I,8970, Öst.-Ung. Auss. I, no. 212. But cf. Grey to Asquith, 5.10.08. cited in Bridge, p. 113.
50. GD.26, p. 108. Rich & Fisher, pp. 577-8. This growing dependence on France and Russia also resulted from the end of the Austro-Russian Entente. Cf. F.R. Bridge, 'Izvolsky, Aehrenthal and the End of the Austro-Russian Entente, 1906-8', *Mitteilungen des Österreichischen Staatsarchivs*, BD.28 (1976), pp. 315-62.

CHAPTER 2

1. Ahmad, pp. 24-5. On the wider implication, see: B. Schmitt, *The Annexation of Bosnia, 1908-9* (Cambridge, Mass. 1937), *passim*. F.R. Bridge, *op. cit.*., Ch. 6.
2. Lowther to Grey, 7.10.08, tel. no. 300. Minutes by Tilley and Hardinge. FO/371/550.
3. Buchanan later admitted his support for Bulgaria's enmity to the new regime; see his *My Mission to Russia, and other Diplomatic Memories*, vol. 1 (London 1925) p. 79. Grey sounded very sympathetic towards the new regime both publicly and confidentially. Cf. his public speech at Wooler, Northumberland, and his letter to Asquith, Bridge, *op. cit*., p. 113; also Lowther to Grey, 6.10.08, tel. no. 296, *ibid*., no. 313. Grey to Buchanan, 6.10.08, tel. nos. 51, 53, *ibid*., nos. 319, 320.
4. Clarke (Budapest) to Grey, 6.10.08. no. 37. Minutes, 12.10.08, FO/371/552. Hence Britain also rejected the German suggestion of a guarantee for the remaining territories of the Ottoman Empire. See Lascelles to Grey, 13.10.08, tel. no. 54. BD.V. no. 367 and Minutes in FO/371/552.
5. Grey to Lowther, 12.10.08, tel. no. 335. BD.V. no. 360.
6. Grey to Lowther, 12.10.08, tel. no. 339. BD.V. no. 361. Nevertheless, Grey did not accede to what he termed Izvolsky's 'one-sided' suggestions on this issue. Neither was he moved by Izvolsky's protestation that 'Russia now desired to support Turkey as a barrier against advance'. Rather, he played upon Izvolsky's weak position within Russia, which enabled Britain to reject the Foreign Minister's plan without endangering the understanding with Russia. Japan's resistance to relaxations to Russia at the Straits also played a role. The Germans considered the British attitude to the Straits question as a touchstone of Britain's sincerity towards the new regime. GD,26,9029. Cf. also Holstein's view: Rich & Fisher, *op. cit*., pp. 579-80.
7. Lowther to Grey, 13.10.08, no. 667. FO/371/552.
8. The Armenians were also promised security. For the text of the Treaty of Berlin, see G. Britain, *Parliamentary Papers*, 1878, vol. 83, pp. 690-705; and W.N. Medlicott, *The Congress of Berlin and After* (London 1963, 2nd ed.), *passim*.
9. Grey to Lowther, 13.10.08, tel. no. 344. BD.V. p. 330, n. 1.
10. Lowther to Grey, 15.10.08, tel. no. 327, *ibid*., no. 382.
11. Grey to Lowther, 15.10.08, no. 434, BD.V. no. 383. Grey to Lowther, 16.10.08, tel. no. 358, *ibid*., 388.
12. Grey to Izvolsky, 15.10.08. Pte. Confidential, *ibid*., no. 387.
13. Lowther to Grey, 14.10.08, tel. no. 327, Minute. FO/371/552.

14. Buchanan to Grey, 14.10.08, no. 84. Minutes, 19.10. *ibid*.
15. Lowther to Grey, 26.10.08, no. 365. Secret. BD.V. no. 404.
16. Grey to Lowther, 26.10.08, no. 448, BD.V. no. 406.
17. Grey to Nicolson, 26.10.08. Pte. BD.V. no. 409 (b).
18. Hardinge to Nicolson, 28.10.08. Pte. *Ibid*., no. 414. For an Austrian view: Öst.-Ung. Auss. I, 415, 426.
19. Lowther to Grey, 3.11.08. Pte. GP.70. Buchanan to Grey, 4.11.08, tel. no. 75, very conf. BD.V. no. 427. Same to same, 9.11.08, no. 92, Conf. *ibid*., no. 436. Minutes. FO/371/552. Grey to Lowther, 30.10.08, tel. no. 420, *ibid*. Lowther to Grey, 2.11.08, no. 379, *ibid*. Same to same, 5.11.08, tel. no. 385. Minutes, *ibid*. According to Holstein, Britain pursued this policy in order to avoid a conflict with Russia. Rich & Fisher, *op. cit*., pp. 597-8.
20. Hardinge to Lowther, 1.12.08. Pte. LP. quoted in: Lowe & Dockrill, p. 465. Hardinge to Buchanan, 1.12.08. Pte. HP,13. Nicolson to Grey, 1.12.08, tel. no. 279. BD.V. no. 469. Same to same, 1.12.08, no. 556, *ibid*., no. 470.
21. Buchanan to Grey, 24.11.08, no. 100. Minutes by Tilley and Hardinge, 30.11.08, FO/371/557.
22. Grey to Bertie, 30.11.08. No. 555 (conversation with Cambon), *ibid*.
23. Lowther to Hardinge, 1.12.08. Pte. LP; see also Rodd to Grey, 15.12.08. No. 195, conf. Minute by Mallet, 18.12.08. FO/371/558.
24. Hardinge to Bryce, 4.12.08. Pte. HP,13.
25. Hardinge to Goschen, 1.12.08. Pte. *ibid*.
26. Greene (Bucharest) to Grey, 23.12.08. No. 58. Minute, 28.12.08. FO/371/558.
27. Grey to Hardinge, 13.1.09. Pte. HP,17.
28. Lowther to Grey, 16.12.08. Pte. LP. Whitehead to Grey, 21.12.08. No. 98. Confidential FO/371/558.
29. Hardinge to Buchanan, 29.12.08. Pte. HP,13.
30. Hardinge to Nicolson, 4.1.09. Pte. BD.V. pp. 549-50. Grey to Lowther, 5.1.09. No. 6. FO/371/558.
31. Hardinge to Bryce, 1.1.09. Pte. HP,17. Grey to Cartwright, 6.1.09. No. 4. BD.V. No. 502.
32. Hardinge to Rodd, 1.1.09. Pte. HP,17. Of course, this was only the extreme possibility, because British policy was basically concerned to avoid war: 'We shall strain every nerve to keep the peace of Europe.' Hardinge to Bryce, 1.1.09. Pte. HP. *op. cit*. Grey to Rodd, 8.1.09. No. 6, BD.V. No. 507.
33. But in the same breath Lowther was still very strict in his demand for control over any loan to the new regime to make sure that it was not spent on German war materials. Lowther to Hardinge, 6.1.09. Pte. LP. Lowther to Grey, 12.1.09. Pte. tel., same to same, 12.1.09. Pte. *ibid*. Same to same, 12.1.09. No. 25. Minutes. FO/371/765.
34. Hardinge to Bryce, 29.1.09. Pte. HP,17.
35. Lowther to Grey, 4.2.09. Tel. no. 34. Minutes. FO/371/749.
36. Grey to Nicolson, 4.2.09. No. 132. FO/371/749.
37. Grey to Lowther, 5.2.09. No. 71, *ibid*. Hardinge to Block, 5.2.09. Pte. HP,17.
38. Buchanan to Grey, 3.2.09. No. 13. Minute by Maxwell, 8.2. FO/371/750. Hardinge to Lowther, 6.2.09. Pte. LP.
39. Lowther to Grey, 30.1.09. No. 66. Minutes. 8.2. FO/371/750.
40. Grey to Lowther, 8.2.09. Pte. LP.
41. Grey to Nicolson, 8.2.09. Tel. no. 154. FO/371/750. M. B. Cooper, 'British Policy in the Balkans, 1908-9', in *The Historical Journal* (1964), pp. 258-79.
42. Grey to Lowther, 8.2.09. Pte. LP.
43. *Ibid*., and Lowther to Grey, 8.2.09. Pte. *ibid*. Vambéry to Grey, 9.12.08. Pte. Minutes by Grey, VP,33.

44. Nicolson to Grey, 14.2.09. No. 108. FO/371/750. Grey to Nicolson, 14.2.09. Tel. no. 187. BD.V. No. 568. Hardinge to Nicolson, 16.2.09. Pte. BD.V. pp. 596-7. Nicolson to Grey, 16.2.09. No. 114. FO/371/750. Same to same, 15.2.09. Tel no. 75. BD.V. No. 571.
45. *Ibid*. Minute. FO/371/750.
46. Lowther to Grey, 10.2.09. No. 90. Minutes. 15.2. FO/371/760.
47. Lowther to Grey, 22.3.09. Tel. no. 94. Confidential FO/371/755.
48. Grey to Nicolson, 2.4.09. Pte. BD.V. No. 823. Hardinge to Nicolson, 30.3.09. Pte. *Ibid*., pp. 763-4.
49. Hardinge to de Salis, 29.12.08. Pte. HP,13. Hardinge to Nicolson, 4.1.09. Pte. BD.V. pp. 549-50. Cf. Morley's anxieties over a possible war between the Entente and the Triple Alliance: Morley to Minto, 25.3.09. MP. Eur. D. 573/5.
50. Lowther to Grey, 12.10.08. No. 657. FO/371/560. Same to same, 13.10.08. Pte. BD.V. No. 375. Same to same, 12.10.08. No. 657. Minutes. FO/371/560.
51. Memorandum by Block, 26.10.08. Confidential in: Lowther to Grey, 27.10.08. No. 722.*ibid*., Tyrrell to Lowther, 30.10.08. Pte. LP. Lowther to Grey, 3.11.08. Pte. *ibid*. Hardinge to Lowther, 3.11.08. Pte. *ibid*.
52. Grey to Lowther, 13.11.08. Pte. LP. Same to same, 14.11.08. Pte. *Ibid*. Hardinge to Lowther, 17.11.08. Pte. *Ibid*. Lowther to Grey, 13.11.08. No. 773, BD.V. No. 203. Ed. Add. For a German appreciation of Riza, cf. Rich & Fisher, *op. cit*., p. 565. Holstein thought highly of him.
53. See, especially, speeches by Grey and Asquith, 19 November, 1908, *The Cambridge History of British Foreign Policy*, III, p. 402. P. Knaplund, *Speeches on Foreign Policy, 1904-1914*, (London 1931), pp. 107-8; and Lowther to Grey, 24.ll.08. Pte. LP.
54. Lowther's main explanation for the rise of German influence was the outstanding personality of Marschall, 'the central figure amongst the Ambassadors'. But according to Hardinge, such reasoning was hardly sufficient. Mallet suggested that bribery had probably been used. Lowther to Grey, 6.12.08. No. 835. Minutes. 14.12.08. FO/371/556.
55. Lowther to Grey, 9.12.08. No. 851. FO/371/556. Same to same, 11.12.08. No. 854, *ibid*. Same to same, 16.12.08. Pte. LP. Bertie, however, favoured pecuniary assistance to the new regime, otherwise they would apply to Germany. Bertie to Hardinge, 4.11.08. Pte. BP,180. Hardinge replied that Sir Ernest Cassel would advance money to the Porte and added: 'He, of course, has asked, like all Jews, for his *quid pro quo*.' Hardinge to Bertie, 5.11.08. Pte.*Ibid*. Hardinge, *Old Diplomacy* (London 1947), p. 165.
56. Lowther to Hardinge, 22.12.08. Pte. LP.
57. Same to same, 20.12.08. Pte. LP.
58. Same to same, 29.12.08. Pte. *ibid*.
59. Hardinge to Lowther, 29.12.08. Pte. *ibid*.
60. Cf. F. Ahmad, 'Great Britain's Relations with the Young Turks, 1908-14', *Middle Eastern Studies* (publ. Frank Cass 1966), p. 309.
61. Block to Lowther, 2.1.09. in: Lowther to Grey, 4.1.09. No. 6. Confidential FO/371/766. The Foreign Office, however, was encouraged by Cassel's view which was less pessimistic than Block's, concerning the condition of Ottoman finances. Hardinge to Lowther, 29.12.09. Pte. L.
62. Fitzmaurice to Tyrrell, 11.1.09. Pte. BD.V. No. 211. Ed. Add. It is of interest to compare Fitzmaurice's views with those of the Ottoman Ambassador in Berlin. Cf. DDF.2e ser. T.11.599.
63. Maunsell's report in: Major Symonds to Tilley, 19.1.09. Minutes. 20.1.09. FO/371/766/2681.
64. Lowther to Grey, 14.1.09. No. 29. Same to same, 14.1.09. Pte. tel. FO/371/760.

65. Same to same, 19.1.09. No. 37. Minute. FO/371/748.
66. Hardinge to Bryce, 15.1.09. Pte. HP,17.
67. Hardinge to Goschen, 26.1.09. Pte. HP,17.
68. Lowther to Grey, 25.1.09. No. 50. FO/371/749. Compare with an interesting criticism by Munir Pasha, former Ottoman Ambassador to France (1895-1908), Bertie to Grey, 11.1.09. Pte. BP,180.
69. Mallet, however, was inclined to adopt the 'meddling' policy again. He opposed increasing the customs as they might be utilized as a guarantee for the expenditure for the Baghdad Railway. This was essential: 'Without an understanding about the Baghdad Railway, we should really be fighting the Turkish Battle, but they might not thank us all the same.' He agreed with Lowther that the abolition of the Capitulations must depend on the establishment of good government. Lowther to Grey, 25.1.09. No. 50. FO/371/749. Minutes 1.2.09.
70. Lowther to Grey, 16.2.09. Pte. LP.
71. Lowther to Grey, 19.2.09. No. 110. Minutes by Hardinge and Grey, 24.2.09. FO/371/761. He was not 'patronizing' the Young Turks, since he, on the contrary, encouraged them to come into the open and to take governmental responsibility instead of dictating from behind the scenes. Cf. F. Ahmad, *The Young Turks*, p.38.
72. Block to Hardinge, 17.2.09. Pte. HP,192.
73. *Ibid.*, and Hardinge to Lowther, 23.2.09. Pte. LP.
74. Hardinge to Block, 23.2.09. Pte. HP,17.
75. Lowther to Grey, 26.2.09. No. 129. FO/371/761. Lowther to Gorst, 26.2.09. Pte. LP. Lowther to Hardinge, 2.3.09. *Ibid.* Same to same, 10.3.09. Pte. *ibid.* Lowther to Grey, 16.3.09. Pte. *Ibid.* While Lowther could criticize the CUP for its unconstitutional methods, his Military Attaché reported on the state of 'indiscipline' among the army officers, arising from their membership of the CUP. They had, moreover, been responsible for Kiamil's fall, since many of them had come to the Chamber 'influencing and apparently terrorising' the Deputies. He warned that unless the 'authorities' absolutely forbade military interference in politics, the country would soon be subject to a military *coup d'état*. Col. Surtees to Lowther, 27.2.09. No. 13, in: Lowther to Grey, 1.3.09. No. 141. FO/371/761.
76. Hardinge to Lowther, 23.3.09. Pte. LP.
77. Memorandum by Tilley, The Turkish Revolution and its Consequences, 1.3.09. FO/421/250/13516.
78. Lowther to Grey, 28.2.09. No. 139. Minute by Tilley, 8.3.09. FO/371/761. Tilley's memorandum Minute by Hardinge, 10.4.*ibid.*
79. E.g., Lowther to Grey, 21.9.09. No. 774. FO/371/763. On his experiences, see: R.W. Graves, *Storm Centres of the Near East, Personal Memories, 1879-1929* (London 1933).
80. Lowther to Grey, 18.3.09. No. 196. FO/371/761.
81. Hardinge to Block, 8.4.09. Pte. HP,17. Cf. M. Kent, 'Agent of Empire? The National Bank of Turkey and British Foreign Policy', *The Historical Journal* (1975), pp.367-89.
82. Hardinge to Lowther, 6.4.09. Pte. HP.192.

CHAPTER 3

1. Lowther to Grey, 13.4.09. Tel. no. 107. Minutes. 14.4.09. FO/371/770. Same to same, 14.4.09. Tel. no. 108, *ibid.* Same to same, 14.4.09. Tel. no. 112. Minutes, *ibid.* On the Counter Revolution, see: Lewis, *passim*: Ahmad, *The*

Young Turks, passim; D. Farhi, 'The Şeriat as a Political Slogan – or the Incident of the 31st Mart', *Middle Eastern Studies* (1971), pp. 275-99. For contemporary accounts: W. A. Ramsay, *The Revolution in Constantinople and Turkey, A Diary* (London 1909). E. F. Knight, *op. cit.*, both favourable to the CUP; F. McCullagh, *The Fall of Abdul-Hamid* (London 1910).

2. Asquith addressed a public gathering in Glasgow, *The Times*, 19.4.09. Grey's views in *Hansard*, 22 April, vol. 3, col. 1655. Parliamentary Question by Mr J..C. Wedgwood. For a different interpretation of British policy, cf. Bridge, *op. cit.*, p. 136. Mallet, the Head of the Eastern Department, commented on 'the corrupt Young Turks'. FO/371/757/15783.

3. Hardinge to Lowther, 20.4.09. Pte. LP. But see his letter to Cartwright of the same day, Bridge, p. 139.

4. Lowther to Hardinge, 20.4.09. Pte. LP.

5. Hardinge to Goschen, 27.4.09. Pte. HP,17. Hardinge to Villiers, 29.4.09. Pte. *Ibid*. Hardinge to the King, 28.4.09. Pte. *Ibid.*, 18.

6. Grey to Lowther, 30.4.09. Pte. BD.V. No. 219. Grey to Bertie, 30.4.09. Pte. BP.180. Goschen was the single exception to this view. Goschen to Hardinge, 1.5.09. Pte. HP,17.

7. Hardinge to Lowther, 1.5.09. Pte. LP.

8. Lowther to Grey, 5.5.09. Pte. and 12.5.09. Pte. GP,79.

9. Lowther to Hardinge, 22.6.09. Pte. LP. Fitzmaurice to Tyrrell, 27.6.09. Pte. GP,79. On the Jewish myth, see: B. Lewis, *The Emergence of Modern Turkey* (London 2nd ed. 1968), pp. 211-12, Note 4; and E. Kedourie, 'Young Turks, Freemasons and Jews', *Arabic Political Memoirs* (London, Frank Cass 1974), pp. 243-62. Hohler, the First Secretary, was also a victim of Fitzmaurice's theories. Hohler, *op. cit.*, p. 269. Hardinge, *Old Diplomacy* (London 1947), p. 175. Waugh is more cautious, A. T. Waugh, *Turkey, Yesterday, Today and Tomorrow* (London 1930), pp. 113-14. L. Einstein, *op. cit.*, p. 74. S. Story, ed., *The Memoirs of Ismail Kemal Bey* (London 1920), p. 349.

10. Lowther to Hardinge, 20.7.09. Pte. LP.

11. Lowther to Findlay, 3.8.09. Pte. *Ibid*.

12. Lowther to Tyrrell, 15.8.09. Pte. LP.

13. Hardinge to Bryce, 4.6.09. Pte. HP,192.

14. Block to the Council of Foreign Bondholders, 24.6.09. Minute by Mallet, 29.6.09. FO/371/763/24235.

15. Lowther to Grey, 25.5.09. No. 375. Minutes, 1.6.09. BD.V. No. 270.

16. Lowther to Hardinge, 27.4.10. Pte. LP.

17. Lowther to Grey, 2.8.09. No. 614. Minutes. Same to same, 9.8.09. No. 647. Minutes. Same to same, 22.8.09. No. 890. Minute by Lindsay, 31.8. See also: S. Skendi, *The Albanian National Awakening, 1878-1912* (Princeton 1967), pp. 376ff.

18. Memorandum by Grey, 6.8.09. Secret. BD.IX.i. No. 33. To the French Ambassador, however, Izvolsky spoke pessimistically about the future of the new regime, DDF.2e ser. T,12,244.

19. Hardinge to O'Bierne, 11.7.10. Pte. HP,21. Hardinge regarded Lowther as more competent than Buchanan, Nicolson's ultimate successor. *Old Diplomacy*, p. 130.

20. E.g., Marling to Grey, 19.10.09. No. 860. Minute by Mallet, 2.11. FO/371/1008; Hardinge to Marling, 2.11.09. Pte. HP (PRO).

21. Lowther to Hardinge, 25.5.10. Pte. LP; and same to same, Pte. 29.5.10, published by E. Kedourie, *op. cit.*, pp. 243-62. Cf. Öst.-Ung. Auss. III, 2396.

22. Hardinge to Cartwright, 3.5.10. Pte. HP,21. Hardinge to Findlay, 3.5.10. Pte. *Ibid*. Lowther to Grey, 21.4.10. No. 251. Minutes. 10.5.10. Same to same,

3.5.10. No. 268. Minutes. 14.5.10. FO/371/1007.
23. Lowther to Hardinge, 8.6.10. Pte. LP. Hardinge to Findlay, 31.5.10. Pte. HP,21. Hardinge to O'Bierne, 8.6.10. Pte.*Ibid*. Findlay to Hardinge, 25.5.10. Pte. HP,192. Hardinge to Cartwright, 14.6.10. Pte.*Ibid*. Hardinge to Lowther, 14.6.10. Pte. LP. Lowther to Hardinge, 15.6.10. Pte. LP
24. Hardinge to Goschen, 28.6.10. Pte. HP,21. Hardinge to Lowther, 28.6.10. Pte. LP. Hardinge's despair astonished even Lowther. The situation was after all not so bad: 'We are apt to forget that we are still passing through a Revolutionary period ... there is still a chance, a vague one it must be admitted, that the moderate and reasonable folk may perhaps gain the day.' In fact, Lowther was even happy about the CUP's independent attitude in foreign affairs: 'The pro-German, pro-French or pro-any Power attitude is exaggerated. They are for their own purposes pro-Islam.' Cf. e.g., GD,27,I, 9789. Lowther to Hardinge, 6.7.10. Pte.*Ibid*. Same to same, 19.7.10. Pte.*Ibid*.
25. Hardinge to Lowther, 26.7.10. Pte. LP. It is doubtful whether Hardinge can be considered a Turcophile at this period. Bridge, *op. cit.*, *passim*.
26. Lowther to Grey, 30.7.10. No. 521. Conf. BD.IX.i. No. 161. Lowther to Hardinge, 29.5.10. Pte. Kedourie, 'Young Turks ...'.
27. Findlay (Sofia) to Grey, 22.7.10. Tel. no. 30, Conf. Minutes. FO/371/999. Same to same, 2.8.10. No. 94. Secret,*ibid*. No. 163. Lowther to Grey, 30.7.10. No. 522. Minutes. 9.8.10. FO/371/1012. Same to same, 26.7.10. No. 512. Minute by Grey, 3.8.10.*Ibid*. Same to same, 4.8.10. No. 543. Minutes. 8.8.10. *Ibid*. Same to same, 19.7.10. No. 498. Minute by Norman. 30.7.10. FO/371/ 999. Cf. Dakin, *op. cit.*, p.405.
28. Cartwright to Grey, 12.8.10. No. 137. Confidential. Minute by Norman, 28.8.10. BD.IX,i, No. 172.
29. Grey to Nicolson, 18.8.10. Pte. GP,73. Nicolson to Grey, 24.8.10. Pte. *Ibid*. Bridge, *op. cit.*, *passim*.
30. Lowther to Grey, 6.9.10. No. 635. Confidential BD.IX,i,No. 181. Minutes. 12.9.10. There is too much additional material in the FO archives to doubt the authenticity of this letter, which was questioned by Gooch and Temperley, *ibid.*, pp.vii-viii. See: Same to same, 2.11.10. No. 800. FO/371/1017. Marling to Grey, 19.11.10. No. 838. Minutes. FO/371/1000. Bridge, *op. cit.*, *passim*.
31. Churchill to Grey, 20.9.10. Secret. GP,97. M. Gilbert, *W.S. Churchill*, vol. III: *1914-1916* (London 1971), pp.188-9. Blunt, *My Diaries*, II, pp.335-6 (London 1919). Cf. Earl of Lytton, *W.S. Blunt, A Memoir by his Grandson* (London 1916), pp.124-36.
32. Block to Hardinge, 10.9.10. Minute by Grey, 19.9.10, FO/371/993/33484.
33. Block to Hardinge, 21.9.10, FO/371/994/38775.
34. Babington-Smith to Nicolson, 7.10.10, FO/371/993/36804.
35. Lowther to Grey, 21.9.10, Pte. LP. Same to same, 28.9.10, No. 692. Minutes, 3.10.10, FO/371/993. Same to same, 20.9.10, tel. no. 196. Confidential,*ibid*.
36. Babington-Smith to Nicolson, 7.10.10. Minutes, 10.10.10, FO/371/993/ 36804. When assessing the situation again in 1917, Parker mentioned these causes but regarded the chauvinist policy of the CUP in the Persian Gulf and Mesopotamia as primary. [A Parker], 'The Bagdad Railway Negotiations', *Quarterly Review* (October 1917), pp.511-12.
37. E.g., Lowther to Grey, 21.9.10, no. 672. FO/371/1015.
38. As early as November 1910, Babington-Smith reported that the German loan had strengthened German influence at the Porte. To Nicolson, 30.11.10, FO/371/994/44172.
39. Lowther to Grey, 6.10.10, no. 709. Minutes, 17.10.10, BD.IX.i, no. 188. GD,27,I, pp.239-74. The Germans admitted a growing pro-German orienta-

tion in the CUP but were not yet keen to bring the Porte into the Triple Alliance, *ibid.*, 9794.

40. Lowther to Nicolson, 11.10.10, Pte. LP. Nicolson to Lowther, 17.10.10, Pte. LP. Nicolson to Goschen, 22.11.10, Pte. no. 344. And Lowther to Nicolson, 25.10.10, Pte. LP.

41. Marling to Grey, 22.11.10, no. 844. Minutes, 7.12.10, FO/371/1017. F. Ahmad in his book on the CUP does not refer to this Congress.

42. Findlay to Grey, 7.12.10, no. 158. Secret. Encl. Précis of Dispatches from M. Choublier, French Consul-General at Salonika, to M. Pichon, Minutes, 17.12.10, FO/371/1000. Marling to Grey, 7.12.10, no. 885. Secret. Encl. Geary to Marling, 3.12.10, no. 61. Minutes, 7.12.10, FO/371/1017. Öst.-Ung. Auss. III,2425.

43. Grey to Asquith, 22.12.10, Pte. Minute by Asquith, 30.12.10, FO/800/100.

44. Marling to Grey, 30.12.10, no. 945. Minute by Nicolson, FO/371/1241. Marling, however, had on 20 December a frank interview with Rifaat in which he criticized the new regime in the strongest terms. Marling to Grey, 20.12.10, no. 918. Confidential. Grey to Marling, 13.1.11, no. 14. FO/371/1017.

45. Nicolson to Marling, 9.1.11, Pte. NP.347. Nicolson to Cartwright, 9.1.11, Pte. *ibid.* Nicolson to Goschen, 9.1.11, Pte. *ibid.* Parker's Minute, FO/371/993/36804.

46. Marling to Nicolson, 4.1.11, Pte. NP.374. Same to same, 11.1.11. Pte. Minute by Grey,*ibid.* Marling to Grey, 4.1.11, no. 14. Secret. Minutes, BD.X.ii, no. 6. Same to same, 17.1.11, no. 49. Confidential,*ibid.* X.i, no. 651. Marling's views regarding British retreat in Koweit were also rejected. Cf. same to same, 17.1.11, no. 50. Secret. BD.X.i, no. 652.

47. Nicolson to Hardinge, 12.1.11, Pte. NP,347. Hardinge to Nicolson, 2.2.11, Pte. *ibid.* Vambéry to Grey, 12.3.10, Pte. VP.33.

48. Nicolson to Buchanan, 12.1.11, Pte. NP,347. Nicolson to Goschen, 17.1.11, Pte. *ibid.*

49. Nicolson to Cartwright, 23.1.11, Pte. NP.347. Nicolson to Lowther, 23.1.11, Pte. *ibid.*, quoted partly by Lowe and Dockrill, *op. cit.*, 469-70. Nicolson to Grey, 23.1.11, Pte. NP.347.

50. Lowther to Nicolson, 31.1.11, Pte. LP. Lowther to Grey, 10.2.11, no. 93. FO/371/1017.

51. Lowther to Grey, 22.2.11, no. 121. FO/371/1017. Same to same, 21.2.11, tel. no. 44. Minutes, BD.IX.i, no. 216. For more evidence on the so-called Jewish-Zionist-Freemason plot: Turkey, Annual Report, 1910, in: Same to same, 14.2.11, no. 103. FO/371/1017. Fitzmaurice to Tyrrell, 9.2.11, Pte. GP,80. Lowther to Nicolson, 1.3.11, Pte. LP.

52. Fitzmaurice to Tyrrell, 9.2.11, Pte. GP,80. Marling to Nicolson, 27.6.11, Pte. NP,348.

53. Lowther to Nicolson, 4.4.11, Pte. *ibid.* Goschen to Grey, 1.4.11, tel. no. 10, Minute by Grey, 3.4.11. Nicolson to Cartwright, 3.4.11. Pte. Cartwright to Nicolson, 13.4.11, Pte. BD.IX.i. no. 471. Nicolson to Hardinge, 19.4.11, Pte. NP,348.

54. Grey to Akers-Douglas (Cettinje), 24.4.11, no. 4. FO/371/1228. Bertie to Grey, 15.4.11, tel. no. 34. Minute by Mallet, 18.4.11, *ibid.*

55. Cartwright to Grey, 25.5.11, tel. no. 47. Minutes by Mallet and Nicolson,*ibid.* Bertie to Grey, 27.5.11, tel. no. 68. conf. Minutes, *ibid.*

56. Lowther to Grey, 3.5.11, no. 297, *ibid.* Geary to Lowther, 29.4.11, no. 21. Minute by Macleay, 12.5.11, *ibid.* H. Knatchbull-Hugessen, Memorandum respecting the new regime in Turkey, 16.5.11. Confidential FO/371/1249/9858.

57. Despite the allegation by Braham of *The Times,* that she was prejudiced and her accounts exaggerated. Miss Durham to Spence, 30.5.11, FO/371/1228/ 22229. (Minutes, 8.6.11). Same to same, 4.6.11, *ibid.* /23037/Minutes, 14.6.11. Miss Durham was suspicious of the CUP from the beginning. See her *High Albania* (London 1909), p. 347.

58. Chiefs of the Albanian Insurgents to Grey 12.6.11. Minute by Nicolson, 26.6.11, BD.IX.i, p. 477. Grey to Marling, 10.7.11, no. 188, FO/371/1228. Marling to Grey, 20.6.11, no. 433. Minute by Macleay, 26.6.11, *ibid.* Nicolson's interview with Tewfik, 29.6.11, FO/371/12128/25504. There is no clear evidence that Grey's policy in the Albanian question was influenced by his desire to play the role of a 'defender of a small people' as has been implied by S. Skendi, *The Awakening of Albania, 1878–1912* (Princeton 1967), p. 418.

59. Grey to Marling, 6.7.11, tel. no. 261, FO/371/1228. Buchanan to Grey, 5.7.11, tel. no. 142. Minute by Mallet, 6.7.11, and Nicolson to Cartwright, 24.7.11, Pte. NP.349.

60. Nicolson to Hardinge, 5.7.11, Pte. *ibid.*

61. Nicolson to Lowther, 21.8.11, Pte. LP. Nicolson to Cartwright, Pte. 21.8.11, Pte. NP.347.

62. Lowther to Nicolson, 30.8.11, Pte. *ibid.*

63. Lowther to Grey, 3.10.11, no. 670. Very confidential. Encl. Morgan to Lowther, 28.9.11, no. 79. Minute 18.10.11, FO/371/1262.

64. Hardinge to Lowther, 20.4.09, Pte. LP. Hardinge to Buchanan, 20.4.09, Pte. HP.17. Hardinge to Cartwright, 20.4.09, Pte. *ibid.* Hardinge to Goschen, 20.4.09. Pte. *ibid.* Hardinge to the King, 21.4.09, Pte. *ibid.* 18; and Hardinge to Lowther, 4.5.09, Pte. LP.

65. Hardinge to Cartwright, 4.5.09, Pte. HP.17. Hardinge to the King, 4.5.09, Pte. HP.18; Bertie to Grey, 5.5.09, no. 175. Minute, FO/371/757. Lowther to Grey, 9.5.09, no. 329. Minutes, 17.5.09. *ibid.*

66. Lowther to Grey, 26.5.09, no. 384. Memorandum by T. Hohler, *ibid.* Lowther to Hardinge, 25.5.09, Pte. LP. Block to Hardinge, 16.6.09, Pte HP.192.

67. Lowther to Grey, 30.6.09, no. 505. Minutes, FO/371/757. Same to same, 13.7.09, no. 548, *ibid.*

68. Hardinge to Findlay, 5.10.09, Pte. HP.17.

69. Lindley to Hardinge, 20.12.09, Pte. HP.192. Hardinge to Lindley, 24.12.09, Pte. *ibid.* Hardinge to Lowther, 24.1.10, Pte. LP. Whitehead to Grey, 5.1.10, no. 3. Confidential. Minutes, 17.1.10, BD.IX.i, no. 88.

70. Grey's reply to Buxton's Parliamentary Questions, 28.2.11, *Hansard,* Vol. XXII, cols. 180-1, and his Minutes on Mallet's interview with Tewfik, 15.2.11, FO/371/1241/6314. Nicolson's opinion was that Buxton was 'considerably hoodwinked' by the 'moderate' Young Turks. Nicolson to Lowther, 29.2.11, Pte. BD.IX.i, no. 214. Nicolson to Cartwright, 20.2.11. NP.347. Buxton's letter to *The Times,* 15.2.11. Minute by Grey, 20.2.11, FO/371/1245/6324. For a typical exposition of Buxton's pro-CUP views see: N. Buxton, 'Young Turkey After Two Years', *Nineteenth Century and After* (March 1911), pp. 417-32. Earlier, Tyrrell, in a conversation with the Austrian Ambassador, called Buxton 'an intelligent ass'. Öst.-Ung Auss. I, p. 585. But he was defended by other officials like Parker. FO/371/356/41062, (23.12.07). A complete change in the Balkan Committee's attitude took place only in early 1912. Cf. A.J. Morris, *Radicalism Against War, 1906-14* (London 1972), p. 349.

71. Letter addressed to Mr Graham respecting Babylonia by Willcocks, 14.2.09. Minutes, FO/371/764. For earlier views: Grey to Lowther, 14.11.08, tel. no. 438, BD.V, no. 446. Same to same, 19.11.08, no. 486. *ibid.* no. 454. Grey to

Nicolson, 14.11.08, no. 367, FO/371/764.
72. Hardinge to Lowther, 18.5.09, Pte. LP. Lowther to Grey, 21.5.09, no. 363. Minute by Hardinge, 1.6.09, FO/371/764. Hardinge to Block, 28.5.09, Pte. HP,192. Djevad Bey to Grey, 27.5.09, BD.VI. no. 271. Block to Hardinge, 16.6.09, Pte. HP.192. the Germans believed that Britain wished to establish an Arab Caliphate under her auspices in Egypt and the Arab provinces of the Ottoman Empire; cf. the Kaiser's note in: GD.27.II, p. 585. Öst.-Ung. Auss. II, 164.
73. Lowther to Hardinge, 2.6.09, Pte. LP. Hardinge to Gorst, 21.5.09, Pte. HP.17. On the establishment of the National Bank, see: Memorandum by Block, 3.11.08, in: Lowther to Grey, 10.11.08, no. 764, FO/421/245. Hardinge to Block, 17.11.08, Pte. HP.13. Hardinge to Lowther, 17.11.08, Pte. LP. Hardinge to Bertie, 5.11.08, Pte. HP.13. Block to Hardinge, 8.2.09, Pte. HP.192. M. Kent, 'Agent of Empire?' *op. cit.*
74. India Office to Foreign Office, 26.5.09, FO/371/764/19944. Grey to Lowther, 30.5.09, no. 328. B.C. Busch, *Britain and the Persian Gulf, 1894-1914* (Berkeley 1967), pp. 319-22.
75. Lowther to Grey, 21.6.09, tel. no. 212, FO/371/764. Same to same, 17.8.09, no. 674. Minutes, *ibid.* Marling to Grey, 1.12.09, no. 931. FO/371/765.
76. The Report of the Committee on Mesopotamian Railways was submitted on 24 July, Minutes, 27.7.09, FO/371/762. See S.A. Cohen, *British Policy in Mesopotamia*, pp. 102-22.
77. Grey to Lowther, 18.8.09, no. 245. Secret. BD.VI. No. 272, and Grey to Lowther, 23.9.09, no. 298. In fact, when on 23 September, the Foreign Office officially submitted its conditions for agreement to the 4% Customs increase, these did not include the railway concession to the Gulf. Rather, they stipulated the lifting of the embargo upon Egypt's borrowing powers; the money from the 4% Customs increase was not to be used for the Baghdad Railway; one-third of the loan guaranteed by this increase should be offered for subscription in London; and the Porte must fulfil the terms of 3% increase of 1907. Memorandum communicated to Tewfik, 23.9.09, BD.VI. App. VI. The Gulf line concession was mentioned only verbally. Lowther to Grey, 27.9.09, tel. no. 335. Minute by Hardinge, FO/371/764.
78. Hardinge to Block, 13.12.09, Pte. HP.17.
79. At about this time Hilmi told Marschall 'very confidentially': 'I would rather pay a million or two pounds a year than open the way into the interior of our country to England and British influence by means of a great commercial enterprise controlled exclusively by England.' GD.27.II.9969, 9976 (translation by Dugdale). J.G. Williamson, p. 91.
80. Lowther to Grey, 8.11.09, no. 180. Minute by Hardinge, 10.11.09, FO/31/764. GD, *ibid.* 9971.
81. Grey to Goschen, 28.10.09, no. 266. Secret. BD.VI. No. 277. GD.27.II.9972, and Goschen to Hardinge, 14.12.09, Pte. Minutes by Hardinge and Grey, 15.12.09, FO/371/763/45560.
82. Hardinge to Marling, 2.11.09. Pte. *op. cit.* Same to same, 16.11.09, HP.192. Partly quoted by Lowe & Dockrill, p. 468; and Lowther to Grey, 19.10.09, no. 861. Minutes, 25.10.09, FO/371/763. Marling to Grey, 31.10.09, tel. no. 346. Minutes 1.11.09, *ibid.*
83. Cassel to Hardinge, 20.12.09. Memorandum and Minutes, 21.12.09, BD.VI. no. 309. Hardinge to Goschen, 20.12.09, Pte. HP.17. Hardinge to Block, 13.12.09, Pte. *ibid.* The Germans and the Porte would agree to only 50%. GD.27,II,9988.
84. India Office to FO, 15.3.09, FO/371/768, *ibid.* Same to same, 22.4.09, FO/

371/768/15288. Grey to Lowther, 3.5.09, no. 130, *ibid*. Lowther to Grey, 28.5.09, no. 396. Minutes, *ibid*. Grey to Lowther, 12.7.09, no. 199, *ibid*.

85. Lowther to Grey, 13.10.09, tel. no. 320. FO/371/759. Same to same, 15.9.09, tel. no. 1324. Minutes, Same to same, 21.10.09, tel. no. 343. Lynch to Lowther, 28.10.09, FO/371/760/39912. Marling to Grey, 31.10.09, tel. no. 34. Minutes, 1.11.09. The Kaiser's remarks could always serve as typical for German strong opposition to British claims in Mesopotamia: 'The devil's claws are sticking out! The "sympathy" has business at the back of it.' GD.27.II, p.585. (Translated by Dugdale, vol. III, p.385.)

86. Marling to Grey, 14.12.09, no. 973, FO/371/763. Same to same, 21.12.09, no. 975. Minutes, *ibid*.

87. Lowther to Grey, 14.12.09, no. 967. Very confidential minute by Mallet, 22.12.09, *ibid*.

88. Hardinge to Nicolson, 5.1.10, Pte. BD.VI. no. 316. Hardinge to Gorst, 7.1.10, Pte. HP.21.

89. Goschen to Grey, 8.4.10, no. 99. Very confidential Minutes, BD.VI. no. 342. Same to same, 11.4.10, no. 102. Very confidential Minutes, *ibid*. 334. On the kilometric guarantees cf. Cohen, pp.173-4, note 181.

90. Minute by Grey, *ibid*. p.461. Grey to Lowther, 18.4.10, no. 96. Secret. *ibid*. no. 350. Same to same, 20.4.10, no. 107. Secret. *ibid*. no. 352. Goschen to Grey, 22.4.10, no. 117, Minute by Mallet.

91. Lowther to Hardinge, 19.4.10, LP. Pte. Hardinge to Lowther, 26.4.10, Pte. *ibid*. Lowther was right. Cf. e.g., GD.27.II.9989.

92. Lowther to Grey, 2.4.10, no. 197. Minute by Mallet, FO/371/991. Same to same, 3.5.10, no. 276. Secret. BD.VI. no. 359. Minute by Mallet, FO/371/992. Block to Hardinge, 3.5.10, *ibid*. 16572. GD.27.II.10006, 10072.

93. Grey to Lowther, 13.5.10, tel. no. 103. Secret. BD.VI. no. 336. Gwinner to Cassel, 21.5.10, *ibid*. no. 370. Grey to Goschen, 31.5.10, no. 148. Secret, *ibid*. no. 375.

94. India Office to Foreign Office, 2.8.10, Minutes, 3.8.10, FO/371/1010/28116. Same to same, 11.8.10. Minutes, 12.8.10, *ibid*. /29259/ Lowther to Grey, 10.10.10, no. 720.

95. Alwyn Parker was still a junior clerk at this period, promoted only in 1912, but he was already recognized as an authority on Mesopotamia and the Gulf. Cf. Z. Steiner, *The Foreign Office and Foreign Policy, 1898-1914* (Cambridge 1969), p.145, n. 8.

96. India Office to Foreign Office, 6.9.10. Minutes, 7.9.10, FO/371/1014/32605. Minutes by Parker and Mallet, 20.9.10, *ibid*. /34279/. Lowther to Grey, 30.9.10, no. 694. Minute, Marling to Grey, 15.11.10, tel. no. 249, *ibid*.

97. Marling to Nicolson, 20.13.10, Pte. NP.344.

98. Nicolson to Marling, 12.12.10, Pte. *ibid*.

99. Nicolson to Goschen, 26.10.10, Pte. NP.344. Same to same, 20.2.11, Pte. Nicolson to Lowther, 20.2.11, Pte. NP.347. Lowther to Grey, 14.2.11, tel. no. 38. Minutes BD.X.ii. no. 12.

100. Cohen, pp.200-02.

101. M.K. Chapman, *Great Britain and the Bagdad Railway, 1888-1914* (Northampton, Mass 1948), *passim*.

102. Nicolson to Lowther, 6.3.11, Pte. LP. Nicolson to Goschen, 6.3.11, Pte. NP,347. Nicolson to Cartwright, 6.3.11, Pte. *ibid*. See also: Fitzmaurice to Tyrrell, 9.2.11, Pte. GP.80. Fitzmaurice now adopted a hard line in these matters. Compare his views before the Revolution. Same to same, 12.4.08, Pte. BD.V. *op. cit*. He was accused by the CUP of inciting MPs to vote against Hakki on the Railway question. GD.27.II, 10030.

103. *Hansard*, Vol. XXII, cols. 1300, 1328-9. Lowther to Grey, 22.3.11, no. 184. Minute by R. Macleay, 27.3.11, FO/371/1233.
104. India Office to Foreign Office, 3.3.11. Minutes, 4.3.11, FO/371/1231/7880. GD.27.II,10022, 10024. Hardinge to Nicolson, 29.3.11, Pte. BD.X.ii. no. 25. R.C. Lindsay, Turkish Aggression in the Persian Gulf. Memorandum prepared for the CID, 6.3.11. Minutes, FO/371/1245/8629. Hardinge to Bertie, 5.4.11, Pte. BP.180. For German encouragement of the Ottoman resistance to British claims, see, e.g., GD.27.II,10032-3. J.G. Williamson, *op. cit.*, pp. 78-110. Hardinge to Morley, 9.3.11, MSS. Eur.D. 573/26. MP. Same to same, 23.2.11, Pte. Same to same, 11.4.11, Pte. *ibid*.
105. India Office to Foreign Office, 29.3.11. Minutes 4.4.11, FO/371/1233/12463. L. Smith (Board of Trade) to Mallet, 7.4.11, *ibid.* /12979/. Minutes GD. 31.1146ff. The Germans informed the Porte that the agreement of the Baghdad Railway Company must be obtained. GD.31.1148. J.G. Williamson, p. 95.
106. However, the release of the Bahreinese brought relief to the Foreign Office which was already contemplating vigorous action. Lowther to Grey, 25.3.11, tel. no. 66, confidential. Minute by Nicolson, FO/371/1233. Grey to Lowther, 27.3.11, tel. no. 74, *ibid*. Same to same, 7.4.11, tel. no. 91, *ibid*. Lowther to Grey, 11.4.11, no. 241. Confidential. Minutes, 19.4.11, *ibid*. Nicolson to Lowther, 16.4.11, Pte. LP.
107. Extracts from the Minutes of the 110th Meeting of the CID, held on 4.5.11, FO/371/1245/18946. (=CAB/38/18). Hardinge, now Viceroy of India also supported a tough line: cf. Hardinge to Morley, 11.4.11, MP. *op. cit.* Cohen, p. 209.
108. Nicolson to Lowther, 2.5.11, Pte. LP. Lowther to Nicolson, 10.5.11, Pte. *ibid*. Lowther to Grey, 12.5.11, no. 328, FO/371/1245.
109. Lowther to Nicolson, 24.5.11, Pte. LP.
110. Viceroy to Secretary of India, 8.4.11, GP.98. Hardinge to Nicolson, 16.5.11, Pte. NP.348. Grey to Hardinge, 16.5.11, Pte. in: Lowe & Dockrill, pp. 468-9. Nicolson to Hardinge, 19.5.11, Pte. *ibid*. and Grey's speech at the Meeting of the CID, 26.5.11, CAB/38/18. Hardinge to Nicolson, 9.6.11, Pte. NP.38. Morley to Hardinge, 7.4.11, Pte. MP.
111. Persian Gulf. Secret, Report of the Standing Sub-Committee of the CID, 14.7.1, FO/371/1234/29868. Minute by A. Parker, BD.X.ii. p. 45. (Ed. Note). Memo communicated to Tewfik, 29.7.11, Confidential BD. *ibid.* no. 34. Nicolson to Hardinge, 27.7.11, Pte. NP.349. Nicolson to Buchanan, 1.8.11, Pte. *ibid*. GD.31.11470ff. Hardinge felt the new proposals 'enormously' strengthened Britain's position in the Gulf. Hardinge to Crewe, 20.7.11, Pte. C/19.CP.
112. Marling to Grey, 22.7.11, no. 514. Minute by Norman, 28.7.11, W. Willcocks, *Sixty Years in the East* (London 1935), p. 249. Hardinge to Morley, 25.5.11, Pte. MP. *op. cit*

CHAPTER 4

1. For background see: C.J. Lowe and F. Marzari, *Italian Foreign Policy, 1870-1940* (London 1975), Ch. 6. W..C. Askew, *Europe and Italy's Acquisition of Libya 1911-1912* (Durham, N. Carolina 1942); D. Dakin, *ibid.*, pp. 422ff.
2. Rodd to Grey, 31.7.11, no. 117. Conf. minute by Crowe, 9.8.11, BD.IX.i. no. 222. Same to same, 4.9.11, no. 138. Conf. minutes, 11.9.11, (also minute by Norman, FO/371/1251), *ibid.*, no. 224.

3. Grey to Rodd, 29.2.11, tel. no. 178. BD. *op. cit.*, no. 250.
4. Minute by Nicolson, 28.9.11, FO/371/1251/38167. Grey to Lowther, 3.10.11, tel. no. 357, *ibid.*
5. Rodd to Grey, 30.9.11, tel. no. 76. Minutes, 2.10.11, BD.IX.i. no. 256. Nicolson to Cartwright, 2.10.11, Pte. BD. *ibid.* no. 267.
6. *Ibid.*
7. Kitchener to Grey, 2.10.11, tel. no. 23. Minutes, 3.10.11, FO/371/1252. Same to same, 22.10.11, Pte. GP,47. Grey to Kitchener, 3.11.11, Pte. *ibid.* Kitchener to Grey, 5.11.11, Pte. *ibid.*
8. Hardinge to Nicolson, 15.10.11, Pte. NP,351.
9. Minutes by Nicolson and Grey, 16.10.11, BD. *op. cit.,* no. 287. Lowther to Grey, 14.10.11, no. 718. FO/371/1253. Nicolson to Cartwright, 16.10.11, Pte. NP,351. Lowther to Nicolson, 18.10.11, LP.
10. Cartwright to Grey, 28.10.11, tel. no. 117. Very confidential Minute by Vansittart, 30.10.11, FO/371/1255.
11. Granville to Grey, 20.10.11, no. 328. Minute by Mallet, 24.10.11, FO/371/1254.
12. Nicolson to Cartwright, 30.10.11, Pte. NP,351.
13. Lowther to Grey, 7.11.11, tel. no. 305. Minutes, 8.11.11, FO/371/1256. Grey to Lowther, 3.11.11, no. 301, *ibid.*
14. Rodd to Grey, 5.11.11, tel. no. 140, *ibid.* Nicolson to O'Beirne, 8.11.11, Pte. NP,351. Nicolson to Rodd, 9.11.11, Pte. *ibid.* GD,30,I,10920.
15. Lowther to Nicolson, 8.11.11, Pte. LP. Lowther to Grey, 7.11.11, no. 796. FO/371/1257. On Churchill's sympathy towards the Porte, cf. R.S. Churchill, *W.S. Churchill, vol. II: Companion. Part 2: 1907-1911* (London 1969), pp. 1369-1371. Churchill to Grey, 4.11.11, Secret. *ibid.*, pp. 1369-70. But on 26 September, he supported Italy. Churchill to Nicolson, 26.9.11, BD.IX.i. no. 240. Bridge does not mention the letter to Grey: *op. cit.*, p. 181.
16. Grey to Rodd, 14.11.11, Pte. BD.IX.i. no. 308. Nicolson to Lowther, 14.11.11, Pte. LP. Grey's recent biographer ignores his policy on Tripoli question prior to 14 November. K. Robbins, *Sir E. Grey* (London 1971), p. 265.
17. Benckendorff to Grey, 26.11.11. Minutes, 28.11.11, BD. *op. cit.*, no. 322.
18. Hardinge to Nicolson, 30.11.11, Pte. NP.352. On Hardinge's earlier fears, cf. Hardinge to Crewe, 12.10.11, Pte. C/19. CP. Crewe to Hardinge, 10.10.11, Pte. C/23. CP.
19. Lowther to Nicolson, 29.11.11, Pte. LP. *Hansard*, Vol. XXXII, cols. 102-5. Sykes also complained about the public's entire ignorance as to the nature of British policy towards the Porte.
20. Cartwright to Grey, 7.12.11, tel. no. 132. BD. *op. cit.*, no. 343. Confidential minutes by Vansittart, 8.12.11, FO/371/1259. Bridge, *op. cit.*, p. 181.
21. Cartwright to Grey, 3.1.12, tel. no. 1. Minute by Vansittart, 4.1.12, FO/371/1524. Rodd to Grey, 3.1.12, tel. no. 1. Minutes, BD. *op. cit.*, no. 354.
22. Nicolson to Buchanan, 12.3.12, Pte. NP.354. Bertie to Grey, 13.3.12, no. 129. Minute by Norman, 15.3.12, FO/371/1523. Lowther to Grey, 20.3.12, no. 233. Minute by Vansittart, 25.3.12, *ibid.* Grey to Rodd, 29.3.12, no. 67, *ibid.*
23. Lowther to Grey, 18.4.12, tel. no. 98. Minute by Mallet, 19.4.12, FO/371/1531. Buchanan to Grey, 20.4.12, tel. no. 160, *ibid.* Lowther to Grey, 22.4.12, tel. no. 16. Minute by Mallet, 22.4.12, *ibid.* Grey to Rodd, 19.4.12, no. 81, BD.IX.i. no. 395. *Hansard*, House of Lords, Vol. XI, cols. 922-4. GD.30. II.11104, 11107, 11109.
24. Lowther to Grey, 18.5.12, no. 425. Minute by Mallet, 23.5.12, Admiralty to Foreign Office, 31.5.12. Minutes by Mallet and Grey, 3.6.12, FO/371/1535/2334. Admiralty to Foreign Office, 29.6.12, Conf. Encl. Italian Occupation of

Aegean Island and its Effect on Naval Policy, Secret. 20.6.12, BD.IX.i. no. 430. Albertini, *op. cit.*, I, pp. 360ff.

25. R. Bosworth, 'Britain and Italy's Acquisition of the Dodecanese, 1912-1915', *The Historical Journal* (1970), pp. 683-705. BD.IX.i. nos. 446, 508. BD.IX.ii. cf. 96.ii. An Italian-British conflict was exactly what the Germans were hoping for: GD.36.I.13995. Öst.-Ung. Auss. IV.3538.

26. Memorandum on the Effect of a British Evacuation of the Mediterranean on Questions of Foreign Policy, 8.5.12, BD.IX.ii. no. 386. Grey to Kitchener, 8.5.12, Pte. *ibid*. no. 387. Kitchener to Grey, 19.5.12, Pte. *ibid*. no. 390. Nicolson to Bertie, 23.5.12, Pte. NP.356. Nicolson to Hardinge, 18.7.12, Pte. *ibid*. 357. S. R. Williamson, *The Politics of Grand Strategy* (Cambridge, Mass. 1969), Ch. 11. P.G. Halperin, *The Mediterranean Naval Situation, 1908-1914* (Cambridge, Mass. 1971), Ch. 2.

27. Bertie to Nicolson, 16.5.12, Pte. & Conf. BP.180. Bertie to Grey, 18.6.12, tel. no. 81. Conf. Minute, 19.6.12, FO/371/1495. Rodd to Grey, 16.6.12, no. 161. Minute by Nicolson, 21.6.12, BD.IX.i. no. 413. Nicolson to Lowther, 24.6.12, Pte. LP.

28. For background: E.C. Helmreich, *The Diplomacy of the Balkan Wars, 1912-1913* (Cambridge, Mass. 1938), E.C. Thaden, *Russia and the Balkan League, 1912* (Pennsylvania 1965).

29. Bax-Ironside to Nicolson, 23.10.12, Pte. Most conf. BD. *ibid*. no. 525. Cartwright to Grey, 5.12.11, no. 205. Conf. Minute by Grey, 11.12.11, *ibid*. no. 528. Lampson to Grey, 12.12.11, no. 129. Minute by Maxwell, 27.12.11, *ibid*. no. 530. Bridge, *op. cit., passim*.

30. Nicolson to Lowther, 5.2.12, Pte. LP. Grey to Bertie, 7.2.12, no. 51. conf. BD. *op. cit.*, no. 547. Same to same, 3.2.12, no. 53. *ibid*. no. 366.

31. Nicolson to Hardinge, 22.2.12, Pte. NP.353. Bax-Ironside to Nicolson, 26.2.12, Pte. and most conf. BD. *op. cit.*, no. 555. Nicolson to Buchanan, 27.2.12, Pte. NP.354. Lowther to Nicolson, 28.2.12, Pte. LP.

32. Bax-Ironside to Nicolson, 14.3.12, Pte. and Secret. tel. BD. *op. cit.*, no. 558. Same to same, 14.3.12, Pte. and most conf. *ibid*. no. 559. *ibid*. App. V. Nicolson to Cartwright, 18.2.12, Pte. *ibid*. no. 560. Minute by Nicolson, 6.4.12, BD.IX.ii. App. II. Nicolson to Lowther, 11.6.12, Pte. LP.

33. Nicolson to Lowther, 18.3.12, Pte. NP.354. Minute by Norman, 15.3.12, in: Bertie to Grey, 13.3.12, no. 129. FO/371/1492. Same to same, 20.3.12, tel. no. 49. Minute by Mallet. Nicolson to Buchanan, 26.3.12, Pte. NP.354.

34. Lowther to Nicolson, 20.3.12, Pte. BD. *op. cit.,* no. 561. Lowther to Grey, 15.3.12, no. 220. Conf. minute by Mallet, 20.3.12, *ibid*. no. 383. Townley to Grey, 11.3.12, no. 15. Very conf. minute by Mallet, 18.3.12, FO/371/1492.

35. Nicolson to Hardinge, 18.4.12, Pte. NP.355. Grey to Nicolson, 22.4.12, Pte. *ibid*. Nicolson to Lowther, 29.4.12, Pte. LP. Also: BD.IX.ii. App. II. p. 1008.

36. Lowther to Nicolson, 24.2.12, Pte. LP. Same to same, 1.5.12, Pte. *ibid*.

37. O'Beirne to Nicolson, 16.5.12, Pte. BD.IX.i. no. 569. Nicolson to O'Beirne, 21.5.12, *ibid*. no. 570. Nicolson to Goschen, 13.5.12, Pte. NP.355. Same to same, 31.5.12, Pte. *ibid*. Cartwright to Nicolson, 23.5.12, Pte. *ibid*. 356.

38. Skendi, *passim*. They demanded: (1) Albania to be made a single Vilayet. (2) Instruction to be in Albanian using Latin alphabet. (3) Albanian functionaries for Albania and the language of the courts to be Albanian. (4) Military service in peacetime to be in Albania.

39. Grey to Buchanan, 26.8.12, no. 284. Very confidential. BD.IX.i. no. 655. Minute by Grey, FO/371/1482. Grey to Barclay, 26.8.12, no. *ibid*. Bertie to Grey, 23.8.12, tel. no. 102. BD. *op. cit.,* no. 649.

40. Thaden, *op. cit.,* pp. 103-4. *idem*. 'Montenegro: Russia's Troublesome Ally,

1910-12', *Journal of Central European Affairs* (1958), pp.111-33.
41. Marling to Grey, 26.8.12, tel. no. 336. Minutes, 27.8.12, FO/371/1482. de Salis to Grey, 10.8.12, no. 29. Minutes. BD. *ibid*. no. 606. Bertie to Grey, 29.8.12, tel. no. 110, *ibid*., no. 669. Marling to Grey, 12.9.12, no. 779. Confidential minutes, 24.9.12, FO/371/1497. Miss Durham to Nevinson, 4.9.12, FO/371/1497/39179. Marling to Grey, 10.9.12, no. 772, *ibid*.
42. India Office to Foreign Office, 17.10.11, FO/371/1236/40988. Government of India, 12.10.11. Minutes, 18.10.11, *ibid*. Lowther to Grey, 22.11.11, No. 949. Minutes, 30.12.11. Same to Same, 1.12.11, tel. no. 328. Minutes.
43. Lowther to Grey, 23.1.12, tel. no. 9. Minute by Parker, FO/371/1484. Board of Trade to Foreign Office, 12.1.12, *ibid*./1723. GD.31.11480, 11482.
44. Nicolson to de Bunsen, 27.3.12, Pte. NP.354. Nicolson to Buchanan, 27.3.12, Pte. *ibid*. Buchanan to Grey, 27.3.12, tel. no. 121. Confidential. BD. *op. cit.*, no. 44. Aide-Memoire communicated by Tewfik Pasha, 15.4.12. Minutes, 23-25.4.12, BD.X.ii. no. 47. Parker to Djevad, 18.4.12, Pte. *ibid*. no. 48. Joint Minute by Hirtzel and Parker on the Turkish Government Memorandum, 24.2.12, to Lowther, 13.5.12, Pte. *ibid*. Same to same, 1.4.12, Pte. Busch, *op. cit.*, p.330ff.
45. India Office to Foreign Office, 7.3.12. Minute by Mallet, 11.3.12, FO/371/1490/10200. Government of India to Crewe, 15.2.12, no. 24. Secret. *ibid*. Admiralty to India Office, 2.4.12, *ibid*./18365. India Office to Foreign Office, 2.412, FO/371/1492/14179.
46. Hardinge to Nicolson, 14.5.12, Pte. NP.355. Foreign Office to India Office, 16.5.12, FO/371/1484/16000. India Office to Foreign Office, 21.5.12, Minute by Parker, 22.5.12, *ibid*./21766/. Foreign Office to India Office, 30.5.12, *ibid*.
47. Hardinge to Nicolson, 14.5.12, Pte. NP.355. Foreign Office to India Office, 16.5.12, FO/371/1484/16000. India Office to Foreign Office, 21.5.12, Minute by Parker, 22.5.12, *ibid*./21766/. Foreign Office to India Office, 30.5.12, *ibid*. Grey to Tewfik, 18.7.12, Confidential. BD.X.ii. no. 55. The Board of Trade also insisted on a specific tariff for cotton goods; but the Foreign Office decided not to include this point in the general reply lest a new matter thus be introduced into negotiations, which were considered chiefly political in nature. Instead, the demand was included in a separate letter to the Porte.
48. Nicolson to Lowther, 24.6.12, Pte. NP.355. Nicolson to Marling, 22.7.12, Pte. NP.357. GD.31.11496.
49. Ostrorog to P.C. Sarell (British Consul, Dunkirk and at Constantinople 1883-1901), 31.8.11. Sarell to Crowe, 7.9.11. Minutes by Maxwell and Mallet, FO/371/1262. Sarell to Crowe, 11.10.11, *ibid*. 41976. Minutes by Mallet, (14.10.11) and Grey (20.10.11). Later Ostrorog changed his mind and condemned the CUP: L. Ostrorog, *The Turkish Problem* (London 1919). In fact, Lowther had meanwhile also changed his opinion, owing to the détente between the Government and opposition in Constantinople. He now concluded that since the CUP was the only organized body in the Empire, its members should not be overthrown but rather persuaded to moderate their views and come to an agreement with the opposition. He favoured the return of Kiamil to power, albeit not through British encouragement. Neither did he blame the Porte for putting up a fight for Tripoli. Nicolson to Cartwright, 16.10.11, Pte. NP.351. Lowther to Nicolson, 18.10,11, LP. Lowther to Grey, 20.10.11, no. 741. FO/371/1262.
50. Communication from Tewfik Pasha, 31.10.11, BD.IX.i. App. IV. Memorandum by Grey (written by Nicolson and approved by Asquith), 2.11.11, *ibid*. Nicolson to Hardinge, 2.11.11, Pte. NP.351. Grey to O'Beirne, 3.11.11, no. 286. Most Secret. BD. *ibid*. pp.780-1. Minute by Nicolson, 2.11.11, *ibid*.

Thaden wrongly believed in Britain's sincerity to conclude an alliance with the Porte once the Tripoli War was over. Thaden, p. 51. Grey to Churchill, 9.11.11, Pte. M. Gilbert, *Winston Churchill, Companion*, I.2, pp. 1370-1. Asquith to the King, 2.11.11, Pte. in: Lowe and Dockrill, vol. III, p. 470. DDF.3e ser. T.1.53. Marschall was aware of the Ottoman proposal for alliance, GD.30.I.10912.

51. Churchill to Grey, 4.11.11, Secret. GP.87. (Also in M. Gilbert, *ibid*. II,2, pp. 1367-70). Djavid to Churchill, 29.10.11. Churchill to Djavid, 19.11.11. W. Churchill, *The World Crisis*, (London 1923), p. 480. Öst.-Ung. III,2667.
52. Hardinge to Nicolson, 2.11.11, Pte. NP.352.
53. Lowther to Nicolson, 12.6.12, Pte. LP. Magnus, *Kitchener*, (London 1958), p. 230. Kitchener to Grey, 2.6.12, Pte. BD.X.ii. no. 392.
54. Ostrorog to Sarell, (n.d.), minutes by Norman, Parker and Nicolson, 11-12.12.11, FO/371/1263/49300.
55. Lowther to Grey, 12.2.12, no. 133. FO/371/1491. Grey to Lowther, 19.2.12, no. 66. Lowther to Grey, 12.2.12, no. 133. Minute by Norman, 20.2.12. At the beginning of August 1911, the Foreign Office had refused to publish the reports of HM's Consuls in the Ottoman Empire for 1910, as they might give 'great umbrage' to the Porte. Their despatches were 'in nearly every case ... severely critical of the Young Turk regime and of the policy of the Committee.' The Commons were informed that such a publication would not achieve 'any useful purpose' and MPs were advised to find consolation in the already published Consular trade reports. Parliamentary question by McCallum Scott, 3.8.11. Minutes, 1.8.11, FO/371/1261/31416.
56. Lowther to Grey, 19.2.12, no. 144. Minute by Norman, 28.2.12, FO/371/1491. N. Buxton also signed the Memorial. Same to same, 23.1.12, no. 63. Minute by Parker, 6.2.12, *ibid*.
57. Lowther to Grey, 27.3.12, no. 255. FO/371/1493. Lamb to Lowther, 11.3.12, no. 39. Minute by Mallet, 12.4.12, *ibid*. Same to same, 18.4.12, no. 324, *ibid*. Same to same, 24.5.12, no. 435. Minute by Norman, 10.6.12, FO/371/1495. Lewis, *op. cit.,* p. 221ff.
58. Parliamentary Question by McCallum Scott, 25.3.12. Minute by Norman, 23.3.12, FO/371/1493. Lowther to Grey, 27.3.12, no. 259. Minute by Norman, 1.4.12, *ibid*.
59. Tewfik to Grey, 28.6.12, FO/371/1496/27643. Lowther to Grey, 29.6.12, no. 558. Confidential. Minutes, 2.7.12, *ibid*./27983. Grey to Lowther, 6.7.12, no. 295, *ibid*.
60. Goschen to Grey, 25.6.12, no. 306. Minute by Mallet, 2.7.12, FO/371/1496. Lowther to Grey, 24.6.12, no. 533. Minutes by Norman and Mallet, 3.7.12,*ibid*.
61. Tyrrell to Lowther, 27.4.12, no. 32. Confidential in: Lowther to Grey, 1.5.12, no. 371. Confidential Minutes, 11.5.12, FO/371/1496. Ahmad, *The Young Turks*, pp. 99ff. Lewis, pp. 221ff.
62. Nicolson to Buchanan, 30.7.12, Pte. HP.358. Nicolson to Granville, 30.7.12, Pte. *ibid*. Nicolson to Marling, 22.7.12, Pte. NP.357. Cf. Grey's pessimism: Öst.-Ung. Auss. IV. 3645. The Germans believed that the new Government was pro-British. GD.33.12073.
63. Marling to Grey, 20.9.12, tel. no. 384. Minutes, 21.9.12, FO/371/1499. Nicolson to Hardinge, 19.9.12, Pte. NP.358. Marling to Nicolson, 7.8.12, Pte. *ibid*.
64. Marling to Grey, 31.8.12, tel. no. 352. Minute by Norman, 2.9.12, FO/371/1509. Paget to Grey, 28.8.12, no. 51. Minute, 3.9.12, *ibid*.
65. Dakin has different figures: *The Greek Struggle for Macedonia*, p. 407. Cf. DDF.3e ser.T.3,246.
66. Grey to Marling, 28.8.12, tel. no. 529. BD.*op. cit.* no. 666 (written by Parker).

Grey to Barclay, 31.8.12, tel. no. 55. *ibid*. no. 681 (written by Mallet). Thaden, pp. 104-5.

67. Marling to Grey, 20.8.12, tel. no. 313. Minutes, 21.8.12, BD *ibid*. no. 639. Grey to Marling, 21.8.12, no. 382. *ibid*. no. 646. Grey to Bertie, 21.8.12, no. 407. *ibid*. no. 644. Same to same, 21.8.12, *ibid*. no. 408. *ibid*. no. 645. Grey to Marling, 26.8.12, no. 417. *ibid*. no. 654. Marling to Grey, 1.9.12, tel. no. 358. *ibid*. no. 687.

68. Barclay to Grey, 3.9.12, tel. no. 34. Minute, 3.9.12, FO/371/1509. Buchanan to Grey, 28.8.12, tel. no. 315. Minute, 29.8.12, BD. *op. cit.*, no. 665. Note communicated by de Fleuriau, 28.8.12. Minute by Mallet, *ibid*. no. 680. Grey to Buchanan, 2.9.12, no. 307. *ibid*. no. 691. Same to same, 2.9.12, tel. no. 812. Buchanan to Grey, 3.9.12, tel. no. 325. Minutes, 4.9.12, *ibid*. no. 694.

69. Dering to Grey, 1.9.12, no. 262. Minute, 9.9.12, FO/371/1509.

70. Grey to Marling, 10.9.12, no. 432. *ibid*.

71. Grey to Cartwright, 10.9.12, no. 59. BD. *ibid*. no. 713. p. 687. Notes 7-9 and ed. note, p. 686. Cf. Temperley, 'British Policy Towards Parliamentary Rule ...' *Cambridge Historical Journal* (1933), p. 191, n. 80.

72. Nicolson to Hardinge, 19.9.12, Pte. NP.358. Nicolson to Buchanan, 24.9.12, Pte. *ibid*. Nicolson to Granville, 24.9.12, Pte. *ibid*. Nicolson to Townley, 24.9.12, Pte. *ibid*. Nicolson to Grey, 1.10.12, Pte. *ibid*. Same to same, 4.10.12, Pte. *ibid*. Nicolson to Hardinge, 9.10.12, BD.IX.ii. no. 10. DDF, 3e ser.T.3.430, 438. M. Gilbert, *op. cit., Companion*, II,2, p. 1593. On Hardinge's anxieties in India, cf. Hardinge to Crewe, 8.8.12, Pte. C/20. CP. However, on 13 October, he reassured his chief that with 'gentle handling we need anticipate no serious trouble.' Hardinge to Crewe, 13.10.12, Pte. *ibid*. CP.

73. Grey to Barclay, 25.9.12, no. 29. BD. *ibid*. no. 746.

74. Grey to Marling, 23.9.12, tel. no. 648. *ibid*. no. 735.

75. Lowther to Nicolson, 2.10.12, Pte. LP. Marling to Grey, 25.9.12, no. 810. Minute, 1.10.12, FO/371/1499. Same to same, 30.9.12, tel. no. 414. Minute, 1.10.12, *ibid*. Barclay to Grey, 30.9.12, tel. no. 46. BD. *ibid*. no. 759.

76. Beaumont to Grey, 1.10.12, tel. no. 47. Minute 2.10.12, FO/371/1499. Russell to Grey, 1.10.12, tel. no. 84. Minute, 2.10.12, *ibid*. Paget to Grey, 1.10.12, tel. no. 19. Minutes, 2.10.12, *ibid*.

77. Grey to Lowther, 2.10.12, no. 742, *ibid*.

78. Grey to Bertie, 6.10.12, tel. no. 508. BD.IX.i. no. 780. Same to same, 6.10.12, tel. no. 510. Urgent, *ibid*. no. 781. Grey to Lowther, 7.10.12, tel. no. 726, FO/371/1500. Same to same, 6.10.12, tel. no. 511, *ibid*. no. 782.

79. Nicolson to Granville, 8.10.12, Pte. NP.359. Nicolson to Buchanan, 8.10.12, Pte. *ibid*.

80. Lowther to Grey, 8.10.12, tel. no. 442. Urgent. BD.IX.ii. no. 1. Cartwright to Grey, 8.10.12, tel. no. 98. Confidential Minute. BD.IX.i. no. 797. Grey to Cartwright, 8.10.12, tel. no. 249. *ibid*. no. 799.

81. Grey to Lowther, 11.10.12, tel. no. 770, *ibid*.ii, no. 16. Lowther to Nicolson, 9.10.12, Pte. LP. Lowther to Grey, 8.10.12, no. 835. FO/371/1500.

82. Buchanan to Grey, 9.10.12, no. 301. Confidential minutes, 14.10.12, BD.IX.i. no. 811. Nicolson to Lowther, 14.10.12, Pte. LP. Grey to Buchanan, 21.10.12, Pte. BD. *ibid*. no. 813. In a conversation with Cambon on 16 October, Nicolson admitted that Britain would fully favour an anti-Ottoman line only in the case of Christians (i.e. Armenians) being massacred by Moslems in Asia Minor. DDF. 3e ser.T.4.184.

83. Lowther to Nicolson, 9.10.12, Pte. LP. Lowther to Grey, 10.10.12, no. 848. FO/371/1501. Same to same, 10.10.12, no. 843. Minute, 14.10.12, *ibid*. Same

to same, 10.10.12, no. 842. Minute, 14.10.12, *ibid*. Lowther to Nicolson, 16.10.12, Pte. LP.

84. Dering to Grey, 15.10.12, tel. no. 135. Minute, 16.10.12, FO/371/1526. Grey to Lowther, 15.10.12, tel. no. 790, *ibid*. Grey to Imperiali, 25.10.12. BD. *ibid*. no. 459. For the Treaty of Peace: Rodd to Grey, 2.12.12, no. 378, *ibid*. no. 466.

CHAPTER 5

1. Lowther to Grey, 24.10.12, tel. no. 524. Urgent, Secret and Confidential. FO/371/1502. Grey to Lowther, 25.10.12, tel. no. 855, *ibid*.
2. Grey to Goschen, 28.10.12, no. 271. BD. *ibid*., no. 70. Minutes by Nicolson and Grey, 29.10.12, *ibid*. p. 61. Ed. Note. Nicolson to Cartwright, 29.10.12, Pte. NP.359. Nicolson to Goschen, 29.10.12, Pte. *ibid*. Nicolson to Lowther, 30.10.12, Pte. LP. Hardinge to Crewe, 30.10.12, Pte. C/20. CP.
3. Bax-Ironside to Grey, 31.10.12, tel. no. 111. Minute by Vansittart, 1.11.12. FO/371/1526. Lowther to Grey, 1.11.12, tel. no. 561, *ibid*. Grey to Lowther, 1.11.12, tel. no. 908, *ibid*. Öst.-Ung. Auss. IV. 4227.
4. Fitzmaurice to Tyrrell, 5.11.12, Pte. GP.80. Lowther to Grey, 4.11.12, tel. no. 579. Urgent and confidential. BD. *ibid*. no. 120.
5. Kitchener to Grey, 3.11.12, Pte. BD. *ibid*. no. 113. Lowther to Grey, 4.11.12, no. 931. Confidential encl. Memorandum by Fitzmaurice, Confidential. FO/371/1504. Grey to Kitchener, 14.11.12, Pte. BD. *ibid*. no. 204.
6. Lowther to Nicolson, 20.11.12, Pte. LP. Fitzmaurice to Tyrrell, 5.11.12, Pte. GP.80. Lowther to Grey, 21.11.12, no. 984. Cumberbatch to Lowther, 14.11.12, no. 76. Confidential. Minute by Grey, 4.12.12, FO/371/1507. Syria was considered at the Foreign Office as part of 'greater Arabia'. Bertie to Grey, 24.12.12, no. 539. Confidential. Minute by Tilley, 31.12.12, FO/371/1522. The Germans recognized 'Arabia' as a British sphere of influence, GD. 34.I.12588, 12444.
7. Nicolson to Hardinge, 21.11.12, Pte. NP.360; and Hardinge to Nicolson, 19.12.12, Pte. NP.361.
8. Nicolson to Cartwright, 26.11.12, Pte. NP.360. Cartwright to Grey, 24.11.12, tel. no. 158. Minute by Nicolson, 25.11.12, BD. *ibid*. no. 262.
9. Grey to Cartwright, 18.12.12, no. 105. Secret. BD. *ibid*. no. 394.
10. Lowther to Grey, 7.12.12, no. 1043. encl. Tyrrell to Lowther, 2.12.12, no. 89. Minute, 13.12.12, FO/371/1508. Nicolson to Bax-Ironside, 26.11.12, Pte. BD. *ibid*. no. 286. Bax-Ironside to Grey, 19.11,12, tel. no. 162. conf. Minutes, FO/371/1514. Lowther to Grey, 19.11.12, tel. no. 656. BD. *ibid*. no. 230.
11. Grey to Buchanan, 5.11.12, tel. no. 1176. FO/371/1504. Nicolson to Buchanan, 5.11.12, Pte. BD. *ibid*. no. 135. Grey to Lowther, 5.11.12, Pte and Secret, tel. LP. Nicolson to Goschen, 5.11.12, Pte. NP.359. GD.33.12326. But according to French information Asquith favoured internationalizing Constantinople and Salonika, following the Tangier example, DDF.3e ser. T.4.364, 367.
12. E. David, ed., *Inside Asquith's Cabinet: From the Diaries of Charles Hobhouse* (London 1977), pp. 123-24.
13. *The Times*, 11.11.12, p. 10. Hardinge reacted negatively to this speech: Hardinge to Crewe, 6.12.12, Pte. CP. *op. cit.,* Asquith, however, disliked both Turks and the Balkan Kings. E. David (ed.), *op. cit.,* p. 123 (13.10.12). 'What extraordinary bad luck the Balkan States had in their kings. Montenegro was a

savage, Servia an assassin, and Bulgaria a cosmopolitan financier of the lowest type ...'

14. Parliamentary Questions by Sir J.D. Rees, 5.12.12; 11.12.12, *Hansard*, vol. XLIV, col. 2478, vol. XLV, cols. 449-50. Lowther rejected Churchill's view: Lowther to Nicolson, 4.12.12, Pte. LP. Annual Report for 1912, pp. 7-8 in: Lowther to Grey, 17.4.13, no. 315. FO/371/1837.

15. Lowther to Grey, 8.12.12, Pte. Minutes by Nicolson and Grey, 9.12.12, FO/371/1507/52380. Lowther to Grey, 29.11.12, no. 1009. Minute by Vansittart, *ibid*. 6.12.12. Fitzmaurice warned against an anti-Balkan atrocity campaign as a manoeuvre by Salonika Jews and Austrians to save the town from Greek rule. Fitzmaurice to Tyrrell, 18.12.12, Pte. GP.80. The Balkan Committee, too, was indifferent over the Massacre of Moslems. However, two of its members resigned in protest. H.N. Fieldhouse, 'Noel Buxton and A.J.P. Taylor's "The Trouble Makers" ', *A Century of Conflict*, ed. M. Gilbert (London 1966), p. 180, no. 5. p. 181, n. 2.

16. Grey to Lowther, 15.11.12, no. 523. Minute by Grey, FO/371/1506.

17. Cartwright to Nicolson, 22.11.12, Pte. BD. *ibid*. no. 256. Nicolson to Townley, 19.11.12, Pte. *op. cit.* Nicolson to Hardinge, 21.11.12, Pte. *op. cit.* Nicolson to Buchanan, 19.11.12, Pte. *ibid*. no. 238. Chirol to Nicolson, 18.12.12, Pte. NP.360. Hardinge explained: 'Had the Turks been victorious all along the line, the Muhamedans of this country would certainly have suffered from swelled heads. As things have turned out, they will, I think, be in a chastened form of mind and lose some of their arrogance.' Hardinge to Crewe, 5.11.12, *ibid*. CP. Also same to same, 13.11.12, Pte. *ibid*. CP.

18. Nicolson to Bax-Ironside, 12.11.12, Pte. BD. *ibid*. no. 184. Nicolson to Goschen, 13.11.12, Pte. NP.359.

19. Fitzmaurice to Tyrrell, 18.12.12, Pte. GP.80. Cf. F. Ahmad, p. 114.

20. Lowther to Grey, 11.12.12, tel. no. 715. Confidential Minutes 12.12.12, BD. *ibid*. no. 369.

21. Goschen to Grey, 14.12.12, tel. no. 177, conf. FO/371/1507. Grey to Bax-Ironside, 18.12.12, no. 46. *ibid*. no. 396. Lowther to Grey, 18.12.12, tel. no. 727. Minute by Parker, 19.12.12, *ibid*. no. 393. Same to same, 19.12.12, tel. no. 728. FO/371/1507. Same to same, 20.12.12, no. 1090. *ibid*. no. 402.

22. Lowther to Grey, 22.12.12, tel. no. 731. Minute by Grey, 23.12.12, FO/371/ 1507. Same to same, 23.12.12, tel. no. 732. Minute by Grey, 24.12.12, BD. *ibid*. no. 411. Grey to Lowther, 30.12.12, tel. no. 1127. *ibid*. no. 421.

23. Lowther to Nicolson, 1.1.13, Pte. LP. Lowther, however, rejected the 'exaggerated' version of the *Jeune Turc* concerning the massacres. Lowther to Grey, 13.2.12, no. 120. FO/371/1798.

24. Fitzmaurice to Tyrrell, 6.1.13, Pte. GP.80.

25. Nicolson to Cartwright, 7.1.13, Pte. NP.362. Nicolson to Goschen, 7.1.13, Pte. *ibid*. Nicolson to Hardinge, 9.1.13, Pte. *ibid*. Nicolson to Lowther, 8.1.13, Pte. LP. Grey to Cartwright, 7.1.13, no. 8. BD. *ibid*. no. 465. Grey to Rodd, 9.1.13, tel. no. 13, *ibid*. no. 474.

26. Lowther to Grey, 7.1.13, tel. no. 10. Minutes, 7.1.13, FO/371/1757. Same to same, 7.1.13, tel. no. 11. Minute, 8.1.13, *ibid*. Grey to Lowther, 7.1.13, tel. no. 21, *ibid*. Grey to Bertie, 8.1.13, no. 25. BD. *ibid*. no. 470. Goschen to Bethmann-Hollweg, 15.1.13. GD.34.I.23690.

27. Grey to Lowther, 10.1.13, tel. no. 25. BD. *ibid*. no. 482. Lowther to Nicolson, 9.1.13, Minute by Vansittart, 10.1.13, in: Lowther to Grey, 9.1.13, tel. no. 16. FO/371/1757.

28. Lowther to Grey 17.1.13, tel. no. 28, conf. BD. *ibid*. no. 521. (Minutes, 18.1.13, FO/371/1757), Grey to Lowther, 19.1.13, tel. no. 43. *ibid*. no. 529.

29. Nicolson to Lowther, 4.2.13, Pte. LP. Nicolson to Cartwright, 4.2.13, Pte. NP.362. Nicolson to Goschen, 21.1.13, Pte. *ibid*. Nicolson to Cartwright, 21.1.13, Pte. *ibid*. Nicolson to Bax-Ironside, 22.1.13, Pte. *ibid*. Grey to Bertie, 21.1.13, tel. no. 30. BD. *ibid*. no. 534.
30. Lowther to Grey, 24.1.13, no. 62. conf. FO/371/1788. Same to same, 28.1.13, no. 69. Ahmad, *The Young Turks,* passim.
31. Same to same, 23.1.13, tel. no. 39, *ibid*. no. 545. (Minutes, 24.1.13, FO/371/1788). Same to same, 23.1.13, tel. no. 40. Minutes, 24.1.13, *ibid*. no. 547. Same to same, 24.1.13, tel. no. 42.*ibid*. no. 550. Lowther to Nicolson, 21.1.13, Pte. NP.362.
32. Lowther to Grey, 27.1.13, tel. no. 51. Minute, 28.1.13, FO/371/1788. Nicolson to Goschen, 28.1.13, Pte. NP.362. Nicolson to Buchanan, 28.1.13, Pte. *ibid*.
33. Tyrrell to Lowther, 26.1.13, no. 3 in: Lowther to Grey, 26.1.13, no. 65. FO/371/1788. Same to same, 18.1.13, n. 69,*ibid*. Lowther's information was correct. Shevket and Zeki reported to Wangenheim on the 11th and 12th on their coming *coup*. GD.34. I.12669, 12670.
34. According to Lowther, the Young Turks had taken the French Revolution as their pattern. Annual Report for Turkey, 1912, in: Lowther to Grey, 17.4.13, no. 315, p. 9. FO/371/1837.
35. Lowther to Grey, 25.1.13, tel. no. 43, BD. *ibid*. no. 557. Same to same, 5.2.13, no. 92. Conf. Minute by Norman, 12.2.13, FO/371/1788. Same to same, 13.2.13, tel. no. 87. Minute by Parker, *ibid*. On the realization of his forecast, see: Same to same, 15.5.13, No. 210. conf. FO/371/1783.
36. Same to same, 15.1.13, no. 35, FO/371/1757. Nicolson to Hardinge, 9.1.13, Pte. NP.362. Nicolson to Lowther, 19.2.13, Pte. LP. Lowther to Nicolson, 13.2.13, Pte. *ibid*. Nicolson to Cartwright, 19.2.13, Pte. BD. *ibid*. no. 632.
37. Grey promised the German Ambassador that in the event of a break up of the Asian provinces, German interests would be considered. The Germans, indeed, were determined to look after their interests in both Anatolia and Mesopotamia, though like the British, they primarily supported the Ottoman Empire 'as long as it is at all possible'. GD. 35.13436, *ibid*. 38, 15317, pp. 55, 206, *ibid*. 15343.
38. Grey to Buchanan, 28.1.13, no. 52, *ibid*. no. 564. Grey to Bertie, 31.12.12, no. 635. Bertie to Grey, 30.1.13, no. 48. Minute by Grey, 31.1.12, FO/371/1775. The Foreign Office also accepted Kitchener's advice against allowing the French to build a railway from Rayak to El-Arish, but only to Ramleh, since this might constitute a strategic danger to Egypt, particularly as 'foreign influence' might supersede the Ottomans in the districts between the Euphrates and the Egyptian frontier. Kitchener to Grey, 11.5.13, no. 45. Minute by Vansittart, 19.5.13, FO/371/1813. Grey to Lowther, 6.6.13, tel. no. 245, *ibid*. nos. 88, 153. DDF. 3e ser. T.7.25. GD.38.12725.
39. Lowther to Grey, 2.2.13, no. 82. encl. Cumberbatch to Lowther, 24.1.13, no. 8. Minutes by Norman and Nicolson, 10.2.13, FO/371/1798. Same to same, 25.2.13, no. 156. Minute by Norman, 1.3.13, *ibid*. Same to same, 24.3.13, no. 238. Minute by Norman, 2.4.13, *ibid*. Same to same 7.6.13, no. 504. Minutes, 11.6.13, BD.X.ii. App.III, pp. 825-6. Carnegie to Grey, 26.6.13, no. 346. Minute by Norman, 28.6.13. Cromer to Tyrrell, 2.7.13, Minute 3.7.13, FO/371/1775/30562.
40. Minutes by Norman and Mallet, 3-4.3.13, FO/371/1794/10066. Lowther to Grey, 17.3.13, no. 218. Minute by Norman, 16.4.13, *ibid*. As early as 1910, when Zionists and non-Zionists like Dr Nosig had suggested Jewish colonization in Mesopotamia, Mallet had minuted that the Jews were 'parasites' and

not 'good agriculturalists'. Marling to Grey, 27.12.09, no. 992. Conf. Minutes 3.1.10, FO/371/992. Lowther to Grey, 31.8.10, no. 621. Minutes, 17.9.10, *ibid*.

41. Nicolson to Cartwright, 17.3.13, Pte. BD.IX.ii. no. 728; cf. Hardinge to Nicolson, 24.2.13, Pte. NP.364.

42. Lowther to Nicolson, 10.4.13, Pte. LP. Lowther to Grey, 21.4.13, no. 332. Minute by Norman, 28.4.13, FO/371/1799. Same to same, 13.3.13, no. 198. Minute by Vansittart, 17.3.13, *ibid*. Compare *Hansard,* 29.5.13, vol. LIII, cols. 397-8, 408-410, 378-81, and M. Sykes, *The Caliph's Last Heritage* (London 1915), pp. 464-96, 507-51.

43. Note by Grey, 12.6.13, BD.X.i. App. Memo. by Mallet, 19.6.13. Minute by Grey. Grey to Tewfik, 2.7.13, Secret, *ibid*. In June 1913, the Kaiser remarked cynically on Grey's policy: '... des Pacificator Mundi Grey'. GD.35. 13378, p. 25, n.1. Inside the Cabinet, the Young Turks were left with no support, and were regarded with contempt and hatred: '... the ostensible Cabinet is run by an occult committee who though hybrid Jews and Caucasians, and Cretan Mahommedans, are arbiters of an Asiatic and Ottoman Empire.' E. David (ed.), *Inside Asquith's Cabinet,* p. 135 (26.4.13).

44. Cf. Ahmad, 'Great Britain's Relations', *op. cit.,* p. 323. On the same day on which Mallet composed his memorandum, Pallavicini, the Austrian Ambassador, claimed that under Shevket's rule, Ottoman-British relations were far better than under the Anglophile Kiamil, Öst.-Ung. Auss. VI.7417.

45. Nicolson to Cartwright, 24.6.13, Pte. NP.367. Marling to Grey, 7.7.13, tel. no. 323. Minute by Norman, 8.7.13, FO/371/1833. Same to same, 9.7.13, tel. no. 325. Minute 10.7.13, *ibid*. Same to same, 13.7.13, tel. no. 334. Minute, 14.7.13, *ibid*. Grey to Marling, 16.7.13, tel. no. 329. BD.IX.ii. no. 1151.

46. Nicolson to Buchanan, 29.7.13, Pte. NP.368. Chirol warned that the Hindu nationalists might join hands with the Moslems. Memorandum communicated by Sir V. Chirol, 10.7.13, FO/371/1853/31776. Hardinge to Nicolson, 22.7.13, NP.369. Pte. Marling to Grey, 30.7.13, tel. no. 374. Minute by Norman, 31.7.13. Also: BD. *ibid*. nos. 1228, 1232. GD.36.I.13778, p. 25, n. 2; 13781. Hardinge to Crewe, 31.7.13, Pte. C/21.CP. Hardinge feared the increase in the Balkan Committee's influence. Hardinge to Crewe, 14.8.13, Pte. *ibid*. Two months later he was relieved because of the end of the war. Hardinge to Crewe, 15.10.13, Pte. *ibid*. Also: Crewe to Hardinge, 25.7.13, Pte. C/24. CP. Crewe to Hardinge, 4.9.13, Pte. *ibid*. On Asquith's contempt for Turkey and the bogey of Pan-Islam, cf. E. David (ed.), *Inside Asquith's Cabinet,* p. 140-1 (9.7.13).

47. Buchanan to Grey, 23.7.13, tel. no. 273. BD. *ibid*. no. 1173. Grey to Carnegie, 23.7.13, no. 464, BD. *ibid*. no. 1174. Grey to Marling, 26.7.13, tel. no. 352, BD. *ibid*. no. 1183.

48. Minute by Parker, 25.7.13, approved by Nicolson and Grey, FO/371/1837/ 34768. Asquith was definitely a Turcophobe. Cf. his words at a Cabinet session on 9 July 1913: 'The Turk was impossible anywhere as a dominant race and should go.' E. David (ed.), p. 140-1.

49. Carnegie to Mallet, 23.7.13. Minutes, FO/371/1837/34811. Annual Report for 1912, pp. 7-8 in: Lowther to Grey, 17.4.13, no. 315, FO/371/1837. The Kaiser expected a break up of the Entente. GD.36.I.13778, p. 25, 13781.

50. Marling to Grey, 20.7.13, no. 639. Minute by Norman, 31.7.13, FO/371/1837. Granville to Grey, 15.8.13, tel. no. 13. Minute by Mallet, 16.8.13, *ibid*. Marling to Grey, 15.8.13, tel. no. 407. Minutes, 16.8.13, *ibid*. Grey to Marling, 18.8.13, tel. no. 409, *ibid*. Marling to Grey, 9.9.13, tel. no. 460. Minute by Norman, 10.9.13, *ibid*. Marling was also annoyed by Block's support of the CUP. Marling to Grey, 27.7.13, no 683. very conf. Minutes, 5.8.13, *ibid*.

51. Grey to Bertie, 31.7.13, Pte. Lowe & Dockrille, pp. 476-7. Buchanan to Grey, 18.8.13, tel. no. 307. Minute by Norman, 19.8.13, FO/371/1837. no. 1242. Marling to Grey, 14.8.13, no. 772. Minute by Grey, 22.8.13, FO/371/1841. The protest was only a 'brutum fulmen' as Crewe confessed. Crewe to Hardinge, 18.9.13, Pte. C/24. CP.

52. Nicolson to O'Beirne, 22.9.13, Pte. NP.369. Marling to Grey, 8.9.13, tel. no. 459, FO/371/1841.

53. Same to same, 30.9.13, tel. no. 494, FO/371/1837. Grey to Marling, 30.0.13, tel. no. 472, *ibid*. Grey to Nicolson, 1.10.13, NP.370. Grey to Elliot, 27.9.13, no. 113. BD.X.i, no. 150. Grey to O'Beirne, 13.10.13, no. 349, FO/371/1837. GD.36.I.13868.

54. Marling to Nicolson, 9.10.13, Pte. NP.370. Norman's Minute to Buxton's Parliamentary Question, 16.7.13. FO/371/1841. *Hansard,* 17.7.13, Vol. LV. col. 1404. Marling to Grey, 14.10.13, tel. no. 504, FO/371/1837.

55. For a general background: E. Kedourie, 'Minorities' in: *The Chatham House Version* (London 1970), pp. 286-300. R. Davison, 'The Armenian Crisis, 1912-14', *American Historical Review* (1948), pp. 481-505. R.G. Hovannisian, *Armenia on the Road to Independence* (Berkeley 1967), pp. 28-39. Id. 'The Armenian Question in the Ottoman Empire', *East European Quarterly* (1972), pp. 1-26. The Young Turk point of view presented by Djemal Pasha, *Memories of a Turkish Statesman, 1913-19* (London n.d.), pp. 2421ff.

56. Tyrrell to Lowther, 18.8.09, Pte. HP.192. Bryce to Grey, 21.7.09, Grey Papers, 79, P.RO. Pte., Same to same, 29.7.09, Pte. *ibid*. Washburn to Bryce, 29.7.09, Pte. *ibid*

57. See, e.g., Lowther's survey of unrest in Eastern Anatolia in Lowther to Grey, 9.10.13, no. 847. FO/371/1484. Vansittart minuted that this was 'a bad account'. *Ibid*.

58. Lowther to Grey, 4.12.12, no. 1036. Conf. Minute by Mallet, 27.12.12, *ibid*. Atkin to Foreign Office, 30.10.12. Minute by Vansittart, 5.11.12, FO/371/1520/46286. Same to same, 11.11.12. Minute by Vansittart, 12.11.12, *ibid*./48214.

59. The Balkan Committee to Grey, 29.11.12. Minutes, 2.12.12, *ibid*./51957. Maxwell was Senior Clerk at the Eastern Department, of which Sir Louis Mallet was head.

60. Minute by Mallet, 6.12.12, *ibid*./51597. Lowther to Grey, 29.11.12, no. 1006. FO/371/1520. Friends of Armenia to Grey, 16.12.12, *ibid*./53992.

61. Lowther to Grey, 31.12.12, no. 1229. Minutes, 15.1.13, FO/371/1773.

62. Lady Cavendish to Grey, 16.1.13. Minutes 12.2.13, FO/371/1773/6585.

63. Grey (Mallet) to Lady Cavendish, 4.3.13, *ibid*. Lady Cavendish to Grey, 24.3.13 (letter from Bryce). Minutes 27.3.13, *ibid*./13668. Molyneaux-Seel to Lowther, 22.1.13, no. 2, in: Lowther to Grey, 13.2.13, no. 111.

64. Lowther to Grey, 15.3.13, no. 203. Minute by Norman, 19.3.13, FO/371/1773. Same to same, 17.3.13, no. 219. Conf. Minutes by Norman, 27.3.13, *ibid*.

65. Lowther to Grey, 6.4.13, no. 281. Minute by Mallet, 15.4.13, *ibid*. Same to same, 6.4.13, no. 279. Minute by Norman, 15.4.13, *ibid*. Same to same, 19.4.13, no. 329, *ibid*. Same to same, 24.4.13, no. 343. Minute by Norman, 28.4.13, *ibid*. Grey to Lowther, 29.4.13, tel. no. 199. British Armenia Committee to Grey, 28.4.13. Minutes 2.5.13, *ibid*./19706.

66. Tewfik to Grey, 25.4.13. Minutes 29.4.13, BD.X.i. no. 479. (Minutes by Norman and Maxwell, FO/371/1814). Consultation with Russia was exactly what the Porte wanted to avoid. GP.38 no. 15300. Wangenheim warned

Shevket that British officers might infringe upon the German sphere in the Baghdad Railway. Shevket explained to Wangenheim that the move was meant to persuade Britain of the Porte's sincerity and efficiency, and that since the Ottoman Empire would not break up it deserved to receive back the Aegean Islands. Davison is right in noting the Porte's intention to divide Britain and Russia on this question, Davison, *op. cit.*, 493-4. The Kaiser, as usual suspicious of British intentions, opposed the whole plan, GP. no. 15439, p. 201. Jagow added that it might 'make impossible' ('unmöglich machen') German friendship to the Porte, *ibid.* no. 15304 (19.5.13). Shevket, in order to avoid a rupture with Germany, claimed that he would always feel more German than British, *ibid.* no. 15305. Öst.-Ung. Auss. VI. nos. 8463, 7009.

67. Lowther to Grey, 29.4.13, no. 363. FO/371/1814. Grey to Tewfik, 24.5.13, *ibid.* no. 491.

68. O'Beirne to Grey, 26.5.13, tel. no. 197. Minutes, 27.5.13, BD.X.i, no. 492. Grey to O'Beirne, 28.5.13, tel. no. 424, *ibid.*, no. 495.

69. These (and Mesopotamia) were actually the Kaiser's targets. F. Fischer, 'World Policy, World Power and German War Aims', in: H. W. Koch, *The Origins of the First World War* (London 1972), p. 108.

70. Lowther to Grey, 6.6.13, no. 503, conf., BD. *op. cit.*, no. 503. Minute by Keeling, 11.6.13, FO/371/1814. Minute by Norman, 19.5.13, in: Same to same, 13.5.13, no. 416. *Ibid.* Conf. Fitzmaurice to Tyrrell, 8.5.13, Pte., Grey Papers, 80. GD.38, no. 15324, DDF. 3e ser. vol. 8, no. 144.

71. Buchanan to Grey, 6.7.13, tel. no. 247. Minutes, 7.7.13, BD. *op. cit.*, no. 542. Grey to Buchanan, 9.7.13, tel. no. 508, *ibid.* no. 547. GD.38. no. 15363, note.

72. Nicolson to Cartwright, 8.7.13, Pte., NP.368. Partly quoted in C.J. Lowe and M.L. Dockrill, *op. cit.*, Vol. 3: *The Documents* (London 1972), p. 476.

73. Marling to Grey, 1.7.13, no. 575. Minutes, 8.7.13, FO/371/1814.

74. Marling to Nicolson, 2.7.13, Pte. NP.368. Same to same, 11.7.13, Pte. *ibid.* Marling to Grey, 12.7.13, no. 621. Minute by Nicolson, 24.7.13, BD. *op. cit.*, no. 553. Minute by Mallet, FO/371/1814.

75. Marling to Grey, 22.7.13, no. 641. Minutes, 29.7.13. Fitzmaurice's memorandum 10.8.13, in: same to same, 27.8.13, no. 747, very conf., BD. *op. cit.*, no. 567.

76. Grey's reply to Sir J. Barran, 12.7.13, *Hansard*, Vol. LVI, col. 2229. Compare E. David (ed.), *Inside Asquith's Cabinet*, pp. 140-1.

77. Marling to Nicolson, 1.8.13, Pte., NP.368. Fitzmaurice's Memorandum, 10.8.13, BD.X.i. no. 567. GP.38. nos. 15343, 15346, 15359, 15361. Wangenheim for his part believed that Marling, under Fitzmaurice's influence, and using the Armenian crisis as a pretext, aimed to overthrow the Young Turks and to re-install Kiamil in power. GP.38, no. 15370 (30.7.13). Amongst the Germans only Kühlmann, the German Chargé in London, did not believe that Russia aimed at the annexation of Armenia. GP.38, no. 15397.

78. BD. *op. cit.*, pp. 515-516. Minute by Norman, 7.9.13. Minute by Norman, 7.9.13. Minute by Crowe, 23.9.13, *ibid.* Minute by Nicolson, *ibid.* Nicolson to Granville, 23.9.13, Pte. NP.369.

79. Granville to Grey, 24.9.13, tel. no. 165. FO/371/1814. Minute by Crowe. Marling to Grey, 26.9.13, tel. no. 486. Minutes, 27.9.13, BD. *op. cit.*, no. 568, GP.38. nos. 15383, 15386, 15389, 15390.

80. Same to same, 7.10.13, tel. no. 497. Minutes, 8.10.13, BD. *op. cit.*, no. 569. The Foreign Office was unfavourably impressed by the fact that Said Halim, the Grand Vizier, had no idea of Talaat's suggestion; see same to same, 18.10.13, no. 376. Minute by Oliphant, 27.10.13. Graves, *op. cit.*, pp. 287-88.

81. M.K. Chapman, *Great Britain and the Bagdad Railway 1888-1914, passim*.

82. Minute by Nicolson, 20.11.12. Meeting of the Interdepartmental Committee on the question of oilfields in Mesopotamia and Persia. FO/371/1486/50815. Platt argues that Britain had her 'eyes on Mesopotamia in any future formal or informal partition' and that this was the chief motive in her concession-hunting policy. Platt, *op. cit.*, pp. 195-7.

83. Foreign Office to Admiralty, 13.9.12, Very Conf. FO/371/1486/36674. Marling to Maxwell, 18.9.12, Pte. *ibid*. Foreign Office to Babington-Smith, 28.9.12, *ibid*/40516. See also: M. Jack, 'The Purchase of the British Government's Shares in the British Petroleum Co. 1912-1914', *Past and Present* (1968), pp. 139-168. M. Kent, *Oil and Empire, British Policy and Mesopotamian Oil, 1900-1920* (London 1976), pp. 33-58. Similarly, the Foreign Office later refused to take at face value the assurance that the newly-formed Turkish Petroleum Company (established in August 1912) was predominantly British.

84. Babington-Smith to Foreign Office, 9.10.12, FO/371/1486/42490. Minute by Parker, 15.11.12. Immediate and conf. Minutes by Maxwell and Mallet.

85. Grey to Lowther, 6.12.12, tel. no. 1092. Foreign Office to India Office, 9.12.12, conf. *ibid*./51935. Lowther to Maxwell, 11.12.12, Pte. Minute by Mallet, 20.12.12, *ibid*.

86. Lowther to Grey, 31.3.13, no. 257. Minute by Mallet, 9.4.13, FO/371/1760.

87. Same to same, 21.4.13, no. 336. Minute, 28.4.13, FO/371/1760.

88. Same to same, 21.5.13, tel. no. 238. Minute by Parker, BD.X.ii. no. 76.

89. The bad experience with the National Bank deterred the British Government from supporting any similar initiative. The Foreign Office was also deterred by the 'unpromising' future of the Ottoman Empire. Babington-Smith to Grey, 11.6.13, FO/371/1826/16928. Minutes 14.6.13, Lowther to Grey, 20.6.13, tel. no. 261, Conf. Minutes. Mallet to Grey, 5.11.13, tel. no. 547. Minutes, 6.11.13. Minutes by Crowe and Grey, 30.3.14, FO/371/2127/14256. Waugh to Tyrrell, 16.7.14. Minutes, 20.7.14, *ibid*./32879.

90. Mallet to Grey, 11.3.14, tel. no. 157. Minute, 12.3.14, FO/371/2127. Parker to Hakki, 12.3.14, FO/371/2120/10926. Grey to Mallet, 11.3.14, tel. no. 133 (written by Crowe), *ibid*.

91. Mallet to Grey, 11.3.14, tel. no. 159, *ibid*. Arrangements for Fusion of the Interests in Turkish Petroleum Co. 19.3.14. Minute by Crowe, 20.3.14. BD.X.ii. no. 214. It was also hoped that Britain would obtain preferential rights with regard to Nejd, 'where the establishment of a foreign syndicate would create embarrassment in existing conditions.'

92. Same to same, 9.6.14, tel. no. 328. Minutes by Parker and Crowe, 10.6.14, FO/371/2120. Same to same, 30.6.14, tel. no. 393. Minute by Crowe, 1.7.14, *ibid*. Anglo-Persian Oil Co. to Foreign Office, 2.11.14. Minutes, 6.11.14, *ibid*./66612.

93. Babington-Smith to Foreign Office, 21.10.12, Confidential Minutes, 24.10.12, FO/371/1494/44554. The sensitivity of the Russians was also brought up as an argument against this amalgamation.

94. India Office to Foreign Office, 1.11.12. Minute by Parker, 2.11.12, *ibid*./46326.

95. Fitzmaurice to Tyrrell, 13.2.13, Pte. GP.80.

96. Lowther to Grey, 3.6.13, tel. no. 256. Minutes, 4.6.13, FO/371/2136. Grey to Goschen, 2.5.13, no. 177. BD.X.ii. no. 86. Minute by Parker, 7.6.13, *ibid*. no. 91. Foreign Office Minutes, 10.3.14, FO/371/2122/17902.

97. Minute by Parker, 9.5.13, BD.X.ii. no. 69. Minute by Parker, FO/371/1790/21957. L. Smith to Grey, 16.5.13. Minute by Parker, 17.5.13, FO/371/1710/22525. Minute by Parker, 21.5.13, BD.X.ii. no. 78. GD.37.I.14739.

98. Minute by Parker, 3.12.13, BD. *ibid.* no. 183. Concession pour la Navigation sur le Tigre et l'Euphrates, 12.12.13, BD. *ibid.* no. 188.
99. See: J.B. Kelly, 'Salisbury, Curzon and the Kuwait Agreement of 1899', *Studies in International History*, eds. K. Bourne and D.C. Watt (1967), pp. 249-90.
100. Report on Baghdad Railway and Persian Gulf: The Negotiations with Hakki. Secret, 3.5.13, by Mallet and Hirtzel, BD. *ibid.* p. 114ff. Minute by Parker, 8.7.14, FO/371/2136/31036. Busch, *op. cit.*, pp. 336-340.
101. Minute by Parker, 13.5.13. Minute by Vansittart, 14.5.13, BD. *ibid.* no. 71.
102. Report on Baghdad Railway and Persian Gulf, 3.5.13, *ibid.* Minute by Parker, 5.5.13, FO/371/2136. Lowther to Grey, 15.5.13, tel. no. 233, *ibid.* Same to same, 17.5.13, no. 436. Minute by Vansittart, 21.5.13, *ibid.* Same to same, 15.5.13, tel. no. 232, *ibid.*
103. Grey to Bertie, 21.5.13, no. 322 (also to O'Beirne), BD.X.ii. no. 77. Grey to Goschen, 23.5.13, no. 165, BD. *ibid.* no. 79.
104. Grey to Tewfik, 29.7.13, BD.X.ii. no. 124. Anglo-Turkish Agreement, 29.7.13, *ibid.* But the Anglo-Ottoman agreement could not come into force before the end of the Ottoman-German negotiations, which had not yet started as Djavid was still negotiating with the French, and the agreement remained unfulfilled on the outbreak of War. Minute by Parker, 15.10.13, FO/371/1817/46981.
105. Grey to Mallet, 31.5.14, tel. no. 245, FO/371/2122. Grey to Beaumont, 19.7.14, tel. no. 315. BD. *ibid.* no. 260. For the Anglo-German negotiations see also: GD.37.I, pp. 141-470.
106. Later Parker apologized for not achieving more on the grounds that Grey was 'hampered' by the existence of the Convention of 1903. Parker, *op. cit.*, pp. 523-4. On Parker, see: R.V. Kühlmann, *Erinnerungen* (Heidelberg 1948), pp. 366ff. The Agreement itself in: BD.X.ii. 249; GP.37.I. 14907, 14811.
107. Crewe to Hardinge, 21.8.13. Lowe & Dockrill, p. 128. Cf. S.A. Cohen, *op. cit.*
108. Grey and Nicolson agreed that the matter should be mentioned to Hakki unofficially since in any case the Porte was already suspicious about Britain's connections with these sheikhs. A little later, however, when the Foreign Office learned that the sheikh who had contacted Crow had killed the Porte's representative, had seized the Government's land and did not intend to pay taxes, Grey himself telegraphed to Lowther that this new information put the whole matter in a different light and did not justify Crow's earlier telegrams. Lowther to Grey, 14.3.13, tel. no. 145. FO/371/1799. Crow to Lowther, 12.3.13, Secret. Minutes, 15.3.13, *ibid.* Same to same, 22.3.13, tel. no. 157. Secret. *ibid.* Grey to Lowther, 25.3.13, tel. no. 152, *ibid.*
109. Hony to Lowther, 20.2.13, no. 4. Conf. in: Lowther to Grey, 27.3.13, no. 245. Minutes, 1.4.13, FO/371/1805.
110. Mallet minute on Lowther to Grey, 25.6.13, tel. no. 301, and no. 104. FO/371/1817; Parker minute, 22.9.13, on Marling to Grey, 7.9.13, no. 774. FO/371/1845. Lorimer's views in Lorimer to Lowther, 25.4.13, FO/371/1816; and Lorimer to Marling, 4.8.13, no. 845, FO/371/1845.
111. Crow to Marling, 18.6.13, no. 52. Marling to Grey, 25.9.13, no. 819. Minute by Norman, 8.10.13.
112. Hony to Marling, 18.6.13, no. 18. Marling to Grey, 14.7.13, no. 623. Minutes, 24.7.13, FO/371/1805.
113. Nicolson to Cartwright, 8.7.13, Pte. NP.368.
114. Ryan, *The Last of the Dragomans*, pp. 70-1. Ryan was Acting Chief Dragoman.
115. Lowther to Grey, 4.8.08, Pte. BD.V. no. 205, Ed. Add.

116. Ryan, *op. cit.*, pp. 70-1.
117. Bullard, *op. cit.*, p. 64. Lowther to Hardinge, 29.5.10, Pte. p. 6. LP. For Fitzmaurice's influence on Lowther, cf. Wangenheim's remark on 24 April 1913: '... Sir G. Lowther is a distinguished man, but he is ill and therefore weak. He is not strong enough to free himself from the influence of his First Dragoman.' GD.37.165. Translation by E. T. S. Dugdale, *German Diplomatic Documents, IV* (London 1931), p. 241.
118. Lowther to Nicolson, 19.6.13, Pte. LP.
119. Quoted in Ahmad, *op. cit.*, p. 128. (B. Lewis's translation: *Bulletin of the School of Oriental and African Studies* (1960), p. 147.)
120. Lawrence's description of Lowther as an 'utter dud', and his allegation that Fitzmaurice was responsible for Britain's ineffectiveness, cannot be sustained. *T. E. Lawrence to his Biographer, Liddell Hart* (London 1938), pp. 87-8. Cf. Admiral Fisher's remark on Lowther: 'd—d fool, for not realizing that the Mohammedans hold the key of the world.' Marder, *Fear God*, p. 389. F. Ahmad is incorrect in claiming that Britain pursued two different policies towards the Porte. F. Ahmad, 'Great Britain's Relations with the Young Turks, 1908-14', *Middle Eastern Studies* (1966), p. 309. C. J. Lowe and M. L. Dockrill, *The Mirage of Power*, Vol. 1 (London 1971) pp. 85-8. Grey defended Lowther in a letter to Nicolson, *ibid.*, p. 128.

CHAPTER 6

1. Lady Lowther to Hardinge, 12.4.13, Pte. HP.93. Hardinge to Nicolson, 16.5.14, Pte. NP.367. Nicolson to Goschen, 18.6.13, Pte. *ibid.* Same to same, 24.6.13, Pte. *ibid.* Fitzmaurice to Tyrrell, 3.6.13, Pte. GP.80. Hardinge to Parker, 18.8.13, Pte. HP.93. Lowther to Grey, 1.9.13, FO/371/1845/44565. Grey to Lowther, 17.10.13, *ibid.* Hardinge to Mallet, 21.6.13, Pte. HP.93. Hardinge to Sanderson, 22.5.13, Pte. *ibid.* Lowe and Dockrill, p. 128. Öst.-Ung. Auss. IV. 3773. Magnus, *Kitchener*, p. 224.
2. Mallet to Hardinge, 11.8.13, Pte. HP.93. On Asquith's views, cf. Lowe and Dockrill, p. 128.
3. Minute by Crowe, 13.9.13, FO/371/1845/42686.
4. Minute by Crowe, 23.9.12, Minutes, 24.9.12 and 29.9.12, *ibid*/43461.
5. Marling to Grey, 25.9.13, no. 816. (Article of 22.9.13) FO/371/1845.
6. Crowe could not resist commenting 'Magnificent' when he read this flattering article by a prominent CUP politician. Mallet to Grey, 7.11.13, no. 920. (Article of 1.11.13), minute 18.11.13, *ibid.*
7. Mallet to Grey, 4.11.13, Pte. GP.80. Mallet to Nicolson, 4.11.13, Pte. NP.371.
8. Grey to Mallet, 12.11.13, Pte. GP.80. Mallet to Grey, 20.2.14, tel. no. 116. FO/371/2131. Medical documents attached. A. Ryan, *op. cit.*, p. 86. P. P. Graves, *Briton and Turk* (London 1941), p. 188, argues that Fitzmaurice was transferred to placate the CUP. This was also the view of the Austrian Ambassador, Pallavicini: Öst.-Ung. Auss. VII, 9506.
9. Mallet to Grey, 16.12.13, no. 1008. Minute, 24.12.13, FO/371/2111.
10. Mallet to Grey, 6.1.14, tel. no. 9. BD. *ibid.* no. 193.
11. Mallet to Grey, 30.12.13, no. 1044. Minute by Norman, FO/371/2111. These feelings were mutual: Djemal, *Memories*, p. 103.
12. Nicolson to Hardinge, 15.1.14, Pte. NP.372.
13. Ahmad, pp. 143, 151.
14. Mallet to Grey, 21.5.14, no. 363. Confidential, FO/371/2134.
15. Annual Report for Turkey, 1913, in Beaumont to Grey, 4.12.14, FO/371/

2137/79138. The report was written almost entirely before the outbreak of the European War.

16. *ibid.*
17. *ibid..*
18. Mallet to Grey, 28.10.13, no. 905. Conf. Minute by C. Russell, 11.11.13, FO/371/1845. Same to same, 31.10.13, tel. no. 532. Minute by Crowe, 1.11.13, BD. *ibid.* no. 573. Grey to Mallet, 3.11.13, tel. no. 509. BD. *ibid.* no. 574. Grey to Goschen, 4.11.13, tel. no. 379. BD. *ibid.* no. 575.
19. Mallet to Grey, 13.11.13, no. 934. BD. *ibid.* no. 582.
20. Mallet to Nicolson, 15.11.13, Pte. NP.371. Same to same, 16.11.13, Pte.*ibid..*
21. Mallet to Grey, 18.11.13, no. 939. BD. *ibid.* no. 583. Same to same, 24.11.13, no. 953. Minute by C. Russell, 28.11.13, FO/371/1816. Same to same, 13.11.13, no. 934. Minute by Russell, 24.11.13, FO/371/1815. Cf. GD.38, 15408.
22. Mallet to Grey, 25.11.13, Pte. GP.80.
23. Same to same, 27.11.13, no. 965. Minute by C. Russell, 3.12.13, FO/371/1816.
24. Mallet to Grey, 1.12.13, no. 978. Minutes by Crowe and Grey, 18.12.13, BD. *ibid.* no. 586. Same to same, 2.12.13, Pte. GP.80.
25. Guinness to Grey, 6.12.13. Minutes by Russell and Nicolson, 9.12.13, FO/371/1773. Lady Cavendish to Grey, 9.12.13. Minute, 15-18.12.13, *ibid/*56074. Grey to Lady Cavendish, 18.12.13, *ibid.* N. Buxton, 'The Russians in Armenia', *Nineteenth Century and After* (December 1913), pp. 1357-66.
26. Grey to Mallet, 12.11.13, Pte. GP.80. Mallet to Grey, 2.12.13, Pte. *ibid.*
27. Mallet to Grey, 29.12.13, no. 1048. Confidential. BD. *ibid.* no. 185.
28. Same to same, 31.12.13, no. 1045, BD. *ibid.* no. 587. Minute by Russell, 6.1.14, FO/371/2116.
29. Same to same, 6.1.14, no. 6. Grey to Mallet, 14.1.14, tel. no. 27. Mallet to Grey, 16.1.14, tel. no. 37, FO/371/2122.
30. Smith to Mallet, 10.1.14, nos. 1, 2 in: Mallet to Grey, 30.1.14, no. 59. Minutes, 9-17.2.14. (approved by Nicolson and Grey), *ibid.*
31. Mallet to Grey, 10.2.14, Pte. GP.80. Nicolson to Buchanan, 10.2.14, Pte. NP.372. Mallet to Nicolson, 10.2.14, Pte. *ibid.* Nicolson to Mallet, 16.2.14, Pte. *ibid.*
32. Mallet to Grey, 14.3.14, tel. no. 167. Same to same, 17.3.14, no. 178. Same to same, 14.3.14, no. 174. Minute by Russell, 19.3.14, FO/371/2116.
33. Mallet to Grey, 3.4.14, tel. no. 217. Same to same, 17.4.14, no. 259, *ibid.*
34. Memo by Benckendorff, 16.3.14. Minutes, 17.3.14, FO/371/2116/11895. Mallet to Grey, 7.4.14, no. 233. Minute by Clerk, 16.4.14, *ibid.* Also: BD. *ibid.* no. 595. Same to same, 27.5.14, no. 376. Minute by Russell, FO/371/2116. Beaumont to Grey, 27.7.14, no. 542, *ibid.*
35. Williams to Grey, 18.9.14, *ibid./*51007. (Minutes, 19.9.14.) Mallet to Grey, 23.9.14, tel. no. 842. Minutes, 5-6.10.14.
36. Same to same, 25.9.14, no. 607. FO/371/2137.
37. For background see R.J. Kerner, 'The Mission of Liman von Sanders', *Slavonic Review*, 6 (1927-8), pp. 12-27, 344-63, 543-60. 7 (1928), 90-112. U. Trumpener, *Germany and the Ottoman Empire, 1914-1918* (Princeton 1968), pp. 13-14. F. Fischer, *War of Illusions: German Policies from 1911 to 1914* (London 1977), Ch. 15.
38. Mallet to Grey, 30.10.13, tel. no. 350. BD. *ibid.* no. 376. Goschen to Grey, 1.11.13, no. 400, *ibid.* no. 377. Goschen to Nicolson, 19.11.13, Pte. NP.371.
39. Goschen to Nicolson, 19.11.13, Pte. *ibid.* Nicolson to Goschen, 24.11.13, Pte. *ibid.* Grey to Bertie, 24.11.13, no. 713. BD. *ibid.* no. 378.

40. O'Beirne to Nicolson, 27.11.13, Pte. BD. *ibid*. no. 382. O'Beirne to Grey, 25.11.13, tel. no. 393. Minute by Nicolson, BD. *ibid*. no. 379. (Minute by Russell and Clerk, 26.11.13, FO/371/1847).

41. Grey to O'Beirne, 27.11.13, tel. no. 765. BD. *ibid*. no. 381.

42. O'Beirne to Grey, 26.11.13, no. 367. *ibid*. no. 380. (Minute by Vansittart, 1.12.13, FO/371/1847). Pichon claimed that France disliked any compensation which might entail the beginning of the partition of the Ottoman Empire. Granville to Grey, 29.11.13, no. 588, BD. *ibid*. no. 384. But Cambon, the French Ambassador in London, as Crowe noted, spoke in a different vein. Grey to Bertie, 28.11.13, no. 772. Minute by Crowe, 2.12.13, in: Granville to Grey, 29.11.13, no. 588. BD. *ibid*. no. 384. DDF. 3e serie, T.8.536, 541.

43. O'Beirne to Grey, 1.12.13, tel. no. 398. Secret. BD. *ibid*. no. 385. (Clerk's Minute, 2.12.13, FO/371/1847). Grey to Mallet, 2.12.13, tel. no. 557, BD. *ibid*. no. 387. Grey to O'Beirne, 2.12.13, tel. no. 780, BD. *ibid*. no. 388.

44. Nicolson to O'Beirne, 2.12.13, Pte. BD. *ibid*. no. 393. Nicolson to Goschen, 2.12.13, Pte. NP.371.

45. On Limpus' appointment in 1912, see: Admiralty to Foreign Office, 21.2.12, FO/371/1487/7709. Lowther to Grey, 3.3.12, no. 42. Minutes 4.3.12. Churchill to Grey, 7.3.12, *ibid*/10647. Lowther to Grey, 19.3.12, tel. no. 67. Report by Admiral Williams, 29.4.12. Minute, 30.5.12, FO/371/1487/22853.

46. Mallet to Grey, 5.12.13, Pte. BD. *ibid*. no. 405. Same to same, 6.11.13, tel. no. 550. FO/371/1847. Same to same, 3.12.13, tel. no. 599. Minutes, *ibid*. Same to same, 8.12.13, Pte. NP.371. On Churchill's view: M. Gilbert, *Companion*, Vol. II.2, p. 1780. On the monopoly to Vickers: Öst.-Ung. Auss. VII, 9070.

47. Mallet to Grey, 5.12.13, tel. no. 603. Minutes, 6.12.13, BD. *ibid*. no. 403. Grey to Mallet, 4.12.13, tel. no. 560, BD. *ibid*. no. 398. On German irritation, cf. GD.38.15439, 15449, 15452. Also: Stieve, pp. 14-15. (App. II). DDF, 3e serie. T.8.690. Fischer, 'World Policy', pp. 109-10.

48. O'Beirne to Grey, 7.12.13, tel. no. 404. Minutes, BD. *ibid*. no. 406. Nicolson to Mallet, 8.12.13, Pte. NP.371.

49. Mallet to Nicolson, 8.12.13, Pte. NP.371.

50. Mallet to Grey, 11.12.13, tel. no. 613, BD. *ibid*. no. 416.

51. O'Beirne to Nicolson, 11.12.13, Pte. BD. *ibid*. no. 418. O'Beirne to Grey, 13.12.13, tel. no. 441. Minute by Vansittart, 15.12.13, BD. *ibid*. no. 425. Same to same, 14.12.13, tel. no. 413. Minute by Vansittart, 15.12.13, BD. *ibid*. no. 429. Same to same, 9.12.13, no. 375. Minutes by Vansittart and Crowe, 15.12.13, BD. *ibid*. no. 412. CF. GD. *ibid*. 15483.

52. Nicolson to Townley, 15.12.13, Pte. NP.371. O'Beirne to Nicolson, 11.12.13, BD. *ibid*. no. 418.

53. Mallet to Grey, 12.12.13, tel. no. 617. Minute by Vansittart, BD. *ibid*. no. 419. Grey to Mallet, 12.12.13, tel. no. 577, BD. *ibid*. no. 420.

54. Mallet to Grey, 13.12.13, tel. no. 621, *ibid*. no. 426. Same to same, 14.12.13, tel. no. 623. Minute 15.12.13, *ibid*. no. 428. Same to same, 15.12.13, no. 1010. BD. *ibid*. no. 433. GD.38.15481, 15482, 15492.

55. Mallet to Grey, 10.12.13, no. 998. (Article from 5.12.13.) Minute by Vansittart, 15.12.13, FO/371/1847.

56. Limpus to Mallet, 11.12.13, Greene (Admiralty) to Crowe, 24.12.13. Minutes, 29-30.12.13, FO/371/1847/17988. GD.38.15479. Cf. P.G. Halperin, *The Mediterranean Naval Situation, 1908-1914* (Cambridge, Mass. 1971), pp. 321ff. M. Gilbert, *W.S. Churchill, Companion*, Vol. II, pp. 1631, 1800-2.

57. Goschen to Grey, 31.12.13, Pte. BD. *ibid*. no. 455. Same to same, 1.1.14,

tel. no. 1. Minute by Clerk, 2.1.14, BD. *ibid*. no. 456.

58. Mallet to Grey, 15.12.13, tel. no. 628. Minutes by Nicolson and Vansittart, 16.12.13, BD. *ibid*. no. 430. Nicolson to Goschen, 16.12.13, Pte. NP.371.
59. Grey to O'Beirne, 16.12.13, tel. no. 803. BD.*ibid*. no. 434. Buchanan to Grey, 19.12.13, tel. no. 417. Minutes by Vansittart and Crowe, 20.12.13, BD, *ibid*. no. 440. Goschen to Grey, 19.12.13, Pte. BD.*ibid*. no. 441. O'Beirne to Grey, 18.12.13, no. 384. BD.*ibid*. no. 439. Grey to Goschen, 2.1.14. Pte. BD.*ibid*. no. 457.
60. Buchanan to Grey, 8.1.14, tel. no. 6. Minutes by Grey and Nicolson, 9.1.14, BD. *ibid*. no. 465. Bertie to Grey, 11.1.14, no. 19. Confidential BD. *ibid*. no. 466. Buchanan to Grey, 8.1.14, tel. no. 6. Minutes by Grey and Nicolson, 9.1.14, BD. *ibid*. no. 465.
61. Nicolson to Hardinge, 15.1.14. Pte. NP.372. Nicolson to Goschen, 19.1.14, Pte. *ibid*. F. Stieve, *Izvolsky and the World War* (London 1926), Appendices II-III.
62. Mallet to Grey, 15.1.14, tel. no. 30. Enclosed Memorandum by Tyrrell, 15.1.14, FO/371/1847/2739. Buchanan to Nicolson, 21.1.14, Pte. BD. *ibid*. no. 469. Mallet to Grey, 24.1.14, tel. no. 57. Minute, BD. *ibid*. no. 470.
63. Nicolson to Goschen, 19.1.14, Pte. NP.372. Grey to Buchanan, 11.2.14, Pte. BD. *ibid*. no. 474. Cf. GD.38.15524.
64. Lieut.-Col. Cunliffe-Owen to Mallet, 24.3.14, in: Mallet to Grey, 24.3.14, no. 201. Minute by Russell, 30.3.14, FO/371/1847. Lieut.-Col. Russell to Goschen in: Goschen to Grey, 28.3.14, no. 134, *ibid*. U. Trumpener, 'Liman von Sanders and the German-Ottoman Alliance', *Journal of Contemporary History* (1966), pp. 179-92. Already in April 1913, Wangenheim wrote: 'There cannot be an anti-German Government if the Army is controlled by us.' GD.38.15439, p. 200. Cf. Fischer, 'World Policy ...', pp. 114-16.
65. Grey to Dering, 29.10.13, no. 262. BD. *ibid*. no. 154. GD.34.I.12645.
66. Mallet to Grey, 4.11.13, Pte. GP.80. Same to same, 25.11.13, Pte. BD. *ibid*. no. 165.
67. Same to same, 17.12.13, Pte. BD. *ibid*. no. 174.
68. Mallet to Grey, 17.12.13, no. 1018. BD. *ibid*. no. 173. Minutes, 23.12.13, FO/371/1847.
69. Mallet to Grey, 16.12.13, no. 1011. BD. *ibid*. no. 172. Minutes, 23.12.13. FO/371/1804.
70. Grey to Mallet, 23.12.13, Pte. BD. *ibid*. no. 180. Same to same, 24.12.13, Pte. tel. BD. *ibid*. no. 181. Mallet to Grey, 24.12.13, Pte. GP.80.
71. Same to same, 24.12.13, no. 1034, FO/371/1805.
72. Admiralty to Foreign Office, 10.12.12, FO/371/1522/52889. Grey's earlier comments in Lowther to Grey, 7.6.12, no. 514. Minute, 11.6.13. Admiralty to Foreign Office, 10.7.13. Confidential. FO/371/1781/31917. Grey to Lowther, 24.7.13. no. 229, *ibid*.
73. Mallet to Grey, 14.12.13, tel. no. 626. Minute by Crowe, 15.12.13, FO/371/1522. Same to same, 24.12.13, no. 1030. Minute, 31.12.13, *ibid*. Same to same, 31.12.13, tel. no. 646. *ibid*. Nicolson to Mallet, 8.12.13, Pte. NP.371. Nicolson to Goschen, 16.12.13, Pte. *ibid*. de Bunsen to Grey, 1.1.14, no. 1. Conf. Minute by Norman, 5.1.14, BD. *ibid*. no. 188. Halperin, *op. cit.*, pp. 330ff.
74. Mallet to Grey, 27.10.13, tel. no. 525. FO/371/1522.
75. Mallet to Grey, 29.12.13, no. 1048. Confidential. BD. *ibid*. no. 185.
76. Mallet to Nicolson, 31.12.13, Pte. NP.371.
77. Communication from Tewfik, 30.12.13. Minutes by Crowe and Grey, BD. *ibid*. no. 186.

78. Minute by Crowe, 21.1.14, in: Mallet to Grey, 7.1.14, no. 10. FO/371/2112. de Bunsen to Grey, 12.1.14, no. 14. Confidential. BD. *ibid*. no. 202. Minute by Crowe, 23.1.14, FO/371/2112.

79. Same to same, 13.1.14, no. 15. Minutes, 21.1.14, *ibid*. Same to same, 14.1.14, no. 18. Minute by Russell, 19.1.14, *ibid*. Grey to Mallet, 26.1.14, no. 52. BD. *ibid*. no. 213.

80. Mallet to Grey, 24.1.14, tel. no. 54. Confidential. Minute by Vansittart, 26.1.14, BD. *ibid*. no. 329. Same to same, 20.1.14, no. 31. FO/371/2112. Grey to Mallet, 29.1.14, no. 57. BD. *ibid*. no. 219. Mallet to Grey, 26.1.14, tel. no. 62. Minutes, 27.1.14, BD. *ibid*. no. 212. (Minutes by Vansittart and Clerk, FO/371/ 2112.) Same to same, 28.1.14, Pte. BD. *ibid*. no. 218.

81. Mallet to Grey, 4.2.14, tel. no. 78. Minutes, 3.2.14. BD. *ibid*. no. 226. Nicolson to Goschen, 2.2.14, Pte. NP.372.

82. Mallet to Grey, 4.2.14, no. 70. Minute by Vansittart, 10.2.14, FO/371/2113. De Bunsen to Grey, 4.2.14, tel. no. 19. Minutes, 5.2.14, *ibid*.

83. 'The one thing that I dread in this country is another outbreak of war in which Turkey should be involved – especially at the present moment when the Mahomedan community in India is gradually quieting down and beginning to realize that they have been making fools of themselves.' Hardinge to Nicolson, 5.2.14, Pte. NP.372. The Germans understood this British anxiety. GD.36.II. 14290. Cf. Öst.-Ung. Auss. VII, 9275.

84. Rodd to Grey, 30.1.14, no. 42. Very confidential. BD. *ibid*. no. 221. Minute by Crowe, 10.2.14, FO/371/2113.

85. Grey to Mallet, 9.2.14, Pte. BD. *ibid*. no. 240.

86. Crawford to Tyrrell, 5.2.14. Minutes, 10-11.2.14, FO/371/2114/6089. Mallet to Grey, 6.1.14, tel. no. 10. Minutes, *ibid*. Grey to Mallet, 7.1.14, tel. no. 9, *ibid*.

87. On Jemal's appreciation of Mallet's honesty, see: Djemal Pasha, *Memories*, p. 100.

88. Mallet to Nicolson, 17.2.14, Pte. NP.372. Mallet to Grey, 18.2.14, Pte. GP.80. A week later he claimed that the Germans acquired influence because they were 'consistent'. Mallet to Nicolson, 24.2.14, Pte. NP.372.

89. Mallet to Nicolson, 24.2.14, Pte. *ibid*.

90. Mallet to Grey, 10.3.14, Pte. GP.80. (Partly in BD. *ibid*. no. 257.) Mallet to Grey, 11.3.14, Pte. *ibid*. Same to same, 2.3.14, tel. no. 1512. FO/371/2114. Mallet to Nicolson, 10.3.14, Pte. NP.373.

91. Grey to Mallet, 18.3.14, Pte. GP.80. (Partly in BD. *ibid*. no. 262.) Mallet to Grey, 10.3.14, tel. no. 152. FO/371/2114. Grey to Mallet, 10.3.14, no. 126. *Hansard*, Vol. LIX, cols. 2191-5. On Sir E. Cassel, cf. M. Kent, 'Agent of an Empire?' *op. cit.*

92. Mallet to Grey, 24.3.14, no. 198. Same to same, 27.3.14, no. 206. FO/371/ 2114.

93. Mallet to Grey, 23.3.14, Pte. GP.80.

94. Mallet to Nicolson, 25.3.14, Pte. NP.373.

95. Nicolson to Mallet, 2.3.14, Pte. NP.372. Nicolson to Goschen, 30.3.14, Pte. NP.373. Grey to Mallet, 11.6.14. Pte. GP.80.

96. Mallet to Nicolson, 5.4.14, Pte. NP.373. Nicolson to Mallet, 2.3.14, Pte. NP.372. Nicolson to Townley, 7.4.14, Pte. NP.373.

97. Memorandum by Benckendorff, 21.5.14, Minutes, 24-7.5. FO/371/2114/ 23121. Grey to Buchanan, 10.6.14, no. 216, *ibid*. Grey's memorandum, 9.6.14 (written by Crowe). Memorandum by de Etter, 1.6.14. Minute by Crowe, 3.6.14, *ibid*/25026. Cf. GD.36.II, 14587.

98. Buchanan to Grey, 2.1.14, tel. no. 2. Minute by Clerk, 3.1.14, FO/371/2112.

Mallet to Grey, 4.1.14, tel. no. 7. Conf. Minutes by Vansittart and Clerk, 5.1.14, *ibid*. Mallet to Grey, 31.12.13, no. 1052. Minutes, 6.1.14, *ibid*.

99. Mallet to Grey, 21.1.14, no. 356. Minutes, 27-28.1.14, FO/371/2127.

100. The contract was considered so 'desirable for political reasons' that the Foreign Office reassured Limpus that his chances of promotion in England would not suffer, and the Admiralty agreed to his request to retain six officers for another six months. Mallet to Grey, 26.2.14, tel. no. 126. Foreign Office to Admiralty, 6.3.14, FO/371/2130/8647/14. Mallet to Grey, 8.3.14, tel. no. 148. Same to same, 10.3.14, no. 159. (Enclosure: Said Halim to Mallet, 5.3.14.) Mallet to Grey, 12.3.14, tel. no. 163. Minutes. Admiralty to Foreign Office, 25.3.14, *ibid*/13437. Mallet to Grey, 19.4.14, tel. no. 249. Admiralty to Foreign Office, 21.4.14, *ibid*./17638.

101. Mallet to Grey, 20.5.14, no. 357. Minute by Crowe, 26.5.14, confirmed by Nicolson and Grey, FO/371/2114.

102. *Ibid*.

103. The Anglo-Ottoman Association to the Foreign Office, 24.1.14. Minute by Russell, 26.1.14, FO/371/2127/3721. Same to same, 28.1.14. Minute by Crowe, 31.1.14, FO/371/2128/4327. The Foreign Office refused to allow Lt.-Col. Hawker of the Ottoman Gendarmerie to become the Vice-President of the Association. The President was Lord Mowbray and Stourton: Vice-President F. H. O'Donnell, a former nationalist MP, and included: Lamington, T. Barclay, H. Cox, A. Herbert, W. Guinness and E.N. Bennet. All these names, as Crowe commented, did not inspire confidence since they were associated with 'political fads or extremes.' On the Association's objects see: Same to same, 20.2.14, *ibid*./8171. Int.-Bez. II. 215. Öst.-Ung. Auss. VII. 9551.

104. Buchanan to Grey, 17.5.14, tel. no. 114. Minute by Crowe, 18.5.14, FO/371/2114. Buchanan to Nicolson, 14.5.14, Pte. NP.374. Cf. with the report of the German Ambassador, GD.36.II. 14595. Int.-Bez. I.3. 26, 27.

105. Marling to Grey, 21.9.13, tel. no. 475. Minute, 22.9.13, FO/371/1844. Grey to Rodd, 22.9.13, tel. no. 271, *ibid*. Dering to Grey, 15.10.13, tel. no. 177. Minute by Crowe, 16.10.13, *ibid*. Dering to Grey, 15.10.13, tel. no. 178. Minutes, 16.10.13, BD.X.II. no. 151. Grey to Bertie, 22.10.13, no. 629. BD. *ibid*. no. 152.

106. Rodd to Grey, 6.6.12, no. 377. Conf. Same to same, 6.12.13, tel. no. 218. BD. *ibid*. no. 167. (Minutes, 8.12.13, FO/371/1844.) Grey to Rodd, 11.12.13, tel. no. 366. BD. *ibid*. no. 168. Mallet to Grey, 16.12.13, no. 1011, *ibid*. no. 172. (Minute by Crowe, 24.12.13, FO/371/1804.) Rodd to Grey, 11.12.13, tel. no. 220. Same to same, 13.12.13, tel. no. 222. Minutes, 15.12.13, *ibid*. no. 170. Same to same, 14.12.13, no. 348. Minute by Norman, 29.12.13. Nicolson to Townley, 15.12.13, Pte. NP.371. GD.36. II. 14214, 14237.

107. Mallet to Grey, 29.12.13, no. 643. Very confidential. Minutes, 30.12.13, FO/371/1844. Same to same, 29.12.13, no. 1048. Confidential. BD. *ibid*. no. 185.

108. Rodd to Grey, 11.1.14, no. 18. Minutes, 21.1.14, FO/371/2112. Bertie to Grey, 9.9.13, tel. no. 126. Minutes, 10.9.13, BD. *ibid*. no. 147. Nicolson to Mallet, 10.11.13, Pte. NP.372.

109. Mallet to Grey, 28.1.14, tel. no. 65. Conf. Minute, 28.1.14, FO/371/2112.

110. Nicolson took a more balanced view, although he too had doubts about Italy's sincerity: '... we cannot forget [he wrote to Mallet] that we were equally emphatic in regard to the evacuation of Egypt, and we are still there and likely to remain there for some generations, unless we are turned out by force.' He now saw the possibility of an agreement between the Smyrna-Aidin Railway

Co. and M. Nogara the Italian representative. Nicolson to Mallet, 19.1.14, Pte. NP.372. Grey to Rodd, 28.1.14, no. 33. Confidential. BD. *ibid*. no. 217.

111. Mallet to Grey, 2.2.14, tel. no. 78. BD. *ibid*. no. 226.

112. Mallet to Grey, 1.2.14, tel. no. 72. Minutes, 2-3.2.14. Minutes by Crowe, FO/371/2117. Nicolson and Grey, 31.1.14, FO/371/2117. Grey to Mallet, 16.2.14, no. 80. *ibid*. Cf. DDF. 3e ser. T.9. no. 327.

113. Mallet to Grey, 10.2.14, tel. no. 94. BD.X.ii. no. 199. Same to same, 21.2.14, tel. no. 118, FO/371/2117. Mallet to Grey, 28.2.14, tel. no. 129. Same to same, 4.3.14, tel. no. 139. Minute, 5.3.14. *ibid*.

114. Mallet to Grey, 4.3.14, no. 145. Minute by Crowe, 11.3.14, confirmed by Grey, *ibid*. Same to same, 10.3.14, Pte. GP.80.

115. Convention initialled between the Smyrna-Aidin Co. and the Ottoman Government, 7.5.14. Minute by Crowe, 1.5.14, FO/371/2119/20441. Final signature, 29.7.14, *ibid*./34983. Agreement between Smyrna-Aidin Co. and the Italian Syndicate, 19.5.14, *ibid*./22739. Mallet to Grey, 2.7.14, tel. no. 404. Minute by Parker, FO/371/2119. Grey to Rodd, 23.7.14, no. 211, *ibid*. Rodd to Grey, 18.7.14, no. 270. Minute by Crowe, 27.7.14, *ibid*. Beaumont to Grey, 31.7.14, no. 546, *ibid*.

116. This included (a) the revenues of the local Evkafs to be utilized by the local Moslem councils; (b) local military service; (c) Arabic to be the medium of instruction in schools in areas where Arabic-speaking people were the majority; (d) all officials in the Arab provinces to be acquainted with Arabic. Marling to Grey, 25.9.13, no. 818. FO/371/1845.

117. Mallet to Grey, 29.10.13, no. 904. Minute, 11.11.13, FO/371/1848. (Also Clerk's remark on Fitzmaurice's participation in writing this letter: 'pure Fitzmaurice', he commented at one point.)

118. Mallet to Grey, 21.1.14, tel. no. 117. Very confidential. BD.X.ii. p. 833. Same to same, 24.2.14. no. 117. Minute by Russell, 3.3.14, BD. *ibid* pp. 833-4. Grey to Mallet, 16.3.14, no. 135, *ibid*. Merchants of Cairo to Grey, 8.3.14. Minute by Russell, 10.3.14, 4. Mallet to Grey, 9.3.14, tel. no. 153. Confidential, *ibid*.

119. Kitchener to Grey, 6.2.14, no. 22. Secret, BD. *ibid*. p. 827. Same to same, 14.2.14, tel. no. 7. Confidential, *ibid*. Same to same, 21.3.14. Minute by Russell, 21.3.14, *ibid*. p. 830. Same to same, 23.3.14, tel. no. 176. Minute by Russell, Same to same, 2.4.14, tel. no. 213. E. Kedourie, *England and the Middle East, 1914-21* (London 1956), pp. 47-50. id. *In the Anglo-Arab Labyrinth: The McMahon-Husayn Correspondence and Its Interpretations, 1914-1939* (Cambridge 1976), Ch. 1.

120. Busch, *op. cit.*, pp. 340-5.

121. India Office to Foreign Office, 9.2.14. Enclosure 4. Memo by Major A.P. Trevor, Political Agent, Bahrein and Captain W. Shakespear, Political Agent, Koweit. FO/371/2123/6117. Foreign Office to India Office, 7.3.14, Enclosure, Minute by Parker, and Grey, 7-8.3.14, *ibid*/10244. Foreign Office's Memo concerning HMG's attitude to Ibn Saud, 9.3.14, made by A. Hirtzel, P. Cox and A. Parker to Hakki, *ibid*/10596. See also: G. Troeller, *The Birth of Saudi-Arabia: Britain and the Birth of the House of Saud* (London, Frank Cass 1976).

122. India Office to Foreign Office, 4.4.14, FO/371/2123/15023.

123. Foreign Office to India Office, 6.4.14 (drafted by Clerk and Crowe), FO/371/2123. Mallet to Grey, 4.5.14, tel. no. 276, *ibid*. Foreign Office to India Office, 4.6.14, FO/371/2124/23753.

124. Mallet to Grey, 12.5.14, no. 335. Minutes by Parker, Crowe and Grey, 18-19.5.14, FO/371/2124. Foreign Office to India Office, 4.6.14, *ibid*./23753.

125. Parker emphasized that he always strongly opposed the contacts between

British Political Agents in the Gulf and Ibn Saud. Mallet to Grey, 18.3.14, no.
193. Minute by Parker, 31.1.14, BD. *ibid.* pp. 827-8. Same to same, 23.3.14,
Pte. GP.80.
126. Same to same, 15.5.14, no. 346. Minutes, 22.5.14, FO/371/2124.
127. Memo by Lt.-Col. H. Jacob: A Plea for a New Policy in the Yemen. Minute by
Crowe, 30.5.14, FO/371/2134/22608.
128. Mallet to Grey, 23.6.14, tel. no. 376. Minutes. Same to same, 29.6.14, tel. no.
391. Same to same, 11.7.14, tel. no. 306.
129. Fitzmaurice to Tyrrell, 8.5.13, Pte. GP.80. He admitted to following here
an idea put forward by H.H. Johnston, 'The Final Solution of the Eastern
Question', *Nineteenth Century and After* (March, 1913), p. 544.
130. Mallet to Grey, 21.12.13, no. 1023. Minutes, 29-30.12.13, FO/371/2136.
131. Hough (Jaffa), 29.4.14, no. 33. McGregor (Jerusalem), 30.4.14, no. 31. in:
FO/371/2136. Mallet to Grey, 12.5.14, no. 329 (signed by Russell and Crowe,
19.5.14), FO/371/2136. See also: N. Mandel, 'Turks, Arabs and Jewish Immigration into Palestine, 1882-1914', *St. Antony's Papers, No. 17* (Oxford 1965),
pp. 77-108. Y. Ro'i, 'The Zionist Attitude to the Arabs 1908-14', *Middle
Eastern Studies* (1968), pp. 198-242. N.J. Mandel, *The Arabs and Zionism
Before World War I* (University of California Press 1976).
132. Sokolow to Grey, 7.7.14. Minutes, 9-10.7.14. Crowe to Sokolow, 14.7.14,
FO/371/2136/30841.
133. Mallet to Grey, 6.7.14, no. 497. FO/371/2136. Mallet to Grey, 1.7.14, Pte.
GP.80.
134. Beaumont to Grey, 20.7.14, no. 520. Minute by Russell, 28.7.14, FO/371/
2136.
135. Nicolson to Buchanan, 30.6.14, Pte. NP.374. Same to same, 14.7.14, Pte.
NP.375. (Partly in BD.X.ii. App. I.) Nicolson to de Bunsen, 6.7.14, Pte. *ibid.*
Nicolson to Buchanan, 28.7.14, Pte. BD. *ibid.* no. 239. Cf. *The Outbreak of
War*, German Documents collected by K. Kautsky (N.Y. 1924), nos. 45, 71,
256. U. Trumpener, *op. cit., passim.*

CHAPTER 7

1. A considerable number of the documents relating to this chapter were published
(sometimes in full, but without the minutes) in, Miscellaneous nos. 13.14
(1914), Cds. 7628, 7716. Documents relating to the *Goeben* and *Breslau* affair
can be found in: E.W.R. Lumby (ed.), *Policy and Operations in the Mediterranean, 1912-1914* (London 1970), pp. 431-62.
2. Ahmad, 'Great Britain's Relations ...' *op. cit.*, pp. 323-4. Cunningham, 'The
Wrong Horse? ...' *St. Antony's Papers*, no. 17 (1965), pp. 56-76. See also:
Nicolson's and Grey's constant praise quoted in Chapter 6. But see: P.P.
Graves, *Briton and Turk, passim.* Sir E. Pears, *Forty Years ...* pp. 344ff. Ryan
defended Mallet but could not resist writing: 'If he had a fault it was that he was
too mercurial, oscillating between the deepest depression and comparative
optimisim.' Ryan, *op. cit.*, pp. 96-7, 108-10. Ryan was Second Dragoman and
later Acting Chief Dragoman at Constantinople. For recent references to
Mallet's high reputation, see: Z.S. Steiner, *The Foreign Office and Foreign
Policy, 1898-1914* (Cambridge 1969), pp. 105-6. Z.A.B. Zeman, *A Diplomatic
History of the First World War* (London 1970), pp. 51-3. But not D. Dakin, *The
Unification of Greece, 1770-1923* (London 1972), p. 241.
3. Graves, *op. cit., passim.* Cunningham, *op. cit.*, p. 72. Magnus, *op. cit.*, pp. 224-6.
The Times, 24.8.17. Mallet's apologia, 27.8.17, FO/371/3060. See also an

adaptation of Mallet's arguments, the apologia of 1917, in F. Cunliffe-Owen, 'The Entry of Turkey into the War: The Action of H.M. Embassy', *National Review* (November, 1931), pp.611-22. Grey, *Twenty-Five Years* (London 1935), Vol. III, pp.127-8. House of Commons Debates, 21 October 1915, 5th Series, Vol. LXXIV, cols. 1970-1. H. Nicolson, *Lord Carnock* (London 1930), p.428. For the German Alliance, see: Trumpener, *op. cit.,passim*. Howard, *The Partition of Turkey, passim*. F.G. Weber, *Eagles on the Crescent: Germany, Austria, and the Diplomacy of the Turkish Alliance 1914-1918* (Cornell 1970), pp.60ff.

4. Y.T. Kurat, 'How Turkey Drifted into World War I', *Studies in International History*, eds. K. Bourne and D.C. Watt (London 1967) p.293. Ahmad curiously denies, without any proof from Ottoman sources, the existence of a pro-German faction, claiming that the main body was the pro-Entente faction. Kurat has made clear the prominence of the pro-German faction, *op. cit.*, p.297. Ahmad, *op. cit.*, p324. See also: D.A. Rustow, 'Enver Pasha', *Encyclopedia of Islam*, II, p.699. Enver told Wangenheim on 22 July: '... a small minority in the Committee ... wanted an alliance with Russia and France ...' 'The majority of the Committee, headed by the Grand Vizier with Talaat Bey, Halil and himself, did not want to become vassals of Russia and was convinced that the Triplice was stronger than the Entente and would be the victors in a world war ...' quoted by Albertini, *The Origins of the World War of 1914*, III, pp.611-12. Djavid, the Minister of Finance, presented the only real objections to Enver's policy. When informed of the alliance on 1 August he 'vigorously' argued against this 'fatal mistake'. Trumpener's claims, that Germany was not predominant at the Porte and that Enver acted only as a result of 'Ottoman self-interest', are not very convincing, *op. cit.*, pp. 16-20. This view has been recently repeated by H.S.W. Corrigan, 'German-Turkish Relations and the Outbreak of War in 1914: A Re-Assessment', *Past and Present*, (1967), 144-152. Cf. Also: F.G. Weber, *op. cit.*

5. But note that neither Giers the Russian Ambassador, nor Bompard the French Ambassador, who were both at the time in Constantinople, had any idea of what was going on between the Germans and the Ottomans. *The Outbreak of War, op. cit.*, nos. 117, 141, 256, 285, 320, 411, 508, 517, 547, 733.

6. Nicolson's interview with Tewfik, 1.8.14. Grey to Beaumont, 6.8.14, no. 522. FO/371/2137. Same to same, 3.8.14, tel. no. 333. *ibid*. The Porte had in fact intended to use them in the struggle between the Entente and their enemies, and on 1 August Enver and Talaat had suggested to Berlin that they transfer the *Sultan Osman* to a German port. Trumpener, p.24. This fact has been over-looked by R.R. James, *Church – A Study in Failure* (London 1970), p.58, no. 1, and by Z.Z.B. Zeman, *op. cit.*, p.51. Cf. Churchill's biography, *Companion to Vol. II*, Part 2, p.1992. M. Gilbert, *W.S. Churchill*, Vol. III, 1914-1916 (London 1971), pp.191ff.

7. Beaumont to Grey, 3.8.14, tel. no. 476. FO/371/2137. Same to same, 7.8.14, tel. no. 493, *ibid*. Grey to Beaumont, 4.8.14, tel. no. 337. *ibid*.

8. A suggestion which Grey rejected for fear that the British Naval Mission, if withdrawn, would be replaced by a German Mission. Beaumont to Grey, 7.8.14, no. 495, *ibid*. Grey to Beaumont, 8.8.14, tel. no. 345, *ibid*.

9. Beaumont to Grey, 6.8.14, tel. no. 489, *ibid*. Same to same, 7.8.14, tel. no. 492, *ibid*. *The Outbreak of War, op. cit.*, nos. 751, 775, 795.

10. A.J. Marder, *From the Dreadnought to Scapa Flow*, Vol. II (1965), pp.20-41. Lumby, *op. cit.*, pp.131ff. On 4 August, Enver ordered that German and Austrian warships be allowed to enter the Straits without hindrance. *The Outbreak of War, op. cit.*, no. 852. U. Trumpener, 'The Escape of the Goeben and

Breslau: A Reassessment', *Canadian Journal of History* (1971).
11. Armstrong and Whitworth to Foreign Office, 11.8.14, Minute, FO/371/2137/ 38132.
12. Minute by G.R. Clerk, 11.8.14. Minutes by Crowe and Nicolson,*ibid*./39189.
13. Kurat, pp.303-4. Grey to Beaumont, 13.8.14, no. 524. FO/371/2138. Tewfik to Grey, 13.8.14, Minute, FO/371/2138/38756. Beaumont to Grey, 13.8.14, tel. no. 536. Minutes, 14.8.14, by Oliphant, Clerk and Crowe, FO/371/2138.
14. Beaumont to Grey, 15.8.14, tel. no. 545, *ibid*. Same to same, 15.8.14, tel. no. 546, *ibid*.
15. Beaumont to Grey, 15.8.14, no. 564. Encl. Col. Cunliffe-Owen; Military Attaché, 13.8.14, no. 28, *ibid*.
16. Churchill to Beaumont, 15.8.14, Pte. tel. GP.80. Cf. Gilbert, pp.194-5. Mallet reported that Enver was 'very much pleased' with Churchill's message. Mallet to Grey, 18.8.14, tel. no. 554, FO/371/2138.
17. Quoted by Taylor, *The Struggle for Mastery in Europe* (Oxford 1954), p.534.
18. Beaumont to Grey, 16.8.14, tel. no. 547, FO/371/2138. Grey to Roberts etc., 17.8.14, tel. no. 21, *ibid*. Grey to Beaumont, 17.8.14, tel. no. 382, *ibid*.
19. Mallet to Grey, 17.8.14, tel. no. 555,*ibid*. Grey to Mallet, 18.8.14, tel. no. 391, *ibid*.
20. Minute by Crowe: Situation in Turkey, 16.8.14, *ibid*/40391.
21. Grey to Bertie, 15.8.14, no. 533. (Repeated to Buchanan, 15.8.14, no. 316.) At a Cabinet meeting on 17 August, Crewe and Kitchener expressed some anxiety as to India and Egypt. They preferred that aggression would come from the Ottoman side 'if possible'. C.J. Smith, 'Great Britain and the 1914-1915 Straits Agreement with Russia: The British Promise of November 1914', *American Historical Review* (1965), p.1018. It is interesting to note that the Germans had intended to use Pan-Islamic propaganda against Britain immediately after the German-Ottoman alliance was signed. *The Outbreak of War, op. cit.*, nos. 751, 876.
22. Mallet to Grey, 18.8.14, tel. no. 557, FO/371/2138. Same to same, 18.8.14, tel. no. 560, *ibid*. On the division in the Cabinet, see: Gilbert, p.195.
23. Mallet to Grey, 20.8.14, tel. no. 572. FO/371/2138. Same to same, 21.8.14, tel. no. 310,*ibid*. Same to same, 20.8.14, tel. no. 574,*ibid*. Same to same, 20.8.14, tel. no. 575, *ibid*. Same to same, 21.8.14, tel. no. 583, *ibid*.
24. Minute to tel. no. 557, 19.8.14, FO/371/2138. Gilbert, p.196.
25. Minute by Parker, 20.8.14, Urgent. Minutes BD.X.ii. p.420. Ed. Note.
26. Hobhouse recorded Grey's views on 21 August: '... he [Grey] told that there was an increasing struggle between pro- and anti-Germans. He thought the pro-Germans would win because while the others threatened Enver performed assassinations ...' E. David (ed.), *Inside Asquith's Cabinet*, p.183.
27. Buchanan to Grey, 21.8.14, tel. no. 311. Minute, 22.8.14, FO/371/2138. Mallet to Grey, 21.8.14, tel. no. 591. Minute, 22.8.14, *ibid*.
28. Mallet to Grey, 23.8.14, no. 599. Same to same, 23.8.14, tel. no. 596, *ibid*. Beaumont to Grey, 13.8.14, no. 560. Confidential. Minutes, *ibid*.
29. Mallet to Grey, 23.8.14, tel. no. 602, *ibid*.
30. Mallet to Grey, 25.8.14, tel. no. 617. Minute, 26.8.14, *ibid*. Grey to Mallet, 26.8.14, tel. no. 435,*ibid*. Parker had convinced the Foreign Office that granting economic freedom to the Porte would have no real influence on the question of Ottoman neutrality. No concessions should be made to them without a *quid pro quo*. Mallet to Grey, 26.8.14, tel. no. 620. Minutes, 27.8.14, *ibid*.
31. Same to same, 26.8.14, tel. no. 628. FO/371/2138. Same to same, 27.8.14, tel. no. 632,*ibid*. Grey to Mallet, 24.8.14, tel. no. 438, *ibid*. The MilitaryAttaché opposed the forcing of the Dardanelles in favour of a landing in the Persian Gulf

or Syria. Mallet to Grey, 27.8.14, tel. no. 630. *ibid.* Gilbert, pp. 197-9.

32. Mallet to Grey, 27.8.14, tel. no. 634, FO/371/2138.

33. Mallet to Grey, 28.8.14, tel. no. 639, Minute, 29.8.14, *ibid.*

34. India Office to Foreign Office, 26.8.14. Minutes by Clerk and Grey, *ibid./* 43829. Foreign Office's letter for publication in India. Hardinge to Chirol, 19.8.14, Pte. HP.93. Same to same, 27.8.14, Pte. *ibid.* On the other hand, Hardinge reported that the Indian Moslems urged the Porte to be strictly neutral. Hardinge to Crewe, 13.8.14, Pte. C/22. CP.

35. Mallet to Grey, 27.8.14, tel. no. 635. Minutes, 28.8.14, *ibid.* Barclay to Grey, 27.8.14, tel. no. 52, *ibid.* Bax-Ironside to Grey, 28.8.14, tel. no. 70, *ibid.*

36. Mallet to Grey, 28.8.14, tel. no. 642, *ibid.* Grey to Mallet, 29.8.14, tel. no. 461, *ibid.* Same to same, 29.8.14, tel. no. 462, *ibid.* The British were suspected long before by the Germans and Austrians for their willingness to annex 'Arabia', e.g., Öst.-Ung. Auss. VIII. 10674. Also: Crewe to Hardinge, 14.8.14, Pte. C/24. CP.

37. Grey to Washington, 31.8.14, tel. no. 370. FO/371/2138. Grey to Mallet, 31.8.14, tel. no. 473, *ibid.*

38. Mallet to Grey, 30.8.14, tel. no. 653, *ibid.*

39. Mallet to Grey, 31.8.14, tel. no. 658, *ibid.*

40. Mallet to Grey, 1.9.14, tel. no. 663, FO/371/2139. Same to same, 1.9.14, tel. no. 672. Confidential. *ibid.* Same to same, 1.9.14, tel. no. 661, *ibid.*

41. Hirtzel to Clerk, 31.8.14, Minutes, *ibid.* Foreign Office to India Office, 1.9.14, Secret. *ibid/*44923. In Egypt, Cheetham thought he was following the proper line when he sent one of his intelligence officers to tell Aziz Ali that he had the 'highest' authority to inform him that Britain could not support the idea of a 'United Arabian State' with money and armaments since it was 'most inopportune'. However, Kitchener minuted: 'All depends on how Turkey acts ... If Turkey breaks out action in Arabia under our auspices would naturally follow.' Cheetham to Grey, 24.8.14, no. 143. Secret Minute. 5.9.14, FO/371/2139.

42. Mallet to Grey, 2.9.14, tel. no. 679, *ibid.* Grey to Mallet, 4.9.14, tel. no. 493, *ibid.*

43. Mallet to Grey, 3.9.14, tel. no. 685, *ibid.* On 1 September, too, Kitchener and Churchill ordered preparations for military and naval operations for the seizure of Gallipoli. Gilbert, *op. cit.*, pp. 202-3.

44. Mallet to Grey, 4.9.14, tel. no. 692, *ibid.* For a fuller discussion of the Indian point of view see: S.A. Cohen, *op. cit.*, pp. 336ff.

45. Mallet to Grey, 5.9.14, tel. no. 707. FO/371/2141. Mallet to Grey, 6.9.14, tel. no. 710, *ibid.* Mallet did not know that on 4 September, Grey and Churchill had committed themselves to Greece. They instructed Admiral Kerr, the Head of the British Mission, to commence 'strictly private and secret' discussions with the Greek authorities as to the correct policy against the Porte in the event of war, but not to provoke the latter in the meantime. On earlier contacts with Greece, Smith, pp. 1019-20. Gilbert, p. 204. Grey to Elliot, 4.9.14, tel. no. 171. Secret. FO/371/3141. First Lord of the Admiralty to Elliot, 4.9.14, tel. no. 170. Most Secret. *ibid.*

46. Mallet to Grey, 6.9.14, tel. no. 715, confidential, *ibid.*

47. Mallet to Grey, 7.9.14, tel. no. 717, *ibid.* Grey to Mallet, 8.9.14, tel. no. 521, *ibid.* Mallet to Grey, 8.9.14, tel. no. 727, *ibid.*

48. Churchill initially rejected Mallet's views: '... if Mallet thinks he is dealing with a Government amenable to argument, persuasion, and proof of good faith, he is dreaming', quoted by Gilbert, pp. 207-8.

49. Grey to Mallet, 9.9.14, tel. no. 538. Secret and Urgent, FO/371/2141. Mallet to

Grey, 10.9.14, tel. no. 738. urgent, *ibid*. Same to same, 11.9.14, Pte. tel. confidential. GP.80. Same to same, 11.9.14 (third letter of the same day), *ibid*. Same to same, 12.9.14, tel. no. 756, FO/371/2141. Grey to Mallet, 12.9.14, tel. no. 556. Secret, *ibid*. Same to same, 12.9.14, Pte. tel. GP.80.

50. Mallet to Grey, 13.9.14, tel. no. 766. Minute by Clerk, 14.9.14, FO/371/2141. Grey to Mallet, 14.9.14, tel. no. 558, *ibid*. Same to same, 15.9.14, tel. no. 782. Confidential. Minutes, 16.9.14, *ibid*. Mallet seemed to be encouraged by the fact that Giers too was trying his best to keep the Porte neutral. Cf. Lowe and Dockrill, *op. cit.*, p. 382, n. 79.

51. Mallet to Grey, 9.9.14, tel. no. 732, FO/371/2141. Same to same, 9.9.14, tel. no. 735. Minute by Clerk, *ibid*. Same to same, 9.9.14, tel. no. 736, *ibid*. Same to same, 10.9.14, tel. no. 741, *ibid*. Same to same, 12.9.14, tel. no. 763, *ibid*. Same to same, 14.9.14, tel. no. 770. Minutes, 15.9.14, *ibid*. The Capitulations had been first granted to Britain by the Sultan in 1675, and up to 1809 they were unilateral. In that year they were reaffirmed by the Treaty of the Dardanelles and acquired a bilateral character. Minute by Clerk, 12.9.14, in: Mallet to Grey, 11.9.14, tel. no. 754, *ibid*.

52. Mallet to Grey, 14.9.14, tel. no. 770, *ibid*; and Mallet to Grey, 15.9.14, tel. no. 785. Very Confidential, *ibid*.

53. Minute, 15.9.14, and Grey to Mallet, 15.9.14, tel. no. 560, *ibid*.

54. Minutes, 16.9.14. Grey to Mallet, 16.9.14, tel. no. 562, *ibid*.

55. Trumpener, *op. cit.*, pp. 39-44.

56. Mallet to Grey, 17.9.14, tel. no. 801. Minutes, 18.9.14, FO/371/2141. Same to same, 18.9.14, tel. no. 807, *ibid*.

57. Grey to Mallet, 23.9.14, tel. no. 581, *ibid*. Cf. Smith, *op. cit.*, p. 1023. K. Robbins, 'British Diplomacy and Bulgaria, 1914-15', *Slavonic and East European Review* (1971), p. 568.

58. Churchill to Grey, 23.9.14, Pte. GP.88, quoted also in: Churchill, *The World Crisis, 1911-14*, pp. 492-3. Cf. Crewe's impression: '... Louis Mallet must have been the most unenviable man in the public service these last two months. He seems to have done very well, speaking with due plainness to the Grand Vizier ...' Crewe to Hardinge, 2.10.14, Pte. C/24. CP. Also: Same to same, 29.10.14, Pte. *ibid*. When on 1 November Churchill welcomed Enver's coup, Grey replied that Churchill 'was always wanting to drag the whole world into the quarrel.' E. David, ed., *Inside Asquith's Cabinet*, p. 194 (1.11.14); Also p. 183.

59. Mallet to Grey, 23.9.14, tel. no. 840, FO/371/2141. Same to same, 23.9.14, tel. no. 841. Minutes, 24.9.14, *ibid*. Grey to Mallet, 24.9.14, tel. no. 586, *ibid*. Mallet to Grey, 26.9.14, Pte. GP.80. Same to same, 27.9.14, tel. no. 875. Minutes by Clerk and Nicolson, 28.9.14, FO/371/2141. Same to same, 28.9.14, tel. no. 884. Minutes, *ibid*. Same to same, 21.9.14, tel. no. 823, *ibid*. A Territorial Division was expected in Egypt on 26th. Minute by Kitchener, 22.9.14, *ibid*. G.P.O. to Foreign Office, 20.9.14, Minute by Oliphant, FO/371/2142/5125. Mallet to Grey, 22.9.14, tel. no. 830. FO/371/2142. Same to same, 23.9.14, tel. no. 839. Minutes, 24.9.14, *ibid*. Same to same, tel. no. 843, *ibid*. Grey to Mallet, 25.9.14, tel. no. 588, *ibid*. Mallet to Grey, 25.9.14, tel. no. 852. Minutes, 26.9.14, *ibid*. G.P.O. to Foreign Office, 25.9.14, Minute, 27.9.14, *ibid*./53201.

60. Mallet to Grey, 16.9.14, tel. no. 796. FO/371/2142. Grey to Mallet, 20.9.14, tel. no. 574, *ibid*. Mallet to Grey, 21.9.14, tel. no. 825, *ibid*. Elliott to Grey, 21.9.14, tel. no. 227, *ibid*. Mallet to Grey, 24.9.14, tel. no. 844, confidential, *ibid*. Grey to Mallet, 25.9.14, tel. no. 594, *ibid*.

61. Mallet to Grey, 18.9.14, tel. no. 805, *ibid*. Grey to Mallet, 25.9.14, tel. no. 587.

Minute by Nicolson, 26.9.14, *ibid*. India Office to Foreign Office, 26.9.14, Minute by Crowe, 29.9.14, *ibid*./53604. Hardinge to Crewe, 9.9.14. Pte. C/22. CP.

62. Viceroy to India Office, 15.9.14, Secret, *ibid*/51580. India Office to Foreign Office, 21.9.14, Secret and Immediate. *ibid*. News from Turkey was carefully censored by the Indian Government. Hardinge to Crewe, 17.9.14, Pte. C/22. CP. Ryan was more concerned about Pan-Islam. But he too envisaged the establishment of a 'new system' of tribal administration in Arabia and Meso-potamia, which would be dependent on British support and replace existing Ottoman rule. Memorandum by Ryan in: Mallet to Grey, 22.9.14, no. 604. Confidential. FO/371/2142.

63. Kitchener to Cheetham, 24.9.14, tel. no. 219, Secret, *ibid*. Cheetham succeeded Kitchener in Cairo.

64. Minute by Crowe, The Arabs and Turkey, 26.9.14, FO/371/2139/53671. Cf. S.A. Cohen, *op. cit.*, pp. 336ff. In the Cabinet, Grey still claimed that the situation was 'obscure', whilst the rest of his colleagues thought a 'vigorous offensive' ought to be taken by his bringing Bulgaria, Greece and Roumania into the Entente. Smith, *op. cit.*, p. 1025.

65. Mallet to Grey, 27.9.14, tel. no. 880. Minutes by Clerk, Nicolson and Grey, FO/371/2142. Same to same, 27.9.14, tel. no. 879, *ibid*. Same to same, 28.9.14, tel. no. 885. Minute, 29.9.14, *ibid*. Same to same, 29.9.14, tel. no. 890. Minutes, 30.9.14, *ibid*. Grey to Mallet, 30.9.14, tel. no. 615, *ibid*. Mallet to Grey, 1.10.14, tel. no. 904. Minutes, 2.10.14, *ibid*. Grey to Mallet, 2.10.14, tel. no. 627, *ibid*. Mallet to Grey, 3.10.14, tel. no. 917. *ibid*. Same to same, 3.10.14, tel. no. 923, *ibid*. Grey to Mallet, 4.10.14, tel. no. 638, *ibid*. Same to same, 4.10.14, tel. no. 635, *ibid*.

66. Mallet to Grey, 1.10.14, tel. no. 910, *ibid*. Grey to Mallet, 2.10.14, tel. no. 624, *ibid*. Mallet to Grey, 4.10.14, tel. no. 928, *ibid*. Same to same, 4.10.14, tel. no. 931. Minutes, 5.10.14, *ibid*.

67. Mallet to Grey, 6.10.14, tel. no. 939. Minutes, 7.10.14, *ibid*. Grey to Mallet, 7.10.14, tel. no. 644, *ibid*. Mallet to Grey, 7.10.14, tel. no. 944. Same to same, 10.10.14, tel. no. 952. Minutes, 11.10.14, *ibid*. Grey to Mallet, 11.10.14, tel. no. 659, *ibid*. Smith, *op. cit.*, p. 1027.

68. Mallet to Grey, 11.10.14, tel. no. 958. Minute, 12.10.14, *ibid*. Same to same, 12.10.14, tel. no. 959. Minutes, *ibid*. Grey to Mallet, 13.10.14, tel. no. 663, *ibid*. Mallet to Grey, 12.10.14, tel. no. 962, *ibid*. Same to same, 12.10.14, tel. no. 963. Minutes, 13.10.14, *ibid*. Viceroy to India Office, 14.10.14, Secret. Minutes, FO/371/2142/59744. Grey to Mallet, 17.10.14, tel. no. 681. FO/371/2142. E. David, (ed.), *Inside Asquith's Cabinet*, p. 194 (2.10.14).

69. Admiralty to Foreign Office, 21.10.14, Secret. Minutes, 22.10.14, FO/371/62013. Grey to Mallet, 23.10.14, tel. no. 698. FO/371/2142. Viceroy to India Office, 21.10.14, Secret. Minute, 22.10.14, *ibid*. Grey to Mallet, 30.10.14, tel. no. 724A, *ibid*.

70. Mallet to Grey, 7.10.14, tel. no. 941, *ibid*. Same to same, 7.10.14, tel. no. 942. Minute, 8.10.14, *ibid*. Grey to Mallet, 10.10.14, tel. no. 655, *ibid*. Grey's declaration to the Cabinet on 2 November that Britain 'must finally abandon the formula of "Ottoman integrity", whether in Europe or in Asia', was no more than a formal approval of what amounted to a *de facto* abandonment of that formula after August 1914; quoted in W.A. Renzi, 'Great Britain, Russia, and the Straits, 1914-15', *Journal of Modern History* (1970), p. 5, n. 23. The Cabinet, however, had already agreed to such an abandonment on 2 October. K. Robbins, *op. cit.*, p. 568. Smith, *op. cit.*, p. 1025.

71. Resident at Aden to Viceroy, 30.9.14, Minute 1.10.14, FO/371/2142/54700.

Mallet to Grey, 5.10.14, tel. no. 936. Minute by Clerk, 6.10.14, FO/371/2142.

72. Mallet to Grey, 22.9.14, no. 604, *ibid*. Memorandum by Ryan, in: Mallet to Grey, 22.9.14, confidential, *ibid*. Memorandum by Fitzmaurice, 11.10.14. Minutes, 13.10.14 (Oliphant, Clerk, Crowe and Nicolson), FO/371/2142.

73. Grey to Mallet, 10.10.14, tel. no. 656, *ibid*. Mallet to Grey, 12.10.14, tel. no. 965. Minute by G.H. Nicolson, 13.10.14, *ibid*. Same to same, 12.10.14, tel. no. 966, *ibid*. Same to same, 12.10.14, tel. no. 967. Minute, 13.10.14, Mallet to Grey, 14.10.14, tel. no. 976, *ibid*. Same to same, 14.10.14, tel. no. 979. Minute, 15.10.14, *ibid*. The Consuls in Beirut, Damascus and Jerusalem reassured the Foreign Office that there was little or no enthusiasm at all amongst the local population either over preparations for war against Britain and her Allies or for a campaign against Egypt. Only in Palestine were anti-British feelings reported to exist amongst 'certain classes' of Moslems, but even there a 'large part' of the population hoped for a British occupation. *Ibid*.

74. Cheetham to Grey, 26.10.14, tel. no. 223. Minute by Oliphant, 27.10.14, *ibid*. Same to same, 28.10.14, tel. no. 228, *ibid*.

75. Mallet to Grey, 15.10.14, tel. no. 968, *ibid*.

76. Mallet to Grey, 28.10.14, tel. no. 1081. Minute by Crowe, 29.10.14, *ibid*.

77. Viceroy to India Office, 28.10.14. Minute by Oliphant, 29.10.14, *ibid*./64904. India Office to Foreign Office, 28.10.14. *ibid*./64873. Neither was Hardinge prepared, as Fitzmaurice had suggested, to use Shia resentment against the Porte as a propaganda measure for the dismemberment of 'Turkish Arabia' since Indian Moslem 'opinion' was 'almost entirely' Sunni. Viceroy to India Office, 31.10.14, Secret. *Ibid*./66303.

78. Captain G.F. Clayton informed Aziz Ali on 26 October that it was 'out of the question' for Britain to assist any movement against 'a Power with whom she was at peace', but she certainly acquiesced in anti-Ottoman propaganda. Cheetham to Grey, 15.11.14, no. 177. As for Talib, by early December, the Foreign Office finally realized that he was 'certainly a rascal, but a very dangerous one.' This led Clerk to the conclusion that: 'He will now be against us, and, unless we are lucky enough to kill him fairly soon, can do much harm.' India Office to Foreign Office, 1.12.14. Minute approved by Crowe, Nicolson, Grey and Kitchener, 2.12.14, *ibid*./77724. On Koweit's firm support: S.G. Knox, Resident in the Gulf to the Government of India, 25.8.14. Memorandum by W.G. Grey, 22.8.14, FO/371/2144.

79. Cheetham to Foreign Office, 31.10.14, no. 233. Foreign Office to Cheetham, 31.10.14, no. 303.

80. Trumpener, pp. 48-51, 53. Kurat, pp. 307-8, 311. See also: Crawford to Tyrrell, 26.11.14, FO/371/2143/77254.

81. Mallet was to mention Rahmy's 'anti-German' attitude and his 'dismay' of war with Britain a few years later in 1917 to defend his belief in the 'Moderates'. He believed that neither he nor his Consul at Smyrna had been deceived by Rahmy. The truth was that Mallet had been misled into believing that Rahmy was as 'powerful' as he had been immediately after the 1908 Revolution. Heathcote-Smith (Smyrna) to Mallet, 12.10.14, no. 125. Confidential, *ibid*. Mallet to Heathcote-Smith, 15.10.14, tel. no. 91. Confidential, in: Mallet to Grey, 16.10.14, no. 651. Confidential, *ibid*. Mallet to Grey, 28.10.14, no. 659, *ibid*. Heathcote-Smith, 17.10.14, no. 129, *ibid*. Mallet's apologia, 24.8.17, Confidential FO/371/3060. Ahmad, *The Young Turks, passim*. Rahmy is not mentioned by either Kurat or Trumpener.

82. Mallet to Tyrrell, 16.10.14, Pte. GP.80.

83. Buchanan to Grey, 20.10.14, tel. no. 538. Minute, 21.10.14, FO/371/2143. Mallet to Grey, 21.10.14, tel. no. 1020. Minutes, 22.10.14, *ibid*. Same to same,

21.10.14, tel. no. 1024, *ibid*. Mallet learned from a Greek source that 'certain extremists' had decided on an attempt on his life. Grey sent Mallet one of his usual possibly somewhat exaggerated encouragements, pointing out that he was 'full of admiration' for his courage, and praised the 'character, resources and ability' that he had shown throughout. Mallet to Grey, 19.10.14, Pte. and Conf. Very Secret, GP.80. Grey to Mallet, 20.10.14, Pte. tel. *ibid*.

84. Mallet to Grey, 12.10.14, tel. no. 1033. FO/371/2143. Same to same, 23.10.14, tel. no. 1037, *ibid*. Same to same, 23.10.14, tel. no. 1039. Conf. *ibid*. Grey to Mallet, 24.10.14, tel. no. 705. *ibid*. Mallet to Grey, 24.10.14, tel. no. 1048. E. David, (ed.), *Inside Asquith's Cabinet*, p. 194, (23.10.14).

85. Same to same, 26.10.14, tel. no. 1063, FO/371/2143. Same to same, 27.10.14, tel. no. 1071. Conf. Minute, 28.10.14, *ibid*. Same to same, 27.10.14, tel. no. 1073. Minutes, 28.10.14, *ibid*. Grey to Mallet, 28.10.14, tel. no. 716. *ibid*. Same to same, 28.10.14, tel. no. 714, *ibid*.

86. Trumpener, pp. 54-5. Kurat, p. 312-3.

87. Mallet to Grey, 29.10.14, tel. no. 1087, FO/371/2143. Same to same, 29.10.14, Pte. and Conf. GP.80.

88. Mallet to Grey, 29.10.14, tel. no. 1089, Conf. FO/371/2143.

89. Consul-General Roberts (Odessa) to Grey, 29.10.14, tel. no. 76. Minute by Clerk, *ibid*. Cf. Gilbert, p. 215. Hardinge to Crewe, 22.10.14, C/22, CP.

90. Buchanan to Grey, 29.10.14, tel. no. 571. FO/371/2143. Same to same, 30.10.14, tel. no. 576, *ibid*. Grey to Buchanan, 29.10.14, tel. no. 938, *ibid*. Grey to Mallet, 30.10.14, tel. no. 727, *ibid*. Nevertheless, on the 29th, Grey stated that 'Unless Grand Vizier is strong enough to arrest and punish those responsible for this outrage and to make immediate reparation to Russia, I do not see how war can be avoided, but we shall not take the first step.' Grey to Mallet, 29.10.14, Pte. tel. GP.80.

91. The Foreign Office announcement to the Press, 30.10.14, FO/371/2143/65795.

92. This was in fact the contention of the peace party, as Crawford had been told by the Ministers Boustani and Mahmud Pasha. Crawford to Tyrrell, 26.11.14, FO/371/2143/77254.

93. Mallet to Grey, 31.10.14, tel. no. 1097. Minute, 2.11.14, FO/371/2143. General Maxwell to Kitchener, 2.11.14, no. 233E, *ibid*. Buchanan to Grey, 31.10.14, tel. no. 584, *ibid*. On that day, Asquith wrote: 'Few things would give me greater pleasure than to see the Turkish Empire finally disappear from Europe ...' quoted by Gilbert, p. 216.

94. Mallet to Grey, 4.11.14, tel. FO/371/2143/67911. Grey to Mallet, 4.11.14, tel. no. 349. Minute by Grey, 5.11.14. Minute by Nicolson, 31.10.14, *ibid*.65802. R. Grey (Cairo) to Clerk, 14.12.14, *ibid*. Note on Turkish Diplomacy and the rupture between Turkey and the Allied Powers by P.P. Graves, 12.12.14, *ibid*./87312. Hardinge commented: 'How extraordinary it is that Turkey should have gone to war with us, who after all, are the only Government in existence that attach any value to the maintenance of Turkey as an independent Mahomedan power.' Hardinge to Crewe, 5.11.14, Pte. C/22. CP.

95. Mallet to Grey, 20.11.14, Grey to Mallet, 4.12.14, Cd. 7716.

96. *The Times*, 24.9.17, p. 7. Also cf. Steed to Bourchier, 12.3.15, quoted in: *The History of the Times* (London 1952), Vol. IV, Pt. 1: 1912-20, p. 234.

97. Mallet's apologia, 27.8.17, *op. cit.* Lord Robert Cecil commented that it was a 'powerful' defence.

98. Alan Cunningham, *op. cit.*, p. 72.

99. On 20 July 1919, Curzon suggested to Lloyd George that he appoint Mallet as Ambassador to Rome. The PM refused on the grounds that Mallet had been 'a great failure' at Constantinople, that he 'was not at all an able man, but a stupid

man, that he was wholly unsuited for Rome, where (after Rodd's departure) an Ambassador will be required not only warmly sympathetic to the Italians, but possessing real authority with them and that Mallet could never acquire this position.' Curzon admitted that though Mallet was his friend, he was 'unable to say that I regard him as a man of real ability, resolution or power. I think the reverse.' Balfour Papers, 217, pp. 231-3. I am indebted to Mr B. B. Davis for this information. See also: Sir E. Grey, *Twenty Five Years, 1892-1916*, (London 1935 ed.), Vol. III, p. 128.

CONCLUSIONS

1. Ahmad, 'Great Britain's Relations with the Young Turks ...' *op. cit.*, p. 324.
2. Z. Steiner's assertion that 'a study of the Eastern question will show, I think, the importance of Mallet's contribution', cannot be sustained. *The Foreign Office and Foreign Policy*, p. 106. Cf. also Steiner's later assessment in *Britain and the Origins of the First World War* (London 1977), pp. 119-20
3. Temperley, 'British Policy towards Parliamentary Rule ...' *op. cit.* J. Joll, *Britain and Europe, Pitt to Churchill, 1793-1940* (London 1950), pp. 5-6.
4. M. S. Anderson, *The Eastern Question, 1774-1923* (London 1966), pp. 397-8.
5. Kurat, *op. cit.*, p. 292.

BIOGRAPHICAL APPENDIX

Aehrenthal, Alois, Baron Lexa von (1854-1912). Austrian Minister for Foreign Affairs, 1906-12.

Asquith, Herbert Henry (1852-1926). Chancellor of the Exchequer, 1905-8. Prime Minister, 1908-16.

Babington-Smith, Sir H. (1863-1923). Director of the National Bank of Turkey, 1909-13.

Barclay, Sir George H. (1862-1921). Chargé at Constantinople Embassy, 1906-8. Minister, April-July, 1908. Minister at Tehran, 1908-12; at Bucharest, 1912-18.

Beaumont, Sir Henry, H.D. (1867-1949). Chargé at Cettinje, 1909-10. Counsellor at Athens, 1910-14. Counsellor at Constantinople, 1914. Chargé July-August, 1914.

Benckendorff, Alexander, Count (1849-1917). Russian Ambassador at London, 1903-17.

Berchtold, Leopold Count von (1863-1942). Austrian Ambassador at St Petersburg, 1906-12. Minister for Foreign Affairs, 1912-15.

Bertie, Francis Leveson, Viscount (1844-1919). British Ambassador at Rome, 1903-4; at Paris, 1905-18.

Block, Sir Adam S.J. (1865-1941). Chief Dragoman, 1894-1903. President and Representative of British and Dutch Bondholders in the Council of Public Debt, 1903-29. President of the British Chamber of Commerce from 1907.

Bompard, M. (1854-1935). French Ambassador at St Petersburg, 1902-7; at Constantinople, 1909-14.

Buchanan, Sir George N. (1854-1924). Agent, Consul-General and Minister at Sofia, 1903-8. British Ambassador at St Petersburg, 1910-18.

Buxton, Noel, Baron Noel-Buxton (1869-1948). MP 1905-6, 1910-18. Founded the Balkan Committee (with Lord Bryce), in 1903.

Carrasso, Emanuel (?-1934). Member of the CUP 'inner circle' at Salonica. Grand Master of 'Macedonia Risorta' Masonic Lodge. Deputy for Salonica and Istanbul.

Cartwright, Sir Fairfax L. (1857-1928). Minister Resident at Munich and Stuttgart, 1906-8. Ambassador at Vienna, 1908-13.

Cassel, Sir Ernest Joseph (1852-1921). British financier. In 1898 financed the dams of Aswan and Assiut, the National Banks of Egypt, Morocco and Turkey (1909). Negotiated with the Germans as to the possibility of British participation in the

Baghdad Railway. Personal friend of Edward VII. Disliked by the Foreign Office.

Chirol, Sir Valentine (1852-1929). Director of the Foreign Department of *The Times*, 1899-1912.

Churchill, Sir Winston S. (1874-1965). President of the Board of Trade, 1908-10. Home Secretary, 1910-11. First Lord of the Admiralty, 1911-15.

Clerk, Sir George R. (1874-1951). First Secretary at Constantinople, 1910-12. Senior Clerk at the Eastern Department, 1913-14.

Constans, J.M. (1833-1913). Ambassador at Constantinople, 1899-1909.

Crawford, Sir Richard F. (1863-1919). Customs Adviser to the Ottoman Government, 1904-11. Adviser to the Ottoman Ministry of Finance, 1911-14.

Crewe, Marquess (1858-1945). Secretary of State for the Colonies, 1908-10. Secretary of State for India, 1910-15.

Crowe, Sir Eyre (1864-1925). Senior Clerk in the Foreign Office. Assistant Under-Secretary, 1912-20. Head of the Eastern (and Western) Department, 1913-14.

De Bunsen, Sir Maurice (1852-1932). First Secretary and Chargé at Constantinople, 1897-1902. Paris, 1902-5 (Minister and Chargé). Minister at Lisbon, 1905-6. Ambassador at Madrid, 1906-13; at Vienna, 1913-14.

Djavid, Pasha (1875-1926). Member of the CUP's 'inner circle' at Salonica and Deputy in the Ottoman Parliament. Minister of Finance, June 1909–May 1911. Minister of Public Works, February 1912; Finance, May-July 1912; and again from January, 1913.

Djevad, Bey, Counsellor and Chargé at the Ottoman Embassy in London, 1908-13.

Durham, Miss M.E. (1863-1944). Balkan Correspondent of the *Manchester Guardian, Nation*, etc. Influential at the Foreign Office. Strongly sympathized with the Balkan Christians.

Enver, Pasha (1882-1922). Member of the Central Committee of the CUP, 1908. Military Attaché at Berlin, 1909-11. Fought at Tripoli and the Balkans. Promoted to a General and Minister of War in early 1914.

Ferdinand, Prince of Coburg (1861-1948). Prince of Bulgaria, 1887. King, 1908-18.

Findlay, Sir Mansfeldt de C. (1861-1932). Minister at Dresden, 1907-9; at Sofia, 1909-11; at Christiania, 1911-23.

Fitzmaurice, Gerald Henry (1865-1939). Student Interpreter, 1888. Acting Vice-Consul, Van, 1891-2; at Erzeroum, 1892-3; at Trebizond, 1893. Acting Third Dragoman at the Embassy, 1894-5. Vice-Consul at Smyrna, 1895-6, at Adana, 1896. Third Dragoman, 1897. Consul at Salonica, 1900-1; at the Dardanelles, 1902. British Commissioner for the Aden Frontier Delimitation, 1902. Second Dragoman, 1906. Chief Dragoman, October, 1907–February, 1914. Acting Consul-General at Tripoli, January-June, 1912.

Ghazi Ahmed Mukhtar, Pasha (1839-1918). President of the Senate, 1911. Grand Vizier, July-October 1912.

Giers, Michael de. Russian Minister at Bucharest, 1902-12. Ambassador at Constantinople, 1912-14.

Goltz, Colmar von der (1843-1916). German General. In charge of the reorganization of the Ottoman army, 1883-95, 1908-11.

Goschen, Sir William E. (1847-1924). Ambassador at Vienna, 1905-8; at Berlin, 1908-14.

Graves, Sir Robert W. (1858-1934). Adviser to the Ottoman Ministry of Finance, 1909-14. Inspector-General and Adviser to the Ottoman Ministry of the Interior, 1914.

Grey, Sir Edward, Viscount Grey of Fallodon (1862-1933). Secretary of State for Foreign Affairs, December 1905–December 1916.

Hakki, Pasha, Ibrahim (1863-1918). Legal Adviser to the Ottoman Ministry for Foreign Affairs before the Revolution. After the Revolution, Minister for Education and the Interior, 1908-9. Ambassador to Rome, 1909-10. Grand Vizier, January 1910–September 1911. In charge of the negotiations with the British Government concerning Mesopotamia and the Persian Gulf, 1913-14.

Halil, Bey (Menteshe) (1874-1948). Deputy for Menteshe. Leader of the CUP Parliamentary party and President of the Parliament. Supported Enver's pro-German policy in 1914.

Halim, Pasha, Mehmed Said (1863-1921). Senator after the Revolution. President of the Council of State, 1912. General Secretary of the CUP, 1913. Minister for Foreign Affairs and Grand Vizier, 1913-17.

Hardinge, Sir Charles, Baron Hardinge of Penshurst (1858-1944). Permanent Under-Secretary for Foreign Affairs, 1906-10, 1916-20. Viceroy and Governor-General of India, 1910-16. Ambassador at Paris, 1920-22. Knighted, 1904. Baron, 1910.

Hilmi, Pasha, Hussein (1855-1923). Inspector-General of Macedonia, 1903-8. Minister of the Interior, 1908-9; of Justice, 1912. Grand Vizier, February-December, 1909 (except for the period of the Counter-Revolution).

Hirtzel, Sir Arthur F. (1870-1937). Secretary of the Political Department at India Office, 1909-17.

Izvolsky, Alexander (1856-1919). Minister for Foreign Affairs, 1906-10. Ambassador at Paris, 1910-17.

Jahid, Hussein (1875-1957). Deputy for Istanbul. Editor of the *Tanin*, the CUP organ and influential in political matters.

Jemal, Bey, Ahmed (1872-1922). Member of the CUP Central Committee. Vali of Adana, 1909; of Baghdad, 1911. Military Governor of Istanbul, 1913. Minister of Public Works, 1914; of Marine, 1914.

Kiamil, Pasha, Mehmed (1832-1913). Grand Vizier, August 1908–February 1909, October 1912–January 1913. The most bitter opponent of the CUP.

Kitchener, Horatio Herbert, Earl (1850-1916). C.-in-C. India, 1902-9. Field-Marshal, 1909. Member of the Committee of Imperial Defence, 1909-10. Agent and Consul-General in Cairo, 1911-14.

Liman von Sanders, Otto (1855-1929). General and Head of the German Military Mission for the reorganization of the Ottoman Army, 1913.

Limpus, Admiral Sir A.H. (1862-1931). British Adviser to the Ottoman Ministry for Marine, 1912-14.

Lorimer, J.D. (1870-1914). Political Resident and Acting Consul-General, Baghdad, 1910. Consul-General 1911. Acting Consul-General at Bushire, 1913-14.

Lowther, Sir Gerard Augustus (1858-1916). Ambassador at Constantinople, July 1908–July 1913. Bitter opponent of the CUP.

Lynch, H.F.B. (1862-1913). Writer and senior partner in the firm of Lynch Brothers, Eastern Merchants. Travelled extensively in the area between India and the Mediterranean. Partner in the Euphrates Steam Navigation Company.

Mallet, Sir Louis (1864-1936). Assistant Under-Secretary for Foreign Affairs, 1907-13, and Head of the Eastern Department. Ambassador at Constantinople, October 1913–November 1914.

Marling, Sir Charles M. (1862-1933). Counsellor at Constantinople, October 1908– October 1913. Chargé, October 1909–January 1910; November 1910–January 1911; June–July 1911; July–October 1912; July–October 1913.

Marschall von Bieberstein, Adolf Freiherr (1842-1912). German Ambassador at Constantinople, 1897-1912; at London, 1912.

Mensdorff, Count Albert, Puilly-Dietrichstein (1861-1945). Austrian Ambassador at London, 1904-14.

Morley, John, Viscount Morley of Blackburn (1838-1923). Secretary of State for India, 1905-10. Lord President of the Council, 1910-14. Viscount, 1908.

Nicolson, Sir Arthur, Lord Carnock (1849-1928). Ambassador at St Petersburg, 1906-10. Permanent Under-Secretary, 1910-16.

Norman, Herman C. (1872-1955). Assistant Clerk in the Foreign Office, 1906-14 (in the Eastern Department until 1913). Secretary to the St James Conference, 1912-13.

O'Beirne, H.J. (1866-1916). Counsellor, Chargé and Minister at St Petersburg, 1906-15.

O'Conor, Sir Nicolas, R. (1843-1908). Ambassador at Constantinople, 1898-1908.

Ostrorog, Leon. Legal Adviser to the Porte, 1898-1914.

Pallavicini, Johann Margrave (1848-1941). Austrian Ambassador at Constantinople, 1906-18.

Parker, Alwyn (1877-1951). Junior Clerk, Foreign Office, 1906. Assistant Clerk, 1912. The Foreign Office's expert on the Persian Gulf, Baghdad Railway and Mesopotamia.

Rifaat, Pasha, Mehmed (1860-1925). Ottoman Minister at Athens, 1898-1908. Ambassador at London, 1906-9. Minister for Foreign Affairs, 1909-11. Ambassador at Paris, 1911-14.

Riza, Ahmed (1859-1950). More influential amongst Young Turks in exile than after the Revolution. After 1908 Deputy for Istanbul and President of the Parliament (1908-12). Senator from 1912.

Rodd, Sir J. Rennel, Baron Rennel (1858-1941). Ambassador at Rome, 1908-19.

Ryan, Sir Andrew (1876-1949). Student Interpreter in the Levant, 1897. Vice-Consul, Constantinople and Uskub. Second Dragoman in the British Embassy at Constantinople, 1907. Acting Chief Dragoman, June 1911–July 1912; February 1914–November 1914.

Said, Pasha, Mehmed Kuchuk (1838-1914). First Secretary to Abdul Hamid, 1876. Grand Vizier, 1879, 1882-5, 1895, 1901-3, 22 July–5 August 1908, September 1911–July 1912.

Sazonov, Sergei, Count (1861-1927). Acting Russian Minister for Foreign Affairs, 1909-10. Russian Minister for Foreign Affairs, 1910-16.

Shevket, Pasha, Mahmud (1856-1913). Vali of Kossovo at the time of the Young Turk Revolution. As Commander of the Third Army in Macedonia, defeated the Counter-Revolution in April 1909. Inspector-General of the first three armies. Minister of War in Hakki's Cabinet, January 1910–July 1912. Grand Vizier, January–June 1913.

Talaat, Pasha, Mehmed (1874-1921). Leading member of the CUP. Deputy for Edirne after the 1908 Revolution. Minister for the Interior, July 1909–February 1911. Minister of Post and Telegraph, January–July 1912. Leader of the CUP Parliamentary party. Minister for the Interior, 1913-17.

Tcharykov, M.N. (1855-1930). First Secretary at the Russian Embassy at Constantinople, 1890-3. Assistant Secretary for Russian Foreign Affairs, 1908-9. Ambassador at Constantinople, 1909-12.

Tewfik, Pasha, Ahmed (1845-1936). Ottoman Minister for Foreign Affairs, 1895-1909. Grand Vizier during the Counter-Revolution, April 1909. Ambassador to London, 1909-14.

Tilley, Sir John A.C. (1869-1952). First Secretary at Constantinople, August 1906–August 1908. Granted an allowance for knowledge of Turkish 1907. Again at the Foreign Office, September 1908 (in the Eastern Department until March 1909). Acting Senior Clerk, February 1909. Senior Clerk, 1910 (African Department).

Tyrrell, G.E. (1871-1917). Lieut.-Col. Attached to the Macedonian gendarmerie, 1907-9. Military Attaché at Constantinople Embassy, 1909-13; also at Athens, 1909-11; at Sofia, 1911-13.

Tyrrell, William G., Baron (1866-1947). Senior Clerk and Private Secretary to Grey, 1907-15. A friend of G.H. Fitzmaurice and influential at the Foreign Office.

Vambéry, Arminius (1832-1913). Professor at Budapest University for Oriental Languages. Travelled extensively in the Orient and Central Asia. British Agent at Constantinople.

Wangenheim, Baron von (1859-1915). Minister at the German Mission at Athens, 1909-12. Ambassador at Constantinople, 1912-15.

Willcocks, Sir William (1852-1932). Employed by the Ottoman Ministry for Public Works as Adviser on Irrigation (Mesopotamia), 1900-11.

Zinoview, N. Russian Ambassador at Constantinople, 1898-1909.

INDEX